"ATTENTIVE, INTELLIGENT, RATIONAL, AND RESPONSIBLE":

Transforming Economics to Save the Planet

"ATTENTIVE, INTELLIGENT, RATIONAL, AND RESPONSIBLE":

Transforming Economics to Save the Planet

by John Raymaker and Pierre Whalon

MARQUETTE
UNIVERSITY

PRESS

With gratitude to our long-suffering wives,
Christa and Hélène,

and to the memory of Philip McShane

Cover and text by Rose Design
Cover photo: iStock.com/ RomoloTavani

Library of Congress Cataloging-in-Publication Data

Names: Raymaker, John, author. | Whalon, Pierre W., 1952- author.
Title: Attentive, intelligent, rational, and responsible : transforming
    economics to save the planet / John Raymaker, Pierre Whalon.
Description: Milwaukee, Wisconsin : Marquette University Press, 2023. |
    Includes bibliographical references and index. | Summary: "The great
    philosopher and theologian Bernard Lonergan is best known for his
    transcendental method, but he considered his most important work to be
    in macroeconomics. The authors lift up his innovative theory as a model
    of his method, and they propose developments in both fields"-- Provided
    by publisher.
Identifiers: LCCN 2023001932 | ISBN 9781626000605 (paperback)
Subjects: LCSH: Lonergan, Bernard J. F. | Macroeconomics--Philosophy. |
    Environmental economics--Philosophy. | Economics--Religious
    aspects--Christianity. | Transcendence (Philosophy) | Philosophy,
    Canadian--20th century.
Classification: LCC B995.L654 R3895 2023 | DDC 330.1--dc23/eng/20230413
LC record available at https://lccn.loc.gov/2023001932

∞ The paper used in this publication meets the minimum requirements of the American National Standard for Information Sciences—Permanence of Paper for Printed Library Materials, ANSI Z39.48-1992.

ASSOCIATION
of UNIVERSITY
PRESSES

Contents

LIST OF ILLUSTRATIONS[1]

APPENDICES / 237

---

1. Figures 1–3 concentrate on Lonergan's notion of two circuits in the economy; Figures 4–5 explore the need and possibility of what Lonergan called the redistribution function. Figure 6 shows one of his mathematical explorations.

Foreword

Why Changes in Economics and Environmental Policies are Essential Today

"*Attentive, Intelligent, Rational, and Responsible*": *Transforming Economics to Save the Planet* is a groundbreaking work in economics and theology. John Raymaker and Pierre Whalon have produced a work with two currents that neatly conjoin. The first pivots towards economists and technocrats, and the second pivots towards Lonergan students and scholars. The philosophical theology and economic ideas of the Canadian Jesuit Bernard Lonergan (1904–84) form the superstructure of the book. Its genius lies in the authors' fusing the fruit of their scholarship with Lonergan's ideas without disturbing the flow of their argument. The two scholars detail carefully, but unapologetically, why they've had to draw from a theologian to correct the errors of economists. For, in Lonergan, they find a rich tapestry of economic ideas and "fresh original thinking" that can help resolve some contested issues in economics. They use their ideas, grounded in Lonergan's thought, to illustrate how political economy should work in a new world order. They reappropriate some of the solutions Lonergan offered as correctives to the ignorance of the economic process in his time that led to the collapse of the economy and the Great Depression (1929–41). From these solutions, they develop concrete plans they believe can help contemporary economies, particularly developing nations, to move forward. "We cannot rely on the old political economy: it was democratic but has been found wrong," Lonergan writes. "We cannot rely on the new economics: it is accurate but it can solve real problems only by eliminating democracy. What is needed is a new political economy that is free from the mistakes of the old, a democratic economics that can issue practical imperatives to plain men."[1] Lonergan was convinced that a new system was needed for our collective survival—that the need for creating is manifest when a people's survival requires a system that does not exist.[2] This need for healing and creating in history is the guide post for *"Attentive, Intelligent, Rational, and Responsible": Transforming Economics to Save the Planet.*

Raymaker and Whalon clearly demonstrate some of the ways Lonergan addressed many of the same economic problems we face today. Lonergan spoke of the "badness" of the economic structures and their techniques.[3] He cautioned against our intellectual development outrunning our moral development.[4] He was wary of the rapid destruction of the organic cap of the earth. He warned that our countryside is emptying into cities and our cities, with their "disquieting tendency to neurasthenia," have birthrates below the net reproduction rate. He was concerned that the cities were making "men mere cogs in worldwide depressions and wars."[5] He discerned that a proper response to many of these environmental and economic challenges has to be a global environmental and economic reckoning. He cryptically calls his suggested solution a "Toynbeean Withdrawal and Return." The *withdrawal* is a jettisoning of whatever is unhelpful in human thinking and doing, and the *return* is "the creation of a new environment and culture under the inspiration of new values and new ideals."[6] In many of his works, directly or indirectly, he puts more premium on the economy, which, for him, is a concrete instance of the human good. "It is to be insisted that the good of order

---

1. Bernard Lonergan, *Collected Works of Bernard Lonergan*, vol. 21, *For A New Political Economy*, edited by Philip McShane (Toronto: University of Toronto Press, 1998), 5.

2. See Bernard Lonergan, "Healing and Creating in History," in *A Third Collection: Papers by Bernard J.F. Lonergan, S.J.*, edited by Frederick E. Crowe, S.J. (New York: Paulist, 1985), 100–109, 103.

3. See Bernard Lonergan, "Review of George Boyle, *Democracy's Second Chance*," in *Collected Works of Bernard Lonergan*, vol. 20, *Shorter Papers*, edited by Robert C. Croken, Robert M. Doran, and H. Daniel Monsour (Toronto: University of Toronto Press, 2007), 157.

4. Lonergan, "Healing and Creating in History," 100.

5. Lonergan, review of *Democracy's Second Chance*, 157.

6. Ibid., 158.

is not some design for Utopia, some theoretic ideal, some set of ethical precepts, some code of laws, or some super-institution. It is quite concrete. It is the actually functioning or malfunctioning set of "if—then" relationships guiding operators and coordinating operations. It is the ground whence recur or fail to recur whatever instances of the particular good are recurring or failing to recur."[7] Such was Lonergan's philosophic-economic program for a new world order. But unfortunately, for some odd reasons, the influence of this intellectual giant of the last century was limited more to philosophy and theology than to economics. Even more disappointingly, his economic manuscripts were published only posthumously. The late Phil McShane (1932–2020) was motivated to correct these lapses and produced an economic theory that is very much Lonerganian.[8] He put a lot of energy into steering scholars, young and old, in that direction. While I am not sure of the extent of McShane's influence here, Raymaker and Whalon's masterpiece is very much in line with McShane's vison of what a genuine Lonerganian economic manuscript ought to look like.

In the years following the housing bubble and subprime mortgages meltdown that triggered the financial crisis of 2007–2009 and the first Great Recession of the new millennium, I attended a conference on sustainability and political economy in Copenhagen, Denmark (2015). In my audience were scholars from various fields in the humanities and with a wide range of interests in political economy and sustainability. Many were unfamiliar with Lonergan's work. Some had not even heard the name of this philosopher-theologian who developed a revolutionary idea in economics in the twentieth century. My apprehensions about their lack of familiarity with the ideas of Lonergan were allayed near the end of my presentation. It was then that I became aware, from the many questions posed to me, of the possibilities Lonergan's work might offer to economists, particularly in lieu of what Lonergan says about the main

---

7. Bernard Lonergan, *Collected Works of Bernard Lonergan*, vol.14, *Method in Theology*, edited by Robert M. Doran and John D. Dadosky (Toronto: University of Toronto Press, 2017), 49.

8. See Phil McShane, *Economics for Everyone: Das Jus Kapital* (Vancouver, BC: Axial Publishing 2017).

variants of traditional market economy, modern transactional economy, and giant or multi-national corporations that he understood to be ideologically driven. Not only does Lonergan castigate these ideologies in an intellectually satisfying way, but he also speaks with equal erudition about the errors of the physicists who for years proclaimed the necessary laws of nature but only turned to speaking about statistical probabilities fifty years later. His assessment of the errors of the physicists coheres with his assessment of the errors of economists who, in like manner, first spoke of the ironclad laws of economics but eventually renounced them and turned "their hand to advising bureaucrats on the probable results of this or that course of action."[9] We glean from Lonergan how the net result of such classical thinking, in economics in this case, led to the division of social activities into two realms: the profitable and the unprofitable. The former was entrusted to the "beneficence of intelligent self-interest" while the latter's residue was handed over to the state.[10]

The profitable and the unprofitable realms of social activities, for Lonergan, are ideologically-driven. He discovered that they present us with "an economic system that runs only by fits and starts and with a political system overloaded with the ever-mounting residue of unprofitable business."[11] The good news is that Lonergan worked out a soteriological solution for the ideology he sometimes labels "basic sin." Although Lonergan offered a solution to the basic sin of economics, he never had time to develop it. The realities of contemporary global society cry for such a development and prompt us to ask: How does Lonergan's economics fit the new world global financial market? Does his economic theory adequately address how we can overcome the limitations of those social and economic engineers who are content with making the masses seem like raw materials of rich people's economic propaganda? *"Attentive, Intelligent, Rational, and Responsible": Transforming Economics to Save the Planet* answers

---

9. Bernard Lonergan, "Revolution in Catholic Theology," in *Collected Works of Bernard Lonergan,* vol. 13, *A Second Collection,* edited by Robert M. Doran and John D. Dadosky (Toronto: University of Toronto Press, 2016), 195–201, 198.

10. Bernard Lonergan, "Review of Harry M. Cassidy, Ph.D., *Social Security and Reconstruction in Canada,*" in *Shorter Papers,* 168–70, 168.

11. Ibid.

these questions and many more. In fact, the book is a development of the solution Lonergan offered for the basic sin of economics. Not every book comes well-primed and well-timed. This one surely is. The connection Raymaker and Whalon make between what they package as Lonergan's "Copernican Revolution" in economics and Lonergan's "philosophical premises"—the Generalized Empirical Method and Functional Specialty (GEM-FS)—will be of essential benefit to specialists and non-specialists alike. It can help in resolving some of "the tragedies that mere technical interpretations of economic policies have provoked."

The financial crisis of 2007–2009 was the first global financial crisis of the millennium and the first of my generation. But it did not take long before the Coronavirus pandemic of 2020 foisted upon us another global financial crisis. This means that in just over a decade my own generation has already seen two global financial crises, both with deleterious consequences. Nature has a way of making a comeback, especially when the lessons of the past are not heeded. Lonergan determines that what is responsible for the human failure to heed warnings of the past are "a darkening of the intellect and a weakening of will."[12] Even the billionaire Bill Gates has observed how in 2020 the pandemic forced the world to rethink what is acceptable for many of our activities.[13] But there is "a profound difference between diagnosing a malady and proposing a cure."[14] Lonergan says what we need is "a cure and not a wheelchair."[15] If the post-Coronavirus financial crisis came multifaceted, it is largely because we have often passed off a wheelchair for a cure. In Raymaker and Whalon's assessment, the post-Coronavirus financial crisis has resulted in environmental degradation, collapse of democracies, inequities in distribution of wealth, economic meltdown, and inflation. They also determine that the developing nations have been more hard-hit by the crisis—that the developing nations face, to a greater degree than their developed counterparts, shrinking values

---

12. Lonergan, "Healing and Creating in History," 101–102.

13. Bill Gates, *How to Prevent the Next Pandemic* (New York: Alfred A. Knopf, 2022), 238.

14. Lonergan, "Healing and Creating in History," 102.

15. Lonergan, review of "Social Security and Reconstruction in Canada," 170.

of their currencies, high food prices, and high energy costs. We need not look too far to validate their claim. In recent years, many developing nations have suffered from catastrophic floods stemming from climate change. In 2022 alone, Pakistan, for example, was hit by melting glaciers and torrential monsoon rains that caused flooding that killed more than 1700 people, displaced tens of millions of people, and resulted in over $30 billion dollars in damage. At the 27th United Nations Climate Change conference, commonly referred to as the Conference of the Parties of the UNFCCC (COP27), in Sharm El Sheikh, Egypt (November 6–18, 2022), the point was made that the developed nations are the largest emitters of greenhouse gases while the poorer developing nations, which contribute minimally to the greenhouse gases, bear most of the brunt. To add to the intrigue, the only leader of a major polluting country to attend the conference was the president of the United States, Joe Biden. Neither President Vladimir Putin of Russia nor President Xi Jinping of China attended. In a nutshell, the post-Coronavirus financial meltdown is a crisis that has been precipitated by the mistaken assumptions of philosophers, economists, and technocrats. Lonergan warned long ago about the complacency toward some long-held principles, cautioning that long-accepted principles are often inadequate and suffer from radical oversights.[16]

If "innovation can solve big problems,"[17] then *"Attentive, Intelligent, Rational, and Responsible": Transforming Economics to Save the Planet* is an innovative work with myriad value. It lays bare the solution offered by a thinker who had a nose for change. With the publication of this work, confining Lonergan's work to philosophy and theology should come to an end. Raymaker and Whalon have led the way in bringing forward in a single work the interface of Lonergan's philosophy, theology, and economics. They call their GEM-FS process-approach a "sandwich" approach. Many that are familiar with Lonergan's work know that apart from a few hints in "Healing and Creating in History," Lonergan scarcely showed how his generalized empirical method (GEM) and functional

16. Lonergan, "Healing and Creating in History," 103.
17. Gates, *How to Prevent the Next Pandemic*, 239.

specialties (FS) are to be applied to economics. Raymaker and Whalon
have helped to make this connection. They show how GEM-FS theory
and praxis reinforce one another. It is not only Lonergan that the two
scholars bring to bear on the subject, however; they also detail the main
macroeconomic theories in the history of economics, in particular the
three major theories of neoclassical economics, Keynesian economics,
and Marxian economics. They fuse these theories with what they retrieve
from Lonergan's careful reading of the economic models developed by
Adam Smith, Karl Marx, John Maynard Keynes, and Joseph Schumpeter,
among others. They intersperse these approaches with Lonergan's balanced critique of both the socialist and capitalist economies. Lonergan
notes, "Obviously socialism is no solution, for that 'nationalization of
capitalist errors' only puts more wealth into the hands of fewer, to redirect careerist from business to palace intrigue and turn citizens into
guinea pigs for the experiments of social theorists."[18]

One of the things Raymaker and Whalon have done clearly well is
take what Lonergan calls *self-appropriation* to a new level. To aid our grasp
of our communal self-appropriation, they rephrase Lonergan's economic
theory in contemporary terms and language, showing how what Lonergan
describes as "the rhythmic flows of an economy still rhythmically cycles
together in the same basic ways they did in ages past." They help us pay
attention to how Adam Smith's "invisible hand" has birthed liberalism,
laissez faire economic theory, and modern-day trickle-down economics.
They also help us understand how Marxian theory and its questionable
approach to economics furthered neoliberalism's economic absurdity and
the "mechanization of humanity." Here, Lonergan's solution is again offered
as an alternative. Not only did Lonergan show how the economy cannot
be divorced from a society's civic institutions, political order, and cultural
traditions, he also adequately accounts for "the normative rhythms of economic development and the conditions of its dynamic equilibrium." Raymaker and Whalon do, in fact, call the Lonergan alternative they propose a
"Third Way." Apart from being an alternative to neoliberalism, this "Third
Way" avoids exploitation and accounts for sustainable development. It is

---

18. Lonergan, Review of *Democracy's Second Chance*, 157–58.

a form of liberation from the mechanization of humanity. Lonergan was, after all, clear that the alternative to socialism and unabridged capitalism has to be a democratic solution with a program of education that is both intellectual and moral.[19]

Lonergan was indeed committed to addressing whatever was inhumane in the economic structure. He wondered whether our economic and social structure might not be "a sick man needing treatment than a dying man awaiting burial."[20] It is this concern about the detached and inhumane approach to economics that Raymaker and Whalon take up, cautioning that the detached and inhumane approaches that provoked economic disasters in the past still linger to this day. Taking into account the evolution of economic theories and practices from Adam Smith to some notable contemporary thinkers, they see the need to apply Lonergan's ethics to the economic process. They package this as a new effort to apply Christian values and ethics to societal problems. Their good judgment tells them that applying this kind of ethics to the economic process will ameliorate the conditions of the poor and marginalized who suffer the most in situations of economic collapse. One of the many innovations that make Lonergan unique is this infusion of ethics into economics. For, Lonergan was motivated by the idea of trying to help people discover their true values as they search for that just economy that gives equal protection and freedom to all. One of the notable events of COP27 was a demand the developing nations made on the richer nations in which they asked the richer nations for support for flood relief and recovery and requested upward of $100 billion per year in climate-related finance. Although the developing nations were clear that the demand is not a request for humanitarian assistance but a call for climate and environmental justice, it is doubtful the richer nations will heed it and be economically just.

What Raymaker and Whalon call "the GEM-FS achievement" is, in fact, their own unique contribution to the fields of economics and Lonergan studies. Where ordinarily Lonergan's theological method

19. Ibid., 158.
20. Ibid.

and philosophy would be studied in isolation from his economic theory, Raymaker and Whalon weave these together, showing that FS and GEM, in so far as they help the religious person, bankers, economists, and scholars distinguish between knowing facts and understanding facts, ought to be considered "imperatives" for promoting economics and individual and communal self-transcendence. Lonergan did not take the field of economics by storm in his lifetime, but *"Attentive, Intelligent, Rational, and Responsible": Transforming Economics to Save the Planet* may well help him do that posthumously. The book does for Lonergan what Lonergan would have liked to do in his lifetime. When he was asked whether Terry J. Tekippe's *The Universal Viewport and the Relationship of Philosophy and Theology in the Works of Bernard Lonergan* coheres with his work, Lonergan affirmed unambiguously that "It illustrates very well an intermediate position between what I had worked out in *Insight* and, on the other hand, the views presented *in Method in Theology*." Were Lonergan alive today, I believe he would affirm that *"Attentive, Intelligent, Rational, and Responsible": Transforming Economics to Save the Planet* illustrates very well the connection he would have liked to make between GEM-FS and his economic theory. A book that interprets Lonergan from the standpoint of his GEM-FS and makes economics a serious part of the religious quest is a rare gift.

In their implementation of Lonergan's macroeconomics, Raymaker and Whalon are convinced that such implementation is integral to the turnaround in economic policies that the times demand. Lonergan wanted "a new political economy that is free from the mistakes of the old," such as the type we see in the state capitalism of some Communist-oriented economies and the "greed of finance-dominated capitalism" in the industrialized West. This is why he worked towards establishing "a democratic economics that can issue practical imperatives to plain men."[21] While Lonergan may not have been the first to suggest a democratic control of economic structures, since Adam Smith and David Ricardo did that before him, he still stands unique in many respects. The reader will be fascinated by how the GEM-FS process approach, which

---

21. Lonergan, *For a New Political Economy*, 5.

centers on the subject-object sides of human knowing and doing, puts a religious face to economics. The authors have used the approach to call for reform of both the capitalist and the socialist economies. They have suggested in the process two new modalities of conversion (economic and environmental), which they modestly call "two communal turnarounds in economic and environmental policies." Their essential argument in this respect is that besides the four conversions (intellectual, moral, religious, and psychic), there is a need for two additional conversions (economic and environmental) to complement the generally accepted four. They are convinced that "Lonergan's work implies a need for an environmental, socially conscious turnaround that would radically change policies to counter climate change for the good of all."

In the final analysis, *"Attentive, Intelligent, Rational, and Responsible": Transforming Economics to Save the Planet* illustrates reasonably and responsibly what Lonergan intended to do with his economic theory. The scholarship is phenomenal. The literature review is sound. The work of leading Lonerganian economic scholars, such as Phil McShane, Michael Shute, Eileen de Neeve, Paul St. Amour, and Pat Byrne, are well-developed and furthered to achieve the book's two stated objectives, i.e., "to develop clear concrete thinking on the part of individuals and of academics such as economists" and "to reflect on Lonergan's perspective as to how an economy actually works." Raymaker and Whalon have demonstrated clearly and distinctly how Lonergan's economic theory overcomes post-Marxian and Post-Keynesian deficiencies. They have shown how this economic theory can advance the new social contract or "the Great Reset" the World Economic Forum initiated to address global relations and contemporary economic crises. Simply put, Raymaker and Whalon have offered Lonergan economic literacy to the emerging global nations. If ever an economist or philosopher or theologian wants an amalgam of Lonergan's works that makes good sense, this is it.

CYRIL ORJI
PROFESSOR OF SYSTEMATIC THEOLOGY
UNIVERSITY OF DAYTON, OHIO

Introduction

IF ECONOMISTS COULD GET THEMSELVES THOUGHT OF AS HUMBLE, COMPETENT PROFESSIONALS ON A LEVEL WITH DENTISTS—THAT WOULD BE SPLENDID.[1]

Every human community has an economy. It is a simple matter of survival: in the short term, it provides daily food and shelter; in the long term, it provides for the next generation. We transform the resources provided by our planet into those necessities specific to our community. The climate crisis—the one that encompasses all the other crises we are facing—is the result of the ways we humans exploit the earth's resources. In other words, our economies threaten the very survival that they should provide.

If the average temperature of the planet continues to rise, it will once again make our lives "nasty, brutish and short." Not just the very poor, for whom that slogan already applies today, but for the race as a whole. This has been increasingly clear since the early 1970s, when Richard Nixon created the *Environmental Protection* Agency. Fifty years later, the earth-warming process has almost reached the point of no return; we humans desperately need to reinvent our economics so as to change the processes by which we survive, and even thrive. This book points toward the wisdom we need so as to address the fundamental challenges facing all of humanity. While the present authors are what some might call religious professionals, we are not proposing a specifically Christian or even religious way forward. The wisdom we need in the present crisis is basic; it touches on economics and on two pressing issues.

First, we take stock of other crises that an inadequate economics has created. The stark divisions in the United States today point to how

---

1. John Maynard Keynes, *Essays in Persuasion*, quoted in Roger Farmer, *How the Economy Works* (Oxford University Press, 2014), 1.

hugely unequal levels of income have pitted us against one another—in the U.S. and across the world. The impact of the financial collapse of 2008 continues. It began with the ways central banks propped up the global economy with unparalleled flows of very cheap money—further complicating ways of combatting the deadly effects of the COVID-19 pandemic.

The second issue involves the present surge in inflation that shows how threadbare is the prevailing view of globalization: as supply lines backed up, demand has led to ever more inflation of our already shaky money.[2] People now increasingly distrust the "creditworthiness" of governments.[3] New thinking is necessary to address these crucial issues.

As distrust has grown, so has people's existential anxiety. Over and over, they have been let down by "authorities." Such figures as politicians, scientists, clergy, and journalists have been steadily losing credibility; this includes economists who have lost what clout they once had. There are many reasons for this. One is the repetition of boom/bust cycles that have adversely affected inordinate numbers of people. Most economists have been taken by surprise by such negative developments. On the other hand, the policies that often enable such events (think subprime mortgages) are blamed on them. Economists tend to be seen as puppet masters behind the scenes who often get their marionettes' strings tangled. "Economics is at its most influential in debates that are technical, far from the public eye, and most like 'fine-tuning' a policy instrument."[4]

Today, fewer and fewer people control the world's wealth. Oxfam International reported that in 2020, 153 billionaires in the world had more wealth than the 4.6 billion people making up 60 percent of the planet's

---

2. As of this writing in 2022 analysts are much worried about a spike in inflation which is driving up interest rates and cancelling any post-COVID global economic recovery. The Inflation Reduction Act signed into law by President Biden on Aug. 16, 2022, remains controversial due to, e. g., its calling for raising $222 billion from a 15% corporate minimum tax. See https://www.investopedia.com/inflation-reduction-act-of-2022-6362263

3. See, for example, https://www.govinfo.gov/content/pkg/GPO-FCIC/pdf/GPO-FCIC.pdf

4. Daniel Hirschman, Elizabeth Popp Berman, "Do economists make policies? On the political effects of economics," *Socio-Economic Review*, Volume 12, Issue 4, October 2014, 779–811: 800. https://doi.org/10.1093/ser/mwu017

population.[5] The 22 richest people in the world now have more wealth than all the women in Africa.[6] Industrialists brag about how "capitalism" has brought millions out of extreme poverty, which is true as far as it goes, but to go from surviving on $1.00 a day to $2.00 is not real progress. A majority of "boats" has risen a little, but no boats have risen in proportion to the huge rising tide of wealth limited to the very rich. The present world situation is undoing even those modest gains of the very poor.[7] There is also a large and growing class of people plagued with "negative wealth," more debt than assets—their assets being in illiquid real estate.[8] They have to work harder to stay ahead of the debt collectors: they have poorer health and are more likely to suffer mental illnesses or addictions to drugs, alcohol and gambling. The rise of new populist leaders promising quick fixes is directly connected to such misery.

Another cause of anxiety about the reliability of money today is so-called fiat money—currency backed by the nebulous "full faith and credit" of a government, or in the case of the Euro, by 19 governments.[9] The development of cryptocurrencies like Bitcoin and Ethereum that do not rely on other currencies or gold is a response to this. Climate change adds to all the other crises. The coronavirus pandemic has only poured more gasoline onto the fire. Among young people age 16 to 25, chronic dread about our planet's future has grown exponentially. This was confirmed in a September 2021 study, "Young People's Voices on Climate Anxiety, Government Betrayal and Moral Injury: A Global

---

5. www.oxfam.org/en/press-releases January 20, 2020.

6. "Wealth" defined as assets, including real estate, minus liabilities. Source: Oxfam, quoted at https://inequality.org/facts/global-inequality/#global-wealth-inequality

7. See Crédit Suisse's 2022 Global Wealth Report.https://www.credit-suisse.com/about-us/en/reports-research/global-wealth-report.html

8. The Federal Reserve's Distributional Financial Accounts data shows that America's top 1 percent holds more than half the national wealth invested in stocks and mutual funds. Most of the wealth of Americans in the bottom 90 percent comes from their homes—the asset category that took the biggest hit during the Great Recession.

9. Fiat money is a government's currency not backed by a commodity such as gold which gives central banks greater control over the economy because they can decide how much money is printed. We believe that what is needed is a monetary system automatically adaptable to the standard of living rather than a fiat one in which a currency's value, not based on any physical commodity, is allowed to fluctuate.

Phenomenon."[10] The relationships between economic policies, planetary environmental degradation and extinction of species has contributed to the overall loss of confidence. Many people have a deep dread as to what is awaiting us in the future.

And fear throttles intelligent thinking.

Only together can we humans remedy the situation, because it is together that we create the economies enabling us to survive. But whom can we trust? The world needs some fresh original thinking. We are writing to suggest that there are resources not yet tapped to help humanity face these interrelated crises. One such resource is Bernard Lonergan's *macroeconomic theory*,[11] a truly original approach to economics, one that seeks to give ordinary people as well as governmental and business leaders ways to organize their finances and economies more effectively, both locally (all economies are first of all local), and at regional, national and international levels. Lonergan's method for economics is partially reflected in his best-known work, *Insight: A Study in Human Understanding*, that helps people become aware of how their mind comes to know what is real.[12] His method, applied to a community of thinkers such as economists, can help them understand and revise in depth their presuppositions—enabling them to collaborate in effective ways that make a real difference. To survive and thrive in the long run we need to

---

10. Caroline Hickman, *The Lancet*, "Planet Health," Dec. 5, 2021. 59 % of respondents were very worried about climate change, rating governmental actions negatively.

11. Our comprehensive approach to Lonergan's lifework addresses toxic corporate policies. See https://functionalmacroenomics.com on efforts that parallel our own. Lonergan noted that ideal conditions whereby theory introduces some level of mutual comprehension is missing. Discontinuities arise. "The better educated become a class closed in upon themselves with no task proportionate to their training. They become effete. The less educated and the uneducated find themselves with a tradition that is beyond their means. . . . The meaning and values of life "are impoverished. The will to achieve slackens. Where once there were joys and sorrows, now there are just pleasures and pains. The culture has become a slum." *Method in Theology*, 1972, 99. *Collected Works of Bernard Lonergan*, vol. 14, (Univ. of Toronto, 1998), 95.

12. Bernard Lonergan, *Insight, A Study of Human Understanding, Collected Works of Bernard Lonergan*, vol. 3, (Univ. of Toronto, 2000). His economic studies antedate *Insight*, and inform it—a point stressed by Patrick Brown, "*Insight* as Palimpsest: The Economic Manuscripts in *Insight*," *The Lonergan Review* Volume 2, Issue 1, Spring 2010, 131–45.

be smarter but also wiser. Wisdom is what allows people to choose well when faced with alternatives: never in the history of the human race have we needed it more. Our book suggests two ways to move forward: first, by developing clear concrete thinking among individuals and communities of scholars such as economists; second, by reflecting on Lonergan's perspective as to how an economy actually works. These two concerns were at the center of Lonergan's lifework.

Despite the fact that Lonergan was a Jesuit, a Roman Catholic priest, this book is not about religious ideas about economics. It is, rather, an introduction to Lonergan's powerful epistemology and how this has affected his innovative economics. If we can think clearly together about our economies, we can improve our common lot, beginning with today's overarching challenge of caring for the climate. To continue blundering on this issue would be humanity's final undoing as a species.

Who is Bernard Lonergan?

Hailed by *Time* Magazine in 1970 as "the finest philosophic thinker of the 20th century,"[13] Lonergan today is remembered more as a theologian. While he certainly was an influential theologian, his own perspective was that his economics was his most important lifework. Despite the 12 Lonergan study centers around the world,[14] and the publication of the 25 volumes of his complete works,[15] Lonergan's influence today tends to be restricted to an informed circle of appreciative admirers. It may be that his thought was too forward-looking, too advanced for postmodern tastes. Yet. we are convinced that he has a lot to offer us in this time of vast inequalities in wealth, of impending climate disasters, of the collapse of some democracies into dictatorships, and of the proliferation of a vague dread that there is nothing to be done—other than the super-wealthy founding colonies for themselves to escape to Mars.

---

13. Cover, *Time* Magazine, April 20, 1970.

14. https://bclonergan.org/lonergan-links/

15. https://utorontopress.com/search-results/?series=collected-works-of-bernard-lonergan

Lonergan's macroeconomics stresses the primordial role of innovation in human progress, which is absolutely essential for dealing effectively with climate change and other threats to human flourishing. Initially, what spurred Lonergan on was his reaction to the Great Depression. Sent out into the streets of Montréal as a young Jesuit, he was shocked to meet some people he knew living on the streets in squalor and misery. He concluded that beyond the greed of individuals, what caused the crash was an ignorance of economic processes.[16] He spent the next twelve years studying economics. He then continued throughout his career to develop his unique perspectives. Besides his expertise in philosophy and theology, Lonergan was also a trained mathematician; he brought math's precision of thought to the task of rethinking economic processes. By 1944, he had finished his first essay on economics (now *CWL* 21) which begins:

> In the introduction to his *General Theory*, Mr. Keynes considers the objection that only the more intelligent type of expert is able to understand the highly abstract theorems of modern economics. His answer is not altogether satisfactory. He says that if practical men such as politicians and bankers and industrialists do not succeed in grasping the issues, then inevitably they will be eliminated. Undoubtedly they will, but so shall we, for they are our leaders.[17]

Lonergan concludes that the problem is clear:

> We cannot rely on the old political economy: it was democratic but has been found wrong. We cannot rely on the new economics: it is accurate but it can solve real problems only by eliminating democracy. What is needed is a new political economy that is free from the mistakes of the old, a democratic economics that can issue practical imperatives to plain men.[18]

---

16. Economic processes include actions that involve the extraction of raw materials and natural resources, as well as the production and sale of goods and services.

17. *For A New Political Economy, Collected Works of Bernard Lonergan*, vol. 21, (Univ. of Toronto, 1998), 3. (Hence *CWL* 21.) Lonergan is here quoting Keynes' *The General Theory of Employment, Interest and Money* (London: Macmillan, 1936), 10.

18. *CWL* 21, 5. By "plain men," he meant "ordinary people." We, writing almost 80 years after *CWL* 21, choose not to paraphrase his text in contemporary usage.

For the rest of his life, Lonergan worked on such "imperatives" for economics and for promoting individual and communal self-transcendence.[19]
His thought is profound; it is not easy to grasp, but it is always directed
toward the concrete, the real. Lonergan was conversant with quantum
physics and the theory of relativity, with the metaphysics of Aquinas and
of Hegel, and with the various schools of phenomenology. Yet, his interest was always focused on what has to be done if humanity is to flourish. The purpose of his economics, he once said, was to help ensure that
"widows and orphans won't starve."[20]

We intend to use Lonergan's macroeconomic analysis as a telling,
far-reaching example of his overall "general empirical method" (GEM)
which is a guide for people to "be attentive, be intelligent, be rational, be
responsible" in life. From this base that applies to individuals, Lonergan
developed a communal version focusing on "functional specialties" (FS),
published in 1972 as *Method in Theology* (*MiT*) and reissued in 1998 as *CWL*
14.[21] Our book combines the *generalized* aspects of Lonergan's method,
"GEM," with his functionally *specialized* (FS) approach in *MiT*. We designate
it as his breakthrough "GEM-FS" achievement.[22] In *MiT*, Lonergan argues
that thinkers are involved in an eightfold division of labor that begins with
research, moves into interpretation, studies histories, argues dialectically
toward a resolution embodied in foundations—a new horizon of basic con-
victions. This leads to fresh doctrines, directives, concepts, policies. These
then require a systematic treatment so as to communicate persuasively with
various audiences. This process then begins anew, always requiring that
each person or group practice being attentive, intelligent, reasonable, and

19. We argue that without self-transcending commitments of some sort, Lonergan's
method cannot be implemented in ways profound enough to redirect present human situations wounded by a self-centered fallen human nature.

20. Quoted in Patrick H. Byrne, "*Ressentiment* and the Preferential Option for the
Poor," *Theological Studies* 54 (1993), 241.

21. *MiT* expands on *Insight*'s study of how individual minds work. It gives a paradigm
for how theologians ought to think collaboratively, but it *is* applicable to other fields of
study. Indeed, when *MiT* appeared in 1972, major theologians criticized it for not really
being theology. We explore and apply *MiT* below in Parts III and IV.

22. John Raymaker, in his books on Lonergan, came up with a "GEM-FS" abbrevia-
tion as a shorthand way of characterizing Lonergan' work in *Insight* and *MiT*.

xxvi   "ATTENTIVE, INTELLIGENT, RATIONAL, AND RESPONSIBLE"

responsible. *Insight* tends to focus on individual persons' rather than groups' development—a focus we extend to groups of thinkers by closely examining and developing *MiT*'s functional approach in two phases.

What is original in Lonergan's economics is that, in conjunction with the method developed in *Insight* and *MiT*, his economics also distinguishes between *knowing* facts and *understanding* facts:

> The facts of the macroeconomy are . . . well known. What is lacking is a clear and precise understanding of the mechanism behind such obvious facts as the relations between expansion and contraction of the economy, employment and unemployment . . . and many other things that are just common knowledge.[23]

We try to apply GEM-FS to Lonergan's two books on economic processes by "sandwiching" the breakthroughs of his better-known *Insight* and *MiT within* the 39-year time period of his two published works on economics, the first in 1944, the second in 1983.[24] Our book is only an introduction to Lonergan's breakthrough method; we only seek to whet readers' appetite for uncovering the rich resources for human flourishing that Bernard Lonergan developed.

Lonergan's Radical Generalization of Economics[25]

Lonergan's dynamic economics model begins with the seemingly obvious fact that all human communities have an economy enabling them

---

23. *Macroeconomic Dynamics: An Essay in Circulation Analysis, Collected Works of Bernard Lonergan*, vol. 15, (University of Toronto Press, 1999), 12. (Hereafter *CWL* 15).

24. One difficulty with correctly understanding Lonergan's macroeconomics is that his two published works on economics, *For A New Political Economy* (University of Toronto Press, 1998: hereafter *CWL* 21), and *CWL* 15, *Macroeconomic Dynamics: An Essay in Circulation Analysis*, were only put together by different groups of his students after his death in 1984. The former manuscript dates from 1944, the latter from his years of teaching economics at Boston College (1976–1983). In between, he wrote *Insight* and *MiT*. There are thus some peculiarities in *CWL* 15, 21 due to the time gap between them and the fact that the books were edited by different editors.

25. The editors of *CWL* 15, page 19, posit that Lonergan's radical generalization of economics "is grounded in a structure of consciousness" which we identify and systematically develop in our GEM-FS approach.

to survive. Their economy supports and influences their culture. He then proposes a "radical generalization"[26] about *all* economies, from hunter-gatherer subsistence economies to modern forms of capitalism, socialism, communism. The generalization is possible because "the productive process itself contains implicit criteria. If these criteria are unknown or ignored, things may go from bad to worse. As many now know, this scenario has already occurred,"[27]—over and over, in fact! Our book presents a condensed version of Lonergan's view on economics with as little mathematics as possible. (In our appendices we do delve into his mathematics for interested readers.) Our hope is that economists will be intrigued enough to investigate further and that other readers will find the thought of Lonergan a source of renewed hope. In this period of history when life and the earth itself face so many threats, a wisdom that can guide resolute action —informed by sound thinking about concrete challenges—has never been more necessary. Bernard Lonergan's time has come!

---

26. Lonergan, *CWL 15*, 9. "Because analysis is an ongoing process, it is subject to revision. In the measure that revision is radical, it involves new concepts and even new definitions . . . The fact of revision displaces the old reliance on essential definitions and gives way to a search for significant basic variables."

27. *CWL 15*, 4.

PART I

Universal Values and Lonergan's Transformational Horizon at the Heart of his Economics

HOW TO EFFECTIVELY APPLY AND EXPAND LONERGAN'S BREAKTHROUGHS IN METHOD

We have set a vast agenda for ourselves: to link Lonergan's writings on the economy with his breakthrough analyses in *Insight*, *MiT* and other works. These can be boiled down to the slogan, "Be attentive, be intelligent, be rational, be responsible." Lonergan argued persuasively that in order to exercise those concretely, "conversion" is needed. We are *not* talking about religious conversions as such nor do we contend that economics can only be reformed by the religiously converted. Rather, what Lonergan meant by "conversion" is an *exercise in freedom*. We will explain this more fully below. Moreover, we shall argue that there is a need for two more "conversions" in GEM-FS, namely, economic and environmental turnarounds.[1]

Recalling historical facts that shaped the major 19th century developments in economic theory and the reactions of Christian leaders to these, we shall examine the tragedies that *mere technical* interpretations of economic policies have provoked. In the main, after Adam Smith there have arisen two opposed (and complex) approaches to economics:

§ Leon Walras (1834–1910) was one of the first economists to apply mathematical techniques, such as simultaneous equations to the economic universe; he was also an early proponent of the marginal utility theory of value. Such a detached but inhuman approach to economics and finance has been one of the means of provoking economic disasters that have adversely affected the poor in rich and developing lands.

§ On the other hand, socialist-communist contentions were modified by the pioneering efforts of the 19th century Protestant Social Gospel and

---

1. We will use the terms "conversion" and "turnaround" interchangeably, since we are concerned that our readers grasp Lonergan's specialized meaning of "conversion" rather than its all too common pejorative use. *The Economics of Happiness*, a 2011 documentary, covers key impacts of globalization on societies, local economies, cultures and ecosystems. It provides ample evidence of the socio-environmental costs of industrialized agriculture and the carbon-intensive global circulation of food. It highlights pressing economic issues such as forced competition and de-regulation, growing indebtedness and the continued subsidization of unsustainable agricultural practices. It challenges the persistent use of economic growth.

of Pope Leo XIII; these gave rise to attempts to apply Christian values and ethics to societal problems.

Taking into account these two approaches to economics,[2] we shall explore and re-evaluate some radical accounts of the history of debt and slavery such as those of David Graeber.[3] We first call attention to Pope Francis' encyclical, *Fratelli Tutti,* and other initiatives.[4] The pontiff has insisted on the need to respond to injustices. In both the 19th and 20th centuries caring leaders have argued that humans need a deeper understanding of economic theories so that they can take concrete actions to improve the situations of the marginalized.

We underscore Lonergan's *implicit* goal of applying ethics to economic processes. As noted, his own interest in economic policy went back to his student days. He was stimulated by a course on ethics in the early 1930's taught by Lewis Watt, the author of *Capitalism and Morality.*[5] Watt was interested in applying the teachings of Pope Leo XIII's social encyclical, *Rerum Novarum,*[6] to the English scene:

Watt related moral principles to what he considered the necessary and ironclad laws of economics. Lonergan was outraged by the way these

---

2. While some observers prefer to contrast positive economics (describing and seeking to explain various economic phenomena) with normative economics, we prefer our own twofold distinction due to the fact that we stress the ethical value aspects of economics.

3. David Graeber, *Debt: The First Five Thousand Years* (New York: Melville, 2013), 331, writes that Hobbes may have been "the opening salvo of the new" devastating moral perspective. When his *Leviathan* came out in 1685, it is not clear what scandalized its readers more: its relentless materialism (Hobbes saw people as basically machines whose actions could be understood by a single principle: that they tended to move toward the prospect of pleasure and away from the prospect of pain), or its resultant cynicism. If love, amity, and trust are such powerful forces, Hobbes asked, "why is it that even within our families, we lock our most valuable possessions in strongboxes?"

4. https://www.vatican.va/content/francesco/en/encyclicals/documents/papa-francesco_20201003_enciclica-fratelli-tutti.html. *Francis published Praedicate evangelium on March 19, 2022 to reorganize and reform the Roman Curia.*

5. Lewis Watt, S. J. *Capitalism and Morality* (London: Cassel & Co., 1929).

6. Maurice Schepers, "Lonergan on the Person and the Economy; Reaching up to the mind of Aquinas," *New Blackfriars*, June 23, 2011, parallels our own goal in this text. As does Schepers, we try to respond to the two-fold challenge emergent in both the object (to promote genuine development in the economic order) and the subject (to work out a coherent explanation of the structure of the human good.)

"necessary and ironclad laws" of economics led British policy-makers to believe that it would have been morally wrong for England to violate the market's laws of supply and demand in order to relieve the Irish famine.[7]

It is due to obvious contradictions in economic policies that have haunted our divided world that we seek to integrate[8] Lonergan's two volumes on economics[9] within the method developed in *Insight* and *Method in Theology*. We do so by reviewing the overall dimensions of Lonergan's work while suggesting ways to apply these dimensions to economic processes—taking into account the evolution of economic theories and practices from the time of Adam Smith to the present.[10] We seek to discern with Lonergan valid alternatives to modern

---

7. Quoted in the "Editors Introduction," to *CWL* 15, xxviii. Lonergan favored government policies that aim at such broad goals as developing (1) within general educational and cultural opportunities, people's economic understanding and their ability to produce; (2) viable economic and social infrastructures. He wanted to facilitate the entry of new businesses of all sizes into production and to ensure that the reinvestment of profits is as broad and as efficient as possible. While governmental and corporate bureaucracies are needed for stable societies, Lonergan notes the limitations of bureaucratic policies. He warned against the harm done by sustained government deficits that are caused by excess imports, exports or international financial flows. In his article "Healing and Creating in History," he calls for creativity on the part of individuals and groups to bring renewal and cultural change so that economic growth will equitably benefit one and all.

8. See McShane, "Grade 12 Economics: A Common Quest Manifesto," in *The Road to Religious Reality* (Axial Press 2012) 60.

9. *CWL* 15 examines anew fundamental variables in economics. It breaks from centralist theory and practice towards a radically democratic perspective on surplus income and non-political control. It explores more fully the ideas introduced in *For a New Political Economy, CWL 21*. McShane and Michael Shute have both treated Lonergan's economics functionally but not systematically *as a process* as we are attempting to do.

10. The 1929 depression was a stimulus for Lonergan's economic research. He read the prominent economists of his day, focusing particularly on Schumpeter's *Theory of Economic Development and Business Cycle*s. This convinced him of the need to explain booms, slumps and crashes in the business cycle. We intend to derive the relevant moral precepts that apply to Lonergan's two volumes on economics. Lonergan drew from the insights of Michal Kalecki and Joan Robinson, two post-Keynesian economists who have had a major impact on economics. On the relation between Robinson and Kalecki's Marxian approach in such areas as investment and innovation, see Peter Kriesler and Geoffrey Harcourt, *Australian School of Business Research*, no. 2010, Econ. 21, Oct. 2009. Robinson was the first to describe macroeconomics as the "theory of output as a whole." We are writing in 2022 when the world is undergoing a series of crises: a war in Ukraine, a pandemic, violent riots

theories on macroeconomics and social movements such as those fore-shadowed by Thorstein Veblen (1857–1929) and Joseph Schumpeter (1883–1950).

Veblen's and Schumpeter's Respective Theories of the Leisure Class and Economic Innovation

Veblen is known for his attempts to imagine a different economy. He espoused a theory that marks a dividing line between classical and modern economics. His lifelong quest was to "marry productivity, technological expertise, scientific advancement, and serviceability to the community." He tried to "update the immigrant farming experience for the industrial age . . . (to) keep the communal spirit of the former while adding the technological wonders of the latter."[11] But such an "updating" by way of digital technology has yet to effectively happen.[12]

Lonergan was most influenced by Schumpeter who is known for his creative-destruction (*schöpferische Zerstörung*) approach to economics—sometimes denoted as "Schumpeter's gale." Schumpeter derived this forceful notion from the work of Karl Marx, but he popularized it as a theory of economic innovation and of the business cycle. According to Schumpeter, the "gale of creative destruction" describes the "process of industrial mutation that continuously revolutionizes the economic structure from within, incessantly destroying

---

in cities across America and even in the halls of the Capitol as well as deadly forest fires and mass flooding. There is an urgent need for global stakeholders to cooperate in this age of crises. The World Economic Forum at its 50th annual meeting in 2020 initiated "The Great Reset" meant to address future global relations, the direction of national economies, societal priorities, and the nature of business models. The Great Reset proposes a new social contract to honor every person's dignity. See www.weforum.org/great-reset. We aim to support this initiative by arguing for the need of economics and environmental conversions or turnarounds.

11. Paul Gleason, "Imagining a Different Economy," March 21, 2021, in *Los Angeles Review of Books*.

12. For possible ways to link Veblen and Lonergan, see Neil Niman, "The Allure of Alternate Reality (and other Games: Toward an Updated Theory of the Leisure Class") *History of Economic Society, Sage Journals*, 2013. Without mentioning Veblen, Lonergan spent years lecturing and writing on how devise an economy that is just.

the old one, incessantly creating a new one."[13] In a way, Lonergan's life work, including his two volumes on macroeconomics (*CWL* 15, 21), is that of a "creative reconstruction"; it stresses the *need of living authentic lives* and of cooperating[14] with those who seek the good. This book attempts to reconcile the processes of the human mind and of communal life with the economic productive processes studied by Lonergan.[15] Lonergan's holistic method can help humanity act in caring, socially-engaged ways so as to transcend the dehumanizing effects of a technology-dominated world. Ursula Le Guin has summarized such abusive processes:

> Technology is the active human interface with the material world. But the word is consistently misused to mean only the enormously complex and specialized technologies of the past few decades, supported by massive exploitation both of natural and human resources.[16]

It is to help undo the exploitation of natural and human resources that we advocate the need for six GEM-FS "conversions" to include two "glocal,"[17] societal (socio-communal) turnarounds based on *CWL* 15, 21 to complement the personal conversions Lonergan stressed in *Insight* and other writings.

---

13. https://en.wikipedia.org/wiki/neoliberalism

14. Lonergan, *Third Collection* (Paulist Press, 1985), 5, 213.

15. Raymaker, *Bernard Lonergan's Method and a Medical Doctor's Approach to Healthcare* (Eugene, OR: Wipf and Stock, 2021) applies Lonergan's lifework as an interdisciplinary process method. It anticipates aspects of this book.

16. https://conversations.e-flux.com/t/ursula-k-le-guin-a-rant-about-technology/3977

17. The word "glocal" stems from Manfred Lange, head of the German National global Change Secretariat, who used it in reference to Heiner Benking's exhibit, "Blackbox Nature: Rubik's Cube of Ecology." John Raymaker's *Pope Francis, Conscience of the World, Building Bridges in a Trouble World*, co-written with Gerald Grudzen (Hamilton Books, 2020) stresses the reality of a glocal economy and its important implications.

Craig Maginnness, *Go Glocal: the Definitive Guide to International Markets* (Lioncrest, 2016), as the title implies, uses "glocal" to focus on profit *not* on ethics as we do. Lonergan's opus implies the need for six turnarounds (six "conversions")—a need which we seek to spell out in Parts III and IV.

Ethically Buttressing Lonergan's *"Transforming Light"*

So as to develop our argument for the need of six GEM-FS turnarounds, we now address two important issues: 1) how to discern[18] what should be done in a world full of injustices? 2) how to help bring about transformations that would benefit all humans? Lonergan is hardly unique in the concern he showed for humanity. Pope Francis' 2020 Encyclical *Fratelli Tutti* is a powerful example of such a concern. But Lonergan is unique in that he devised an integral method to help humans overcome injustices by implementing equitable policies. However, this requires adapting to the "iron laws" of economics.

Richard Liddy, in his *Transforming Light: Intellectual Conversion in the Early Lonergan* notes that Lonergan after his studies of Aristotle and Aquinas in his twenties, "could not just ignore the all-pervasive presence of the sciences in the modern world."[19] Liddy explores Lonergan's pioneering work in economics but does not fully integrate his life-long efforts to address social-concern issues in transformative ways. We aim to interpret Lonergan's two volumes on economics from an ethical standpoint,[20] within the perspective of his career. These two volumes were written *as the enclosing elements* of what we call a *glocal*, dynamic, transformational ethical *"sandwich"*[21] that in principle can help feed the

---

18. Patrick Byrne's *The Ethics of Discernment: Lonergan's Foundations for Ethics*. (Univ. of Toronto, 2017) has many helpful insights into discerning but leaves out economics.

19. Liddy, *Transforming Light*, (Collegeville MN: Liturgical Press, 1993) 149.

20. Jim Morrin and Howard Richards write in their "The Ethical Reconstruction of Economics," *Lonergan Review* 2010_ 0002_0001_0245_0260pdf, 258: "Lonergan's economics requires and facilitates a cultural shift to overcome illusions and restore the authority of reason. Its point . . . can only be grasped within an intellectual framework where human agency is ordered toward ethically valid ends, and in in which rational deliberation in general is ordered toward making responsible decisions." Lonergan begins his "Dialectic of Authority," *A Third Collection*, 5 with the words: "Authority is legitimate power. . . . The source of power is cooperation. . . . The authorities are the officials to whom certain powers (have been) delegated. But authority belongs to the community that has a common field of experience, a common and complementary ways of understanding, common judgements and common aims." It is authenticity that legitimizes power. The same might be said about the authority of economists.

21. Our sandwich approach to GEM-FS is on the analogy of heart and brain—hoping that the two will converge in needed reforms. Just as the heart is a vital organ, while the

world adequately. An important aspect of this is that Lonergan's lifework can only be effective to the extent that the enclosing economic elements (*CWL* 21 and 15) of the "sandwich" be taken as seriously as have been the better-known "fillings" of the "sandwich" (*Insight* and *MiT*). The outer economics *needs* a philosophically-grounded ethical method to be effective.[22] In effect, ours is an "inter-active sandwich" mediating between Lonergan's writings on economics, knowledge and ethics. Our "GEM-FS sandwich approach" presupposes the four personal conversions of *Insight* and *MiT*. But these four, we argue, require *two more communal ethical* turnarounds to help achieve needed glocal reforms in economic and environmental policies. Remedying the oversights in ethics that have stultified economics is a needed preliminary for applying the range of Lonergan's work in *CWL* 15 and 21. Both volumes point toward a need of revising environmental-economic policies to reinforce GEM-FS's overall thrust. We seek to develop that unexplored implication. Our sandwiching efforts occur in Parts III and IV of our text whereby we first dialectically identify the need for changes in economics and its theories; we then suggest foundational ways of doing so.

Holistic Hints from Phil McShane and Terry Quinn

The late Phil McShane wrote us in July 2018 that the time is ripe for a fresh effort in Lonergan studies, and for a new core shift in economics. This "is heuristically much clearer to me now through my laboriously revised structuring of the *lean-forward meaning* of theology" and its "twofold relevance."[23] Our own fresh start in interpreting Lonergan's

---

brain and nerves are a critical organ system, so Lonergan managed to build bridges between sound philosophies and sound policies. There are other analogies we could use to describe the convergence of heart and brain in Lonergan's lifework. *Insight* but especially *MiT* touch on the *heart* of humans "*embodied*" within the "brain" of economic structures explained in *CWL* 15 and 21. GEM-FS upholds the moral precepts of biblical and other sacred writings promoting the dignity of all persons.

22. To a certain extent we accept a laconic saying attributed to Mark Twain: "When the rich rob the poor it's called business. When the poor fight back it's called violence." Our GEM-FS approach avoids this in favor of a viable alternative.

23. See https://www.philipmcshane.org/tinctures/ referring to *Insight*, 766.

economics from a GEM-FS stance, is made within the full context of Lonergan's opus. If today's economic theories are wanting in theoretical and ethical depth, our exploration of Lonergan's economics is partly beholden to McShane's views. With him we see the "need to enlighten *those still stuck in the rut* of "Aristotelian Lonerganism." On a positive note, McShane praised John Benton's site *Bent on Futurology* which can help people reach into the component of "Effective Intervention in the Historical Process."[24] Sadly, on the negative side, McShane recalled that Lonergan failed to have any direct effect in economics in the mid-1940s up to the very end of his life. Now, "We need full international togetherness, as well as 'theories of everything'. Our mistake is not thinking *up* that way."[25]

Terry Quinn has also taken up McShane's challenge. In a shared message, Quinn wrote to McShane that he was following up on his suggestion that economics be part of contemporary religious efforts: "To help get interest going in the new standard model, John Benton and I think that there is a great need of new kinds of locally-and-globally-informed communications efforts to reach various audiences. I am thinking of new kinds of outreach and of 'bearing fruit' not yet worked out but envisioned by Lonergan in *MiT* Chapter 14."

By "sandwiching" Lonergan's twin achievements we primarily refer to the positive side of this book's overall aim. Before touching on the negative side of our sandwich approach, let us note that Lonergan did not view the economic laws that he unveiled (such as his central distinction between the flows of money and credit to investment or consumption) as being *per se* ethical. Still, it is only by reaching its maximum efficiency, he wrote, that an economy can provide for all "with a generous

---

24. Lonergan, *Phenomenology and Logic, CWL*, 18, 306.

25. McShane in a personal message to us. Misinterpretations of economic processes, which Lonergan early on detected, impede reforms of economic systems. Our GEM-FS sandwich interpretation of economics, a precise yet open-ended process, will address imprecisions in due course. It brings into focus inadequate philosophical theories that have failed to understand what transpires in an economy. Abraham Lincoln, Gandhi and Nelson Mandela embodied in their lives geo-political turnarounds adequate to meet head-on otherwise insolvable injustices. They were reformed reformers par excellence, as had been St. Ignatius of Loyola.

hand."[26] Generosity is indeed a desirable trait, but Lonergan knew that humans have to adapt to the inflexible laws of economics, rather than the other way around.[27] The question is how to avoid booms and slumps while raising the standard of living? Generosity can help bring some people out of poverty but not all. Lonergan was indeed influenced by biblical models. The Old Testament prophets asserted that God's blessing would bring about a good standard of living for all. Isaiah's vision of the new earth to come is one of a peaceful, plenteous life, with hearth and home, children, food and drink, and satisfying work (Is. 65:17–23). Observing God's commandments would lead to good economic results, but only if the people acknowledged that all good things come from God (Deut. 28: 11–14). Jesus' teachings reiterate these precepts.

Universal Values and Transformational Horizons[28]

With Lonergan, we are searching for an economics that will ethically raise everyone's standard of living. A comparison may help. Although a main goal of painting is to depict the beautiful in life, artists must occasionally touch on the tragic facts of life. In like manner, we seek to outline both the ideals and the realities of life Lonergan outlined in his writings.[29] In the *outer* facets of our "Lonerganian GEM-FS sandwich" (*CWL* 15 and 21), we examine the various ways Lonergan addressed

---

26. *CWL 21*, 36. In the view of Maurice Schepers, https://www.jstor/stable/43251599, "Lonergan generated a method that meets the exigencies" of a world on the move.

27. This assertion is controversial, of course. That it is shows the extent of the challenge. Those who rightly advocate for economic justice seem to think that economies can be refashioned to achieve that end. Others who seem to understand that the laws of economics must be respected also sweep away such concerns, and show how unrealistic they are as well: economies are above all human.

28. This implies that an economy that is not democratically controlled must be reformed.

29. This goal includes trying to help move communities of thinkers and doers from ungrounded idealisms to *GEM-FS grounded ideals* achieved when people appropriate their basic operations first personally, then interpersonally. Any effort to domesticate economics requires that participants reach deep within themselves and reach out as did, for example, Henry George and Thich Nhat Han.

economic processes, including its dysfunctions. The inner core of our "sandwich" traces ethical ways to remedy dysfunctions. It is important in interpreting Lonergan's lifework to study how his views on the economy, philosophy and theology interface and how these are to be applied in consistent ways. We intend to stress the overlooked ethical implications of his cognitional theory which can be used to critique and urge reforms of capitalist greed,[30] as well as of socialist governments' over-regimentation. The other equally important aspect of our strategic use of the sandwich metaphor refers to *the negative side of reality* such as the fact that today many people, even entire societies, are *trapped by existing forms of unjust* socio-economic situations[31] in which they are caught willy-nilly.

Insight and *MiT* focus on intellectual, moral and religious "conversions." Robert Doran later convinced Lonergan of a need for a "psychic conversion."[32] These four conversions call for changes in a person's conscious direction, away from the trivialization of human life. Often, the harshness of life arises "from the ruthless exercise of power [leading] to despair about human welfare springing from the conviction that

---

30. For Adrial Fitzgerald, realizing a just social order will depend on a minority of persons truly converted and receptive to the promptings of grace—organizing a critical mass of the population to enact non-violent economic stoppages. Resumption of needed mass economic activity would depend on economic restructurings for the ecologically sustainable distribution of what is required for everyone to enjoy a decent standard of living. Since initiatives like "the Great Reset" and "COPS26" propose to mitigate existing social injustices and their ruinous ecological consequences by reforming rather than supplanting capitalism, they may be interpreted as naïve, empty gestures designed to undo or significantly deflate mounting criticism. Our proposals for environmental and economic reforms seek to address Fitzgerald's stern challenge.

31. Nelson D. Schwartz, *The Velvet Rope Economy: how Inequality Became Big Business* (Doubleday, 2020) describes how elites use their status to exclude those of lesser means in all facets of life—leading to divided "communities." Pierre Whalon writes that "If the global economy continues on its present course, there will be a much worse crash than in 2008, or 1929. A concomitant environmental crash will accompany it. To avoid such a catastrophe will require that the biblical norm of a standard of living for all be the benchmark of the maximization of macroeconomic efficiency." Having described the current staggering growth of income inequality, and how the forces creating it are also endangering earth's climate, Whalon discusses the failures of economic theories to guide leaders and the rest of us in making needed, reasonable financial decisions.

32. See William A. Matthews, *Lonergan's Quest: A Study of Desire in the Authoring of Insight* (Univ. of Toronto Press, 2005), 407.

the universe is absurd."[33] Lonergan uses the metaphor of horizon—what concerns people and what they know. What is outside one's horizon is "simply outside the range of one's knowledge and interests: one neither knows nor cares. [...] A horizontal exercise is a decision or choice that takes place within an established horizon."[34] There is also a vertical exercise of freedom by which a new horizon arises. It can be "notably deeper and broader and richer" and still be "consonant with the old and a development out of its potentialities." Lonergan adds that

> The movement into a new horizon involves an about-face; it comes out of the old by repudiating characteristic features; it begins a new sequence that can keep revealing ever greater depth and breadth and wealth. Such an about-face and new beginning is what is meant by conversion. Conversion may be intellectual or moral or religious . . . each is a different type of event and has to be considered in itself.[35]

An intellectual conversion happens when a person rejects "the myth that knowing is like looking . . . and that the real is what is out there now to be looked at."[36] To the contrary, knowing is a compound of experiencing, understanding, judging, and deciding: "The reality known is not just looked at; it is given in experience, organized and extrapolated by understanding, posited in judgment and belief." This conversion acquires "the mastery in one's house that is to be had only when one knows precisely what one is doing when one is knowing."[37]

As our knowledge of the real grows to include human realities, and as we start to cherish human values such as fairness and justice, "we move to that existential moment when we discover for ourselves that our choosing affects ourselves no less than the chosen or rejected objects,

33. *MiT*, 105. (*CWL* 14, 101).

34. *The Lonergan Reader*, Edited by Mark and Elizabeth Morelli, (University of Toronto Press, 1997), 519, 521.

35. *Lonergan Reader*; 521.

36. *MiT*, 238; *CWL* 14, 223. Richard Rorty, *Philosophy and The Mirror of Nature* (Princeton University Press, 1979), 13–14, calls this myth the "Greek ocular metaphor."

37. *MiT*, 239–40. *CWL* 14, 225.

and that it is up to each one to decide for self what he is make of him-self . . . then moral conversion consists of opting for the truly good, even for value against satisfaction when value and satisfaction conflict." That requires continual self-scrutiny of our "intentional responses to values and their implicit scales of preference . . . to listen to criticism and to protest. One has to remain ready to learn from others." Moral knowing is not the same as intellectual knowing; it is attained only by moral persons. "Until one has merited that title, one still has to advance and to learn."[38]

What Lonergan meant by "religious conversion" is not what today's popular images often suggest, namely, a surrender of one's intellect and conscience to some organized religion's irrational dogmas and its manip-ulative leaders. Rather, for him, conversions are *liberations* from error, injustice, hatred and their underlying ideologies. "Religious" conversion is not limited to Christians but it refers to all those who discover them-selves a new horizon, being grasped by concern for others as well as for self. "It is an otherworldly falling in love," coming to view self and others with a transformative "eye of love."[39]

As to Robert Doran's addition of a psychic conversion to Loner-gan's three, the word "psychic" does not refer to its popular meaning of extra-sensory perception, but to the *psyche*, to the life of our feelings: sensation, imagination, fear, delight, joy, sadness, etc., and their relation to our active questioning in order to understand, to judge whether our understanding relates to reality, to taking responsibility for our knowl-edge by acting upon it. Feelings are involved in both modes of being human, of course; yet, in trying to understand, we must push our feel-ings to the background. Psychic conversion helps one exercise one's free-dom through questioning, judging and being responsible—discovering oneself in oneself.[40] Such work will lead to healing which will radiate into all the hard work of the other conversions. It will deeply affect how one lives in the company of others. Before going into detail as to what we

---

38. Lonergan, *Early Works in Theological Method, CWL* 1, Vol. 1, 565.

39. Lonergan was here influenced by William Johnston's use of "the eye of love."

40. *See* Doran, Psychic conversion in "From the Discovery of Lonergan to Psychic Conversion," 1974, Boston College, Lonergan Workshop, 1–49.

mean by conversions in environmental and economic policies—which depend and complement the other four conversions—we shall outline Lonergan's key breakthroughs in cognitional theory, epistemology, and metaphysics. These are needed to underpin and help remedy the societal decline of which Lonergan was quite aware. Far from being a Pollyanna, Lonergan wrote of decline's deeper level:

> Not only do inattention, obtuseness, unreasonableness, irresponsibility produce objectively absurd situations. Not only do ideologies corrupt minds. But compromise and distortion discredit progress. Objectively absurd situations do not yield to treatment. Corrupt minds have a flair for picking the mistaken solution and insisting that it alone is intelligent, reasonable, good. Imperceptibly the corruption spreads from the harsh sphere of material advantage and power to the mass media, the stylish journals, the literary movements, the educational process, the reigning philosophies. A civilization in decline digs its own grave with a relentless consistency. It cannot be argued out of its self-destructive ways, for argument has a theoretical major premise, theoretical premises are asked to conform to matters of fact, and the facts in the situation produced by decline more and more are the absurdities that proceed from inattention, oversight, unreasonableness and irresponsibility.[41]

As for economics, we shall start with some indisputable facts that characterize all economies. Lonergan's revolutionary interpretation of economic processes is a telling example of the validity of his overall method. His GEM-FS procedure is a "bridging catalyst" able to develop an effective economic theory that will give nations and the

---

41. Lonergan, *MiT*, 54–55. *CWL* 14, 53–54. Lonergan analyzed history in terms of progress, decline, and redemption; this quote reflects his realism. Mendo Castro Henriques, "The Lonerganian Revolution in the Understanding of Scientific Research," www:ijcr.eu/ articole/324_02%20Mendo% 20Castro%20 Henriques.pdf writes, "The requirements of a scientific culture cannot be solved by technical instruction. A technician is someone who solves an immediate problem without grasping the complexity of the underlying theoretical process that precede his or her intervention." Lonergan early on realized that the only way to overcome this dilemma is to reexamine the principles of philosophy, economics and theology; we aim to track how he reexamined so as to reintegrate these principles.

global economy tools to bring about the kind of economy that can promote the welfare of both humanity and the earth. This would require that leaders of firms and governments collaborate. Their willingness would be an integral part of a policy turnaround in economics pioneered by Lonergan. First, Lonergan's message must be heard. With Lonergan, we echo Christian social teachings on economic justice. The outer and inner dynamics of our "GEM-FS sandwich" complement and reinforce one another. The inner dynamics explore an ethical praxis to be applied to the economics developed in *CWL* 15 and *CWL* 21.[42] Lonergan's later more detailed approach to ethics was due to his wanting to help people better understand the events that led to the Great Depression of 1929 in specifically economic terms. *CWL* 15 examines such key questions as 1) what is a just family wage for workers; 2) the capitalist process and what Marxists call "realizing surplus," (the difference between the value that living labor creates in production and the wages paid to workers); 3) how capitalists earn a higher profit due to innovations. The innovations motivate new higher rates of investment which lead to increasing rates of capital stock production. However, implicit in this process, are "the unfolding possibilities of recession, depression, or (in Marxist terms) crisis with greater or lesser convulsions . . . even the devastation of the organs of finance."[43]

Our stance complements Gerald Whelan's *Redeeming History: Social Concern in Bernard Lonergan and Robert Doran*. In his review of Whalen's book, Patrick Brown makes two points. First, it is "a biographical account of Lonergan's social concern . . . (but is not a) 'fully-unified

---

42. Lonergan's method, we argue, radically revises Cartesian, Kantian and postmodern presuppositions; based on that radical reform, *CWL* 15, 21 can both be used to foster an ethic that can effectively address the problems holding humans in various forms of unethical economic bondage.

43. *CWL* 15, xliv. The late Phil McShane wrote us that "business people should recognize the need for building in turnover-frequencies in organizing credit etc. Establishment economists are locked into their gross mistakes. A major problem is that most people want to leap to consequences of the basics of philosophy, when what is needed is a macroeconomics that respects both the facts of production and the conducting of good business. We are a long way from a global ethic that parallels the gear-shift car. We are in a world of idiot drivers pretending that progress and well-being (are) a matter of pressing on in first gear, over-heating the engine."

amalgam of both' for it is, too abbreviated and strategically selective to be a full-scale intellectual biography and yet too ambitious and detailed to be a mere overview.[44] *Redeeming History* stresses that Lonergan's life-work was animated by a profound social concern that anticipated what is now known as "the option for the poor." This point may seem implausible to those exposed only to survey-level treatments of *Insight* and *MiT*. But to those who have struggled with Lonergan's writings on history and sociology from the 1930s, or with his two volumes on macroeconomics, it becomes luminously clear that Lonergan's efforts—what he achieved in the realm of theory *"were for the sake of a deepened and ever-more refined type of . . . praxis."*[45] Lonergan's overall theory-praxis[46] method includes his efforts to help free humanity from mistaken economic theories so that the liberating praxis of *Insight* and *MiT* may be realized through the self-transcending efforts of those of good will. Brown's second point is that what is specific to Lonergan's driving social concern is not just the normal Christian concern for improving the condition of those reduced to poverty due to unjust social structures. It is also a form of concern seeking a shift of specifically Roman Catholic social thought away from commonsense eclecticism appropriate to a pre-industrial age into the mode of a rigorous contemporary economic theory. As Lonergan once observed:

> Whether we like it or not, the world has got beyond the stage where concrete problems can be solved merely in the concrete. Economics supplies us with the most palpable example . . . Ideas . . . will build you a shanty but not a house and still less a skyscraper.[47]

---

44. Patrick Brown's review of Gerard Whelan, *Redeeming History* in *Journal of Jesuit Studies*, 2015, Volume 2, Issue 3, 544–46.

45. Brown, in his review of *Redeeming*. "Praxis," activities structured by theory, seeks to consistently integrate one's behavior in view of one's faith and/or beliefs.

46. We later link Lonergan's insights into Christian praxis with his other concerns. Here, we stress that Lonergan's interest in history enabled him to devise a unique trajectory that helped him reach solutions for many issues we address. See also John Raymaker, *Theory-Praxis of Social Ethics: the Complementarity between Bernard Lonergan's and Gibson Winter's Theological Foundations.* (Marquette University, PhD thesis, 1977).

47. Quoted in Brown's review of *Redeeming*, 545.

Or, as Lonergan remarked in 1973, the basic step in helping the poor "is a matter of spending one's nights and days in a deep and prolonged study of economic analysis."[48] Lonergan's "option for the poor," one might say, "was the far-sighted one of working out an explanatory science of economics designed to restructure economic understanding and practice in quite determinate ways with quite distinct moral implications."[49] Brown concludes that the narrative unity of Whelan's book is the broader one of Lonergan's lifelong efforts to construct methodic structures and theoretical frameworks conducive to genuine human progress, not only in the social realm but also in the economic, cultural, political, theoretic, and religious realms. Whelan's last three chapters in *Redeeming History* introduce the thought of Lonergan's disciple, Robert Doran, so as to intimate the salutary practical, social, and cultural potentialities of the methodic and theoretic frameworks Lonergan labored to construct.[50]

In his two volumes on economics, Lonergan argues that production is a process of combining various material and immaterial inputs (plans, know-how) so as to produce consumer goods and deliver services.[51] Economic well-being is created by way of the productive process—that is, all economic activities meant to satisfy human wants and needs. Having

---

48. www.loneranresearch.org/about-bernard-lonergan

49. Home page of the Lonergan Institute in Toronto. We argue that Lonergan has given us guidelines to evaluate economics in our troubled age—now submitted to populist politicians and moneyed interests for whom "monetizing time" is a top priority. Lonergan can help us spiritualize our lives so as to help bring about a sane, ethical society.

50. In the social sciences, framing is a set of concepts and theoretical perspectives on how individuals, groups, and societies organize, perceive, and communicate about reality. Our text reframes some social scientists' "conceptual frames." Lonergan transforms such frames by giving us transcultural, interdisciplinary alternatives that situate issues within their underlying and pervasive ethical and spiritual contexts.

51. In "A von Neumann Representation of Lonergan's Production Model," *Journal of Evolutionary Economics*, Dec. 1992, 2, 269–80, Peter Burley argues that for Lonergan an arbitrary number of fixed capital goods can be accommodated in processes corresponding to a hierarchy of machines making machines. Efficiency "can be seen to entail the abandonment of some capital goods used in earlier processes." This involves incorporating improvements in technology in what Burley calls "the simplest Lonergan-Schumpeter production model. Algorithms for calculating numerical solutions involve only linear programming generalizations of vector difference equations."

noted some of Lonergan's key breakthroughs in economics, we turn to take a closer look at his breakthroughs in *Insight* and *MiT*.

The Originality and Importance of *Insight's* Cognitional Theory

The originality of Lonergan's two major works grew from the influences of many writers in mathematics, physics, philosophy, theology, economics, ethics, and the social sciences. Not the least of these influences was that of Edmund Husserl (1859–1938), a pioneer in the study of science, mathematics and philosophy. Husserl did not coin the term "phenomenology," but he is its father. Phenomenologists attempt to describe human experiences and "things themselves" without metaphysical speculations. Husserl was inspired by Franz Brentano (1838–1917) who himself had tried to adapt Aristotle's work to the modern condition. Brentano reintroduced the Scholastic notion of intentionality into modern philosophy. Husserl expanded on human consciousness "as intentional."[52] Linking conscious intentional operations in all fields of human thinking and endeavors became one of the distinct marks of Lonergan's method while correcting some shortcomings in Husserl's views. Lonergan faulted phenomenology for being too focused on scientific description at the expense of a valid scientific explanation.[53] This resulted in a phenomenological "abstract looking from which the looker and the looked-at have been dropped because

---

52. On the meanings of "intentionality," Michael Vertin, "Intention, Intentionality." *The New Dictionary of Catholic Spirituality.* Michael Downey, ed. (Collegeville, MN: Liturgical Press, 2000): 542–43.

53. Husserl's method brackets away the "natural attitude" so as to have philosophy become a rigorous distinctive science; it insisted that phenomenology is a science of consciousness rather than of empirical things. Lonergan combined these two aspects in his own original way and applied them to all facets of human life. The crucial difference between phenomenology and Lonergan's method is that the former would integrate the several orders of meaning in symbols (somehow intuited) thus reflecting the Kantian grasp of the sensible in *a priori* conditions of knowing. Versus such a Kantian *a priori* of transcendental apperception, Lonergan goes beyond theories of consciousness to the *a priori conditions* of the subject as subject as *prior prerequisite* to any apperception. See Lonergan, *Insight*, 357–59; John Raymaker, *The Theory-Praxis of Social Ethics,* 291.

of their particularity and contingence."[54] Lonergan shows how inquiries in any field of study can be related to actual conditions of life.[55] In *Insight*, he notes that description relates things to ourselves and to our own senses while explanation relates things to one another within a universal viewpoint. Explanatory understanding demands the creation of a theoretical language based on the various differentiations of human consciousness. This basic distinction between description and explanation is central to all of Lonergan's analyses. In the physical sciences, explanatory understanding is made possible by mathematics. In the human sciences including economics, however, mathematics plays only an ancillary role in relation to what and how humans actually understand and how they freely decide.[56]

If Husserl helped bridge Greek and scholastic philosophy with modern philosophy, Lonergan bridges Husserl's abstract approach derived from mathematics with insights into how *all* of us humans in fact use our conscious intentional operations in life. Like Paul Ricœur, Lonergan was interested in the "capable human being." Both men focused on human

---

54. *Insight*, 440.

55. Matthew C. Ogilvie: *Faith Seeking Understanding, The Functional Specialty, "Systematics,"* in *Bernard Lonergan's* Method in Theology, (Marquette Univ. Press, 2011), 39–53, notes that for Lonergan, Immanuel Kant's "Copernican Revolution" was incomplete; although he himself was not a relativist, his incomplete turn to the subject led to forms of relativism. Kant brought the subject into a technically prominent position in philosophy. Lonergan argued that the changes effected by absolute idealism were helpfully addressed by Kierkegaard's stand on faith, as well as by Newman's position on conscience, Nietzsche's will to power, Dilthey's *Lebensphilosophie*, Blondel's philosophy of action and Scheler's emphasis on feeling. (*MiT*, 264; *CWL* 14, 247). These authors differed in emphasis but were united in the belief that "pure reason" does not exist; one must consider how a subject's mind operates. For Lonergan, this means that authenticity cannot be taken for granted; human activity is never "pure." Authenticity is achieved through self-transcendent values. Lonergan noted that his use of "the terms insights and understanding is more precise than . . . *Verstehen*, for it occurs in all fields of knowledge. "It is the active ground whence *proceed* conception, definition, hypothesis, theory, system. This *proceeding*, which is not merely intelligible but intelligent" (*MiT*, 213. *CWL* 14, 201) had provided the ground for his *Verbum* articles written in the 1940's. We closely follow Lonergan on process in knowing-doing—that is, insights occur and are processed in all fields of knowing by a subject. *Process* is at the *center of human knowing on the subject side*, but also at the center of how an economy functions in its productive and exchange phases on *the object side*.

56. *Insight*, 316–21.

abilities, of course, but also on how we humans are vulnerable in our thoughts and activities. Both saw a "human self as an agent responsible for its actions."[57] They rejected claims that the self is immediately transparent to itself or fully its own master. Self-knowledge presupposes one's relations with others in the various spheres of activity one is involved in. Lonergan closely examines the process of coming to self-knowledge in *Insight* which develops a generalized empirical method (GEM)—which combined with functional specialization—enables us to speak of Lonergan's overall method as a GEM-FS process approach. It centers on both the subject-object sides of human knowing and doing.[58]

Having briefly situated the historical genesis of *Insight* and *MiT*, we now give a brief account of Lonergan's cognitional theory so as to bring his majestic, complex work a bit more "down to earth," as it were.[59] Lonergan lists the following as the "basic pattern of operations": seeing, hearing, touching, smelling, tasting, inquiring, imagining, understanding, conceiving, formulating, reflecting, marshalling and weighing the evidence, judging, deliberating, evaluating, deciding, speaking, writing."[60] We are all familiar with these operations. Note that all of them are intentional—a potentially misleading term. One usually thinks of "intentional" as being roughly synonymous with the adjective "deliberate," a point that Lonergan does *not* stress. Rather, he refers to the fact that each of our basic operations *requires an object*. For example, one cannot see without seeing something, nor can one imagine without imagining something, and so on. The "something" in each case is what Lonergan calls the object.

---

57. B. Dauenhaur, D. Pellaueur, "Ricoeur," 2011. https://plato.stanford.edu/entries/ricoeur

58. "To account for disciplines that deal with humans as makers of meanings and values, Lonergan generalized the notion of data to include the data of consciousness as well as the data of sense. From that compound data, one may ascend through hypothesis to verification of the operations by which humans deal with what is meaningful and what is valuable. Hence, a "generalized empirical method" (GEM)." See Tad Dunne, *Internet Encyclopedia of Philosophy*, "Lonergan," under "Origins."

59. John Raymaker and Godefroid Alekiabo Mombula, *Bringing Bernard Lonergan Down to Earth and into Our Hearts and Communities*, (Eugene, OR: Wipf & Stock, 2018).

60. *MiT*, 6. CWL 14, 6.

To say that the operations intend objects is to refer to such facts as that by seeing there becomes present what is seen, by hearing there becomes present what is heard, by imagining there becomes present what is imagined, and so on, where in each case the presence in question is a psychological event.[61]

Operations imply an operator—a subject—ideally, one who is self-transcendent.[62] Lonergan describes a subject's movement through the operations on the empirical, intellectual, rational and responsible levels as being respectively that of experiencing, understanding, judging, deciding. It is through one's four intentional operations that a subject is conscious. Our consciousness expands when from mere experiencing we turn to the effort to understand what we have experienced. In coming to know there emerges within the content of our acts of understanding the question as to whether one is merely dealing with a bright idea or whether one is really on to something; one endeavors to settle what really *is* so. Then when one judges that one has decided correctly as to the facts, one begins to deliberate on what we are to do about this.[63] Every act of knowing involves a pattern of experiencing, understanding, and judging. The fourth level, of deciding, while extremely important, is not constitutive of knowing. We come to know many things without making any decision about what to do with them. The first three patterns in knowing may be summarized as follows:

1) Experiencing. If someone is in a deep coma, or is in a dreamless sleep, he/she cannot come to know anything. Experiencing is necessarily a part of knowing. But, contrary to the claims of empiricist philosophers, experience in itself does not constitute knowledge. What we experience is in itself alone nothing more than scraps of data.

---

61. *MiT*, 7. *CWL* 14, 7.

62. On this point and the importance of "operator" in Lonergan's opus, see below. GEM-FS, a self-transcending process method to problems, favors communal solutions rather than a fixation on individual profits. His approach is consonant with the overall approaches of the world religions and of not a few philosophers and social scientists.

63. *MiT*, 9. *CWL* 14, 13.

2) Understanding. To the data of our experience we put the question, "What is it?" Lonergan calls this the "question for intelligence." Answers come through insights. We have an insight whenever we are coming to understand something. Merely arriving at an insight does not constitute knowledge. Understanding is concerned with "What is it?" questions. We may arrive at correct answers but also incorrect ones.

3) Judging. With regard to an insight, one asks "Is it so?" This is the question for reflection. It is here that one judges whether there are adequate grounds to support our initial insights. The question for reflection is answered with further "reflective" insights that should lead to correct judgments.

Let us expand on these three cognitional operations by noting how Lonergan arrived at his cognitional theory. As explained in *Insight* and *MiT*, GEM seeks to answer three basic questions:

1) "What am I doing when I am knowing?"(the cognitive question). Lonergan explained that in order to know how we come to know anything, we need to pay close attention to our consciousness. He invites each person to become aware of his/her own consciousness and thereby of the mind's processes in coming to know. He observes how people—especially scientists—actually operate when they formulate and verify ideas. Scientists consider given data. In doing so, they are experiencing the first step in knowing. The data are not divorced from how a mind operates as it asks questions so as arrive at answers. Cognitional theory identifies, distinguishes and relates the sets of acts we perform whenever we come to know in mathematics, in the natural and human sciences, or in every day commonsense living.

2) "Why is doing that knowing?" (the epistemological question). *Insight* argues that genuine human knowledge is based on one's personal self-appropriation and an affirmation of one's own rational self-consciousness. Readers are invited to appropriate their own conscious operational acts of experiencing, understanding, judging and deciding—as this occurs in *any* discipline or in everyday life.

3) "What do I know when I am knowing?" (the metaphysical question that transposes Aquinas' cognitional theory into contemporary terms). GEM-FS is a *generalized*, transformative method that can help a person access his/her conscious intentional operations and data of consciousness in ways that interact with other persons in daily life, or when specialists correctly analyze scientific data in *specialized* ways.[64]

The three basic questions must be addressed in that order. Lonergan's GEM began as a cognitional theory influenced by scientific methods of inquiry. Having rejected the Cartesian *cogito ergo sum* in chapter 11 of *Insight*, he invites readers to affirm their own existence—not with a mere *cogito*, but through judgments based on reflective insights. Lonergan then develops an epistemology and a metaphysics that reject both Kant's and Husserl's *a priori* presuppositions.[65] Lonergan also disagrees with Scholastics, as well as with Leibniz and Christian Wolf who both held that epistemology is founded on metaphysics. Having revised taken-for-granted hierarchies in various philosophies, Lonergan transforms the metaphysics of Aristotle and Aquinas within his own original GEM methodical context. His transposition of metaphysics means that a GEM metaphysics depends on one's epistemology which in turn depends on appropriating one's own process of knowing. Such dependent metaphysics, its notion of objectivity,[66] its transcendental integration of heuristic

---

64. Lonergan, *MiT*, 25. *CWL* 14, 27. Tad Dunne raises a fourth basic question: 'What therefore should we do?' It lays out a framework for collaboration, based on the answers to the first three questions"; the fourth question lays a basis for *MiT* as well as for this book. See *Internet Encyclopedia of Philosophy*, "Bernard Lonergan," www.iep.utm.edu/Lonergan

65. Lonergan *ends* by proposing a metaphysics derived from his epistemology, itself resting on a cognitional theory. He does not *begin* from metaphysical theory.

66. For, Lonergan, an adequate analysis of science, far from justifying positivist visions of scientific understanding, reveals the need of a critical realism that coherently integrates all the sciences while addressing the question of God and grounding moral and religious concerns. The key to all this is a critical realism, a change of mind regarding mind itself. GEM metaphysics enables us to talk in a general way about the relationships among the areas explored by disciplines—including the question of the finality of the universe. If the universe is intelligible, if it responds to our questioning—as science presupposes—one must ask "where is all of this heading?" See Richard M. Liddy "Changing Our Minds: Bernard Lonergan and Climate Change," in *Confronting the Climate Crisis: Catholic Theological Perspectives*, (Marquette Univ. Press, 2011), 249–72.

structures as outlined in *Insight*, chapters 12–16, all serve to ground knowledge in general.[67]

Lonergan's Interdisciplinary Method Helps Us Decide Wisely

Our arguments turn on the pivotal point of how Lonergan discovered functional specialization (FS). By definition, FS calls for a division of labor[68] conducted by teams of specialists. Let us amplify a bit more on Lonergan's transformational and integrative discovery which frames issues in the light of deeply *personal attainments*. In the end, nothing can substitute for personally appropriating Lonergan's thought. We can only offer summaries of his major works and outline Lonergan's eight functional specialties[69] (FS). These form a transformational-unifying framework which interrelates many fields of study such as the human and "hard" sciences, ethics, philosophy, religious studies, mathematics etc. It does so by relating them all to the processes of the human mind. Thus, Lonergan transforms and unifies seemingly different approaches to the sciences and other fields of studies—a major breakthrough. Applied to communities of scholars in economics, working within a GEM-FS framework leads to integrating questions of economic justice.[70]

---

67. Lonergan, *Insight*, 372–616.

68. Lonergan's notion of a division of labor differs radically from Adam Smith's.

69. The late Phil McShane preferred to call them "functional collaboration": he was right. However, we see the need to stick closely to Lonergan's own terminology.

70. The first priority in implementing Lonergan's economics is to learn the science, so that it can be properly taught. This is best done in a GEM-FS way. Lonergan once spoke of a hundred years passing before his economic analysis would be implemented. However, since reversing the prevailing course of the economy is an absolutely crucial component of any reversal of the longer cycle of decline, the effort is worth it. As Lonergan wrote (*Insight*, 8) concerning the flight from understanding: "No problem is at once more delicate and more profound, more practical and perhaps more pressing."

Lonergan's "Healing-Creating"[71] Vectors and Judgments of Value

Among the indispensable tools that Lonergan offers us for addressing interdisciplinary issues are his "healing-creating vectors." The "star" for guiding the study of economics on a sound basis is judgments of value.[72] Compassionate hearts, coupled with intelligent, rational and responsible action, are what it takes to resolve the tragic, conflicting issues confronting humanity such as the starvation threatening people in some parts of the planet. Humanity as a whole must "wise up" before it is too late. Lonergan's method helps people become aware of being aware; it helps us become aware of "something" but also aware of who we truly are or might be. Each of us may ask at some point in life "what have I done and failed to do in my life?" Such a determinate procedure may help us find radical ways to overcome what ails us. Today's uncertainties are in no small part due to the processes of mechanization and dehumanization first imposed upon humanity in industrialized nations. In turn, these nations used their industrial prowess to colonize developing nations in Asia and Africa. The implications of colonization are still being worked out in the political and economic dimensions of international life. It must be admitted that these industrial and now post-industrial economies

---

71. Lonergan, "Healing and Creating in History," in a *Third Collection*, edited by Frederick Crowe, 100–09, highlights people's creative movements from below within their own consciousness which Lonergan relates to recent radically-healing movements. He insists on a thorough exploration of *MiT*'s second *healing* phase, beginning with FS 5.

72. Mariana Mazzucato, https://socialeurope.eu/a-new-global-economic-consensus deconstructs several key trends. These include how the financial sector's "casino capitalism" mislabels market speculation as the creation of value rather than the mere extraction of value created elsewhere, and how the real value added by government and public goods and services have been ignored—to the detriment of us all. Ultimately, she notes, we need a more synthetic and integrative view: one that recognizes both how value is created and extracted in the current system, and how this needs to change. She concludes that value depends on vision: "If we cannot dream of a better future and try to make it happen, there is no real reason why we should care about value." She concludes that the ability to value a healthy, sustainable planet, fairness, community and quality of life must be returned to the heart of economics." Mazzucato has also shown how the pandemic has highlighted the deficiencies of economic deregulation and market liberalization; as we do, she argues that a new policy-making paradigm is emerging.

replaced economies based upon slavery, which still exists, principally in the form of human trafficking. In all these cases, traditional notions of value and wisdom have been sorely tested. We humans need to admit that we have gotten too "smart" for our own good; we have sacrificed wisdom. We need to get it back.

How Lonergan Helps us Meet the Threats of a Globalized World

Today's globalization and new technologies present us with rare challenges and opportunities. Ours is a world of instant communication but we are still not sufficiently aware of how our actions can and do impact other human beings. Inequalities between rich and poor, revival of nationalist claims, disputes among religious fanatics, atheists and secularists, further exacerbate our divides. These make it more difficult to implement measures to address human-caused global warming, among other burning issues. Humanity needs transformative bridges that can span divides separating our global communities. Bridge-building requires that we move beyond conventional modes of thinking.

A globalized planet, dominated by self-interested ideologies, needs self-giving persons focused on the common good.[73] We cite many examples of corruption and dishonesty that can only be remedied by the type of transformational actions that Lonergan urges in his writings. With Lonergan we set our sights high, relying principally on his pioneering efforts in developing a "critical realism"[74] in *Insight* and on his use of a

---

73. Some have drawn on Lonergan's notion of the common good to advance notions of altruism. The common good, a product of human dignity, has its personal and social aspects. On the other hand, the common good may be hampered by arbitrary, selfish actions, or when a country such as China seeks to tighten its grip on tech companies while the world comes to rely more heavily on Chinese manufacturing to power the critically-needed transition toward clean energy.

74. See Timothy Walker, "Approaches to Critical Realism: Bhaskar and Lonergan, in *Journal of Critical Realism*, Vol. 16, 2, 111–27. Lonergan notes, *Insight*, 451–53, that "scientists are repelled by the failure of philosophers to reach a single, precise, universally accepted, technical language. They point out the simplicity of this device" and its enormous benefits. "While a scientist is reasonable in entering into the scientific tradition and

universal *"two-phase"* method in *Method in Theology* (*MiT*) that helps us get "inside ourselves" so as to foster cooperation in all fields of life. *MiT*'s two phases are meant to develop the conversions and needed turn-arounds. With this in mind, we seek to deploy *MiT*'s eight interdependent functional specialties (FS) in ways that Lonergan orchestrated and which would underlie changes in economic and environmental policies that we advocate.[75] We shall first place *Insight* in a historical perspective so as to partially answer the question as to why Lonergan endeavored to clarify the mistaken presuppositions not only of philosophers but also (in *CWL* 15 and 21) of prominent economists of various persuasions.

Placing Insight in a Historical, Bridge-Building Perspective by Integrating Three of Lonergan's Breakthroughs

We now focus on three of Lonergan's breakthroughs, namely 1) his study of heuristic structures, 2) his distinction between faith and beliefs and 3) his reconciliation of convergent-divergent components in human knowing.

Lonergan on Heuristic Structures

Insight's study of heuristic structures addresses the importance of Ludwig Boltzmann's classical statistics. As opposed to the familiar division of classical mechanics (Newton), classical statistics (Boltzmann), quantum mechanics (Schrödinger, Heisenberg), and quantum statistics (Bose-Einstein, Fermi-Dirac), *Insight*'s study of heuristic structures demands not a fourfold but a twofold division—classical and statistical:

---

carrying on its work, a philosopher cannot be reasonable on the same terms; he has to become familiar with different traditions; he has to find grounds for deciding between them; and it is the reasonableness of that decision on which will rest the reasonableness of his collaboration with any single tradition."

75. An economics conversion requires that one (primarily economists) recognize that the flow of goods and services involves two stages based on the functional differentiation of the two circuits.

Intelligence either anticipates the discovery of functional relations on which relations between measurements will converge, or else it anticipates the discovery of probabilities from which relative actual frequencies may diverge though only at random.[76]

It may be that just as Boltzmann bridged our incomplete knowledge of a system to classical observations such as temperature and pressure,[77] so Lonergan built heuristic bridges between economics and the deeper implications of intellectual, psychic, moral, and religious conversions to which we add the need for two communal turnarounds in economic and environmental policies. It is in view of this that we seek to integrate Lonergan's twofold-seminal contributions in the fields of method and economics, both of which develop GEM-FS transformative approaches in healing-creating ways.

2. The Roles of Faith and Beliefs in Reinforcing Ethics[78]

Our GEM-FS sandwich approach includes a spiritual dimension, as well as Lonergan's faith-belief distinction. Lonergan succinctly summarizes the issue in *MiT* in his treatment of progress and the manner we can overcome false beliefs. He is not merely concerned with false beliefs but also with "the false believer," and "the manner in which one happened to have accepted erroneous beliefs." Such a person has been coopted by the social surd, biases, etc. False beliefs can prevent one from being oriented to the mystery of love; a loving faith, however, can unite those who have different beliefs. "One has to look into the manner in which one hap-pened to have accepted erroneous beliefs and one has to try to discover

---

76. *Insight*, 91. "The absolute resides not on the level of sensible presentations but in the field of abstract propositions and invariant expressions." (189–90).

77. The mathematician David Bibby has noted that it is likely that Maxwell-Boltz-mann statistics require both kinds of heuristic structure depending on the situation; scientists working in the field are to decide which is appropriate.

78. To fully understand GEM-FS. one must advert to the spiritual, mystic, apophatic which are all integral components of religious conversions. Our approach would allow *CWL* 15 and 21 to be an integrative part of GEM-FS transformations. As to faith reinforcing ethics in the area of economics, Peter Alexander Egom's *Economics of Justice and Peace* (KDP Publishing, 2011) is very useful. He, too, invokes R. H. Tawney on loss of moral norms.

and correct the carelessness, . . . the bias that led one to mistake the false for the true."[79]

On the other hand, beliefs have played a vital role in civilization: "There is progress in knowledge from primitives to moderns only because successive generations began where their predecessors left off." Successive generations could do so, "because they were ready to believe. Without belief, relying solely on their own individual experience and own judgements, they would have ever been beginning afresh. Either ancient attainments "would never be surpassed or, if they were, then the benefits would not be transmitted.[80] Paradoxically, it is knowledge handed on by belief that is responsible for the transmission of science to later generations. Acknowledging this fact is a key facet underlying Lonergan's reconciliation of convergence and divergence.

3. Lonergan's Reconciliation of Convergence-Divergence Issues

While Boltzmann and Lonergan built bridges, E. F. Schumacher was left puzzled in his attempt to do so. In his *Small is Beautiful*, Schumacher writes that G. N. M. Tyrell used the terms "divergent" and "convergent" to distinguish problems which cannot be solved by logical reasoning from those that can. Life is kept going, Tyrell argued, by divergent problems which have to be "lived"[81] and are solved only in death. From this premise, Schumacher argued that physics and mathematics do not recognize divergent problems:

> The physical sciences and mathematics are concerned exclusively with
> convergent problems. That is why they can progress cumulatively,

---

79. *MiT*, 44. Adrial Fitzgerald argues that describing the social surd and evil as a privation of intelligibility by the early Lonergan should be adjusted to align with his later position on the transcendental notion of value as a distinct component of the object of our transcendental yearning—a component which is not reducible to the intelligible.

80. *MiT*, 43. *CWL* 14, 43–4. As with his use of "men" for humans, his reference to "primitives" shows that Lonergan was after all a man of his times. We choose not to amend his text.

81. www.coursehero.com/file/p33feee/G-N-M-Tyrell-has-put-forward-the-terms-divergent-and-convergent-to-distinguish/ referring to Tyrell's *The Personality of Man*.

and each new generation can begin just where their forebears left off. The price, however, is a heavy one. Dealing exclusively with convergent problems does not lead into life but away from it.[82]

Lonergan solves this dilemma. His *Insight* recognizes the convergent problems addressed by scientists, but his *MiT* integrates the processes of conversion with the divergent, existential problems facing humans in everyday life. Lonergan's convergence-divergence approach addresses the need for new policies to confront the threats of environmental collapse and economic chaos. If it is true that life is kept going by divergent problems which are only solved in death and that convergent problems are humanity's most useful invention, we note that the latter do not, as such, exist in reality; they are created by a process of abstraction. A solution to convergent problems is written down and passed on to others, who can apply it without needing to reproduce the mental effort necessary to find it. Tyrell is at a loss on how people should handle divergent problems in family life, economics, politics, education, etc. With Tyrell, we can affirm that mathematics and physical science are concerned only with convergent problems. A GEM-FS approach, however, solves Tyrell's dilemma. GEM, in its treatment of probability, handles divergent series by reformulating problems in such a way that they become convergent. Here, we can highlight one difference between economics and physical science. Mainstream

---

82. For Schumacher, *Small is Beautiful*, (The Greatest Resource-Education), chapter 6, a divergent problem does *not* produce the same answer among various thinkers. Solutions diverge and often produce opposite prescriptions for dealing with them. The example Schumacher gives is the education of children. Persons working on this issue would emphasize the issue of the transmission of learning from one generation to the next. To understand the distinction between convergent and divergent problems may require developing the mathematics of *Insight* to show how to transpose the divergent problems of real-life economics into convergent knowledge. Schumacher's division may be similar to Lonergan's dialectic, but Lonergan assumed progress results from, "a concrete unfolding of linked but opposed principles of change" (*Insight*, 242). This implies convergence in a determinate manner that we don't yet understand. Schumacher argued that the modern economy is unsustainable; we seek to delineate two socio-cultural conversions to complement his argument as a way to wed divergence with viable forms of convergence in addressing economic and environmental problems.

economists cannot reformulate divergent problems due to ignoring the social surd, for example. Acknowledging the existence of the social surd[83] and other problems is essential in economics if it is not to fail in its mission. Lonergan, as noted above, bases his twofold division of heuristic structures on the anticipations of intelligence. Using a different notion of divergence from that used in classical laws, he arrives at the notion of how data converge:

> There is no need to interpret classical laws concretely. They can be statements of elements in an abstract system where (1) the abstract system is constituted by implicitly defined relations and terms, (2) the abstract system is connected with data not directly but through the mediation of a complementary set of descriptive concepts, and (3) the laws of the abstract system are said to be verified inasmuch as they assign limits on which, other things being equal, vast varieties of data converge.[84]

Having indicated three relevant GEM-FS breakthroughs, we turn to examine how Lonergan approaches critical realism—another important factor in laying a basis for GEM-FS' six turnarounds.

---

83. "The will can contribute to the solution of the problem of social surd inasmuch as it adopts a dialectical attitude that parallels the dialectical method of intellect. The dialectical method of intellect consists in grasping that the social surd" cannot be treated "as intelligible. The corresponding dialectical attitude of will is to return good for evil. For it is only inasmuch as men are willing to meet evil with good, to love their enemies, to pray for those that persecute and calumniate them, that the social surd is a potential good. It follows that love of God above all and in all so embraces the order of the universe as to love all with a self-sacrificing love." *Insight*, 721–22.

84. *Insight*, 159. Lonergan is addressing the problem of indeterminism which "is true as a negation of the old determinisms. But indeterminism cannot escape the necessity of methodological assumptions and precepts; it cannot prevent their conjunction in thought with laws and frequencies that are regarded as verified; and so it cannot succeed even in delaying the day when, from a new viewpoint, scientific anticipations once more will envisage a determinate to be known . . . I have offered a unified view that anticipates both the systematic and the non-systematic without excluding in particular cases insight into concrete non-schematic situations" such as the "subatomic order." (161).

How Lonergan's Critical Realism Clarifies the Mistaken Presuppositions of Philosophers and Economists

Lonergan referred to GEM as a critical realism—partially grounded in the Aristotelian-Thomist traditions. Humans can make true judgments of fact and of value. Lonergan's critical realism seeks to ground knowing and valuing in ways analogous to what Kant did.[85] But he avoids both Kant and Husserl's notions of intuition (*Anschauung*). Lonergan considered intuition to be "the same as seeing" which is why he avoided it. His point was that "insights are a dime a dozen and most of them are wrong. You have to have an awful lot of before you get anything that is really considerable."[86] Intuition short-circuits insight and judgment. GEM *radically traces to their roots* the sources of the meanings and values that constitute personality, social orders, and historical developments; it explores the ways such meanings and values are distorted. It proposes a framework for collaboration among disciplines that can overcome basic philosophical misconceptions that negatively affect our lives. It aims to promote sound ways of living. As distinguished from Husserl's phenomenal intentionality, GEM is based on human awareness not only of sensed experiences and feelings but also of other mental acts such as imagining, inquiring, understanding, questioning, hypothesizing, formulating, marshalling evidence, judging and so on. GEM "stands to the data of consciousness"[87] as the empirical method stands to the data of sense. Just as there are data

---

85. *Internet Encyclopedia of Philosophy*, "Lonergan," by Tad Dunne. For Lonergan, his metaphysics, *Insight*, chapters 14–17, reinforce objectivity as treated in chapter 13.

86. *Caring about Meaning*, ed. P. Lambert, C. Tansey, C. Going, (Montreal, Thomas More Inst., 1982), 53. The point Lonergan makes is that "Kant's *Verstehen* is the faculty of judgment. You can get along without understanding and judgment on that basis." What is needed is a critical realism, not mere intuition.

87. The way Lonergan "unobtrusively" introduces the data of consciousness in his canon of selection in chapter 3 of *Insight*, 95, is noteworthy. He notes in the section, "The Restriction to Sensible Data," that in their "essential features" both the data of sense and consciousness have "sensible consequences." Just above that passage he speaks of "a trap for the unwary" as to "grasping the full implications of an "appropriate division of labor." His aim is to show how we can validly transpose private acts into a public domain—a key *Insight* accomplishment.

about the material universe studied in the natural sciences,[88] so there are also data about the working of the human mind available to each of us. From the compound data of sense and of consciousness, one ascends through hypotheses to verification of the operations by which humans deal with what is meaningful and what is valuable: hence, a "generalized empirical method."[89] For Lonergan, the data of consciousness are as ascertainable as are the data of sense in the natural sciences. They are the starting point for the "knowing of knowing": they constitute its justification. Generalizing the notion of data to include the data of consciousness as well as those of sense is pivotal to GEM-FS and to our own procedure in this book which addresses the relations between science, economics, ethics and religion in today's contexts[90] as these affect or are affected by the development of meanings and values.

Insight invites its readers to discover their genuine human knowledge resulting from a personal self-appropriation of one's own rational self-consciousness. It helps readers to become aware of their own fourfold process of conscious intentional operations of experiencing, understanding, judging and deciding. It considers a very wide range of subjects such as philosophy, mathematics, physical sciences, ethics,

---

88. Lonergan stressed that all knowledge has its presuppositions. He replaced Descartes' dualist, would-be presupposition-less *Cogito ergo Sum (I think therefore I am) with* the process of self-affirmation (*Insight*, 344–52).

89. *Insight*, 96.

90. Matthew Lamb, "Orthopraxis and Theological Method in Bernard Lonergan," *Proceedings of the Catholic Theological Society of America* 35: 66–87 (1980) notes that Karl Rahner's first level of reflection and its transcendental experience differs from Lonergan's differentiation between consciousness and knowledge. Lonergan "offers ways to verify the differentiation through a public process of self-appropriation." GEM is applicable to "whole series of basic issues in the sciences and scholarly disciplines." Rahner's first level of reflection is that of a mystagogic theologian. Those "interested in more general theological categories, i.e., categories operative not only in theologizing on the Christian mysteries but also operative in the sciences and other forms of noetic praxis," will find GEM-FS more helpful. Lonergan "transformed method from its empiricist and idealist reifications as sets of axioms, principles or systems into its concrete embodiments in the related and recurrent activities of ongoing communities of knowers and doers in history." His is a framework for a reflectively dialectical orthopraxis critically open to the ongoing procedures and results of empirical and dialectical human sciences and scholarly disciplines. https://ejournals. bc.edu/index.php/ctsa/article/view/2972.

psychoanalysis, literature and theology. Coming to insights in any field has both distinctive and similar patterns. *Insight* helps a reader come to "understand understanding"; it focuses on knowing's dynamic structure, on that structure's invariant patterns shared by all knowers in whatever discipline they might venture. Its program is succinctly if boldly stated:

> Thoroughly understand what it is to understand, and not only will you understand the broad lines of all there is to be understood but also you will possess a fixed base, an invariant pattern, opening upon all further developments of understanding.[91]

Method in Theology's *Eight Functional Specialties* (FS) within Two Phases: How they Handle Notions of the Good

Lonergan's transcendental GEM recognizes all valid insights in scientific and philosophical methods, but it does seek to correct shortcomings. Applying his method worked out in *Insight* to theology, in *MiT* Lonergan reviews the ways theologians think and write. No less a thinker than Karl Rahner criticized it for *not* being truly theological:

> Lonergan's theological methodology seems to me to be so generic that it really fits every science, and hence is not the methodology of theology as such, but only a very general methodology of science, illustrated with examples taken from theology . . . What is specific about Christian theology . . . actually gets lost. While it is ostensibly about theology, *Method in Theology* uses the academic discipline of theology as a specific example of the general work of communities of scholars in any discipline.[92]

---

91. *Insight*, 22.

92. "Some Critical Thoughts on 'Functional Specialties in Theology,'" in *Foundations of Theology,* ed. Philip McShane (Notre Dame Univ. Press, 1972), 194–96. We do not concur with Rahner's appraisal which missed the point that *MiT*'s breakthrough can link theology with the studies relevant to interdisciplinary studies. In his theological writings, Lonergan emphasizes the dynamics of conversion—changes of mind and heart. In reality, head and heart cannot be separated; they are mutually interdependent. Our book focuses in part

In his reply to Rahner, Lonergan focuses on "the good of order," a prominent notion in both *Insight* and *MiT.* The editors of *CWL 15* note this concern; they point to Lonergan's "aggregate, functional, and dynamic analysis of the pure cycle of the productive process of the economic good of order."[93] Lonergan writes that *this good of order*

> Originated by human invention and convention ceases to be an optional adjunct and becomes an indispensable constituent of human living. For the long-run effects of technological advance and new capital formation consist in some combination of increased population, reduced work, and improved living standards. In the course of a century, the differences in all three respects may be so great that any return to an earlier state of affairs is regarded as preposterous and is to be brought about only by violence or disaster.[94]

In *MiT*, after treating notions of the human good, meaning, and religion, Lonergan explains his discovery of the eight functional specialties (FS), namely: research, interpretation, history, dialectic, foundations, doctrines, systematics and communication. Since human

---

on a global or glocal secularity—an approach fitted to the present world's vast complexities. Our GEM-FS "umbrella term" responds to the sacred-traditional and/or secular principles guiding every nation. It appeals to a *universal viewpoint* that Lonergan exemplified throughout his life as he moved from his study of medieval philosophies to embrace modernity. This enabled him to suggest an ethical cure to today's economic conflicts. While today's world events are very complex, for instance, Russia's invasion of Ukraine, Lonergan offers a global vision to address the complexities of today and tomorrow, even as background issues keep changing.

93. Lonergan, *CWL* 15, 117. See https://functionalmacroeconomics.com/theoretical-breakthroughs-of-euclid-newton-hilbert-einstein-and-lonergan/ The site helps readers gain an appreciation of Lonergan's "Modern Macroeconomic Field Theory" by relating his lifework to historically significant advances such as Euclidian geometry and Hilbert's implicit definitions, etc.

94. *Insight*, 239. Today, government and businesses use QR matrix barcodes (machine-readable optical labels containing information about the items to which they are attached). They yield a new economic mode to digitally connect people, things, and places. The QR Code economy now permeates economic and social operations. See www.prnewswire.com/news-releases/wechat-releases-new-report-on-the-qr-code-economys-fight-against-covid-19-301060807.html Digital authoritarianism is often framed as part of a contest between free and unfree countries. But the tech used to support authoritarian practice is often built by companies based in democratic states.

consciousness is intentional, the interplays between our conscious intentional operations give rise to *MiT*'s "diphase FS method," as we call it, that is, its division of the FS into two phases. In the *mediating phase*, the first four FS deal with the matter as indirect discourse, whereby a scholar learns from the past; in the *mediated* phase, the last four FS develop it as a "direct discourse."[95] This enables theologians (or any team of scholars) to tackle contemporary and future problems much more effectively. It was Lonergan's ability to show the critical importance of the data of consciousness and interrelating these data with the data of the senses in all human activities that helps ensure the viability of the GEM-FS strategy.

Two *Insight* breakthroughs show that 1) our intentional operations are conscious and 2) our data of consciousness are as valid and necessary in all human endeavors as are the data of sense. These two breakthroughs help us understand and personally appropriate our own consciousness. They are also at the base of the mediating and mediated phases spelled out in *MiT*'s eight FS. *MiT* correlates the four levels of our intentional operations—experience, intelligence, rationality, responsibility—in two phases. An important point is that for GEM-FS, operating requires cooperating and collaborating. Cooperation is based on our knowing-doing operations; collaboration is at the heart of *MiT*'s FS. *MiT* outlines ways for specialists to collaborate in steps of a process. This requires that one understands the pivotal difference between the mediating-*creative* phase and mediated-*healing* phase.

Before getting into the details of the two phases, we note that for Tad Dunne, GEM is a new way to "shift from fixed conceptual systems to the ongoing management of change. . . . It provides a new conceptual system based on a higher control over other systems." Dunne adds that morality has moved from its original focus on action "into a variety

---

95. GEM-FS is a heuristic process, seeking understanding; Lonergan's economics offers an alternative to all the one-stage economic models that have so far been proposed. Lonergan knew that there is a lot of opportunity for exploring the two phases of economic models but very little competition in doing so. In a way, the same can be said about *MiT* inasmuch as people are not converted.

of conceptual systems under the heading of ethics." Our own GEM-FS approach focuses on these systems and their associated categories. On this level, concepts lose their rigidity. "As long as investigators are committed to, and explicit about their cognitional theory, epistemology and metaphysics, they will continually refine or replace concepts developed in previous historical contexts."[96]

The Structure of the Human Good and Policy-Making

On the matter of replacing concepts developed in previous historical contexts, one must advert to the fact that Lonergan had to move from the closed system of morality he inherited prior to Vatican II to the more open type of system we are exploring. Even some of Lonergan's students who were exposed to his earlier Scholastic approach have failed to grasp the profound change in Lonergan's post-Vatican II method. It has been noted that Lonergan was mistakenly categorized as a "transcendental Thomist," and therefore rejected as a subjectivist and anti-realist by many Thomist authors and teachers. It is certainly true that Lonergan was deeply indebted to the thought of Thomas Aquinas, but his studies found in Aquinas a theory of knowledge and a kind of realism that was, and still is, at odds with other prevailing Thomist interpretations. Prior to his two studies of Aquinas, he was already deeply influenced by his readings of Plato, John Henry Newman, Hegel, and Marx. These great thinkers prepared him to find in Aquinas ideas that earlier scholars had overlooked—ideas that he would develop into his own unique treatments of knowledge, science, the natural world, history, truth, goodness, and God.[97]

We interpret Lonergan's treatment of "The Structure of the Human Good" in *MiT*[98] to mean that policy-making can help people bridge tensions between principle-based and actual approaches to

---

96. Tad Dunne, "Bernard Lonergan," *Internet Encyclopedia of Philosophy*, https://iep. utm.edu/Lonergan/

97. Patrick Byrne, Dominic Scheuring, Stephen Ferguson in *Oxford Bibliographies*, 24 April 2019.

98. *MiT*, 47–52. *CWL* 14, 47–51.

such critical issues as climate-change,[99] for example. Lonergan did not view his use of terms in depicting the human good as "rigorous." He did link "individual operations" with "social cooperation." For him, the particular good means "any entity, whether object or action, that meets a need of a particular individual." Needs and wants of any kind are met by actualizing one's capacities through operations. One must pay close attention to Lonergan's emphasis that cooperation occurs within institutions by the fulfilling of roles and tasks. The structure of the human good and the good of order both involve realities that are at once individual and social. This implies Lonergan's concern for valuing the good through cooperation. Since the human good is abused in many social practices and that the rise in temperature on all continents and in the oceans is due to such abuse, there is a need for new forms of global cooperation through the two socio-communal conversions or turnarounds we are exploring. In our view, *MiT*'s two phases provide an adequate *way to link and integrate* Lonergan's two volumes on economics with his better-known works on method, philosophy and theology.[100] We turn to explore *MiT*'s first and second phases with a view to later identify their possible roles in societal turnarounds that would effectively promote the human good. As the human good is both individual and social, we argue that personal conversions should lead to turnarounds in public policies.

---

99. John Raymaker and Ijaz Durrani undertook this task in *Empowering Climate-Change Strategies with Bernard Lonergan's Method*, (UPA, 2015). If legitimation one stage of the process of social formation (not a problem of motivating an actor to behave in certain patterns as in popular psychology), "it is possible to understand it as the necessary process of internalizing the communicative network of a society in which the subject both learns and is able to criticize rationally" that network." Max A. Myers, "'Ideology' and 'Legitimation' as Necessary Concepts for Christian Ethics" in *The Journal of the American Academy of Religion*, XLIX, 2, 195. GEM-FS gives us needed criteria to explain why in these apocalyptic times of drastic change, conversion-turnarounds can develop viable policies across the globe to save what can be saved.

100. Raymaker's *Empowering Bernard Lonergan's Legacy* (Lanham, MD, 2013) suggests ways to *better organize a Lonerganian movement to spearhead needed turnarounds* through an International GEM Association (IGEMA) that could guide necessary efforts.

MiT's First Mediating-Creative Phase—the Roles of the First FS in Addressing Issues in Economics.

In *MiT*'s mediating-creative phase, the first level of experience is correlated with research in FS 1. The second level of understanding is correlated with interpretation in FS 2. Here one is called to understand texts, authors and oneself. The third level of judging is correlated with studying the nature of history and with the historical horizons of various historians in FS 3. The fourth level of deciding revolves around a dialectic that explores in FS 4 how one is to exercises one's freedom for what is needed.[101]

This first mediating-creative phase which focuses mostly on the past is followed by the mediated-healing phase concerned with the present and the future. Another principle for the division between the two phases "is derived from the fact that our conscious and intentional operations occur on four distinct levels and that each level has its own proper achievement and end."[102] Lonergan's interdisciplinary method lies in his having shown how the first *mediating-creative* phase and the second *mediated-healing* phase do "interact" both in personal and communal processes. With Phil McShane, Eileen de Neeve,[103] Mike Shute and others, we argue that GEM-FS is radical[104] and broad enough to holistically address the methodological shortcomings in many fields, including economics.

---

101. We partially base our group economics conversions on the principle that "Freedom without Responsibility is Egoism." See "Aquinas' Moral, Political, and Legal Philosophy," *Stanford Encyclopedia of Philosophy*, 2021.

102. *MiT* 133, *CWL* 14, 128.

103. Eileen de Neeve, *Decoding* (2008) suggests that Lonergan saw Marxism as undervaluing the role of entrepreneurship and finance in complex economies. She demystifies economic booms and busts, focusing on the dynamics of production and money. Lonergan flags the differences between capital and consumer goods, showing how our actions can offer the rewards of innovation and growth to everyone. Many economists today urge governments to maintain stable money flows. But in our dominantly market economy, which has the advantage of free choice, finance is by no means mainly controlled by governments. Large private international financial movements occur that can be volatile and disruptive. By thoughtfully decoding the economy, we can learn ways to make economic choices that will benefit everyone.

104. Radical for us means getting at the root of things by way of needed ethical reforms.

How MiT's Second Mediated Healing Phase [105] Is Radical Enough to Help Economics Become an Instrument to Foster the Human Good

GEM-FS can be applied to remedy the present shortcomings of economics.[106] The editors of *CWL* 15 highlight this fact by having *inserted in the middle* of the book his article "Healing and Creating in History" in which Lonergan raises this rhetorical question:

> Is my proposal Utopian? It asks merely for creativity, for an interdisciplinary theory that at first *will be denounced* as absurd, then will be admitted to be true but obvious and insignificant, and perhaps finally be regarded as so important that its adversaries will claim that they themselves discovered it.[107]

GEM-FS is a radical breakthrough method, based on human conscious cognitional activities that have to be personally appropriated. In GEM-FS's mediated-healing phase, beginning with the fourth level of deciding (FS 5), one makes a personal commitment to what Lonergan names a foundational reality. In this second phase, one then proceeds "downwards" to the third level of judging which addresses, in the case of theology, what doctrines may best implement universal values in

---

105. Simply put, in *Insight*, Lonergan revised traditional approaches to method. Since knowledge does not come from on high, 1) Lonergan starts with a person's experience; 2) experience leads to understanding through interpreting; 3) the mind judges and comes to knowledge; 4) one can then *act* upon verified knowledge. *MiT* provides a basis for new approaches to theology—no longer based on imperatives— but on what evolves from experience in accord with the two mediating-mediating phases. See, for example, https://srmarynoonan.wordpress.com/bernard-lonergan-in-a-nutshell/

106. Eileen de Neeve, "Suspicion and Recovery: Ethical Approaches to Economics," *Method Journal of Lonergan Studies* 15, 1997, 33, points out that "the major criticism of a Pareto optimum as a goal is that it abstracts from questions of equity."

107. Lonergan, *Third Collection*, "Healing and Creating in History," 108; *CWL* 15, 106, emphasis in the original. Based on their shared concern that the analysis of modernity as a social formation should be at the center of a sociology that takes seriously its task of enlightening society about itself, Andreas Reckwitz and Hartmut Rosa, *Late Modernity in Crisis,* Suhrkamp, 2021, argue that the best interpretation of today's critical situations should generate utopian horizons for shaping the future—what Lonergan had anticipated in his writings—in a realist, interdisciplinary, attainable fashion.

the present age (FS 6). In the case of economics this third level would focus on implementing effective, *ethical* policies for the good of all. The level of understanding (in FS 7) systematizes efforts to promote the good so as to foster in this present case the practice of economic justice: it requires personal and group ethical commitments. In FS 8, one returns to the first level of experience through communications in ways adapted to various audiences.[108] This return to the level of experience can help people directly address economic injustices in positive, effective ways, specifically by raising the overall standard of living. The linked eight FS open up new horizons for practicing justice.[109]

We do realize that many readers may find it odd, at least, to compare theology as a discipline to say, anthropology[110] or physics. However, in theology as any other science, including economics, researchers have to frame their findings in terms that are logically coherent and that account for the available evidence. In the classicist framework of theology as exemplified by Ludwig Ott, theology was conceived in terms of its formal and material objects, namely God and all things in relation to God.[111] Lonergan, however, takes an original functional perspective towards theology; he conceives it as mediating "between a cultural matrix and the significance and the role of

---

108. On the difficulty of communicating to various audiences, see *Insight*, 585–617.

109. As to the need of new horizons, in science and in human affairs, one may cite the example that prior to the Michelson-Morley experiment there was no empirical evidence that the speed of light is constant in all reference frames. Yet despite this lack, it would still be true. Einstein relied on the Michelson-Morley experiment in developing his theory of relativity as part of the empirical evidence needed to prove his theory. As to the need for new insights, Lonergan wrote: "I believe all discussions of concrete possibility to suffer from a radical ambiguity. For on any concrete issue further insight is always possible, and when it occurs, what previously seemed impossible turns out to be quite feasible after all." (*Insight*, 161). Today, a new horizon is needed to transform economic structures in ways Lonergan suggests in *CWL* 15, 21—a horizon we suggest can be found by deploying needed policy changes in economics and environmental protections.

110. See Pierre Whalon's argument in "Theology and anthropology: can each help the other?" *Anthropoetics* XXVI, no. 2 Spring 2021, http://anthropoetics.ucla.edu/ap2602/2602whalon/

111. See Ogilvie's *Faith Seeking Understanding*, (Marquette Univ. Press, 2001) and Gerard Whalen, "The Continuing Significance of Bernard Lonergan."

a religion in that matrix."[112] This *new* notion means that theology is not identified with a particular religion. Rather, Lonergan conceives theology functionally and dynamically. One of its tasks is to help a religion communicate with a culture. This means that one does theology in ways relevant to a particular cultural context. For a classicist, both culture and theology are conceived statically; theology is to be modeled on views of science and culture as permanently valid: one reflects upon an object's nature. Lonergan is not concerned with this approach. Rather, his empirical notion of culture leads him to reflect on theology's method: theology, like science and culture, is an ongoing cumulative and cooperative task.

It was during the Great Depression that Lonergan began writing on economics. We situate his two volumes on economics within the context of his lifework. There is little direct textual evidence that Lonergan thought of his twin contributions to the theory of economics and to the methodological praxis of philosophy and theology as being interconnected parts of his life-long vision. He does hint at this in his "Healing and Creating in History" article.[113] GEM-FS theory and praxis reinforce one another.[114] Our approach is mirrored in 1) Lonergan's comment in *Insight* that links the economy with technology and polity,[115] 2) Toynbee's account of the "seriation of social responses" in history,[116] 3) our proposal of fostering a just standard of living through ethical policies in economics and for the environment. *Insight* prepared Lonergan for his writing *MiT*. He wanted

---

112. *MiT* xi; *CWL* 14, 3.

113. In his comments on *"The Vocation of Business: Social Justice in the Marketplace,"* *March,* 2011 in *Review of Social Economy* 69 (1):130–33, Roderick J. MacDonald, commenting on "Healing and Creating in History," writes that "both the theoretical and practical aspects of economic life require a grasp of the moral principles that inform and heal the human heart, as well as the economic principles" that will help humans pursue "their own well-being. "We argue that a further problem is that economists tend to misjudge human freedom—a mistake we seek to avoid.

114. Our GEM-FS sandwich is "intellectually digestible." It strives to be an interactive integrator, an interdisciplinary interfaith tool to promote collaborative endeavors of which the world will need for a livable future. It does so by addressing the shortcomings of economics and philosophy so as to mutually correct these as did Lonergan.

115. *Insight*, 234.

116. See Philip McShane,1982 Boston College, Lonergan Workshop, 53–82.

to develop his method based on the normal intellectual operations of theologians, and to make explicit how these conscious, intentional operations *function* in a theologian.[117] *MiT* seeks to implement the inherent impetus *all* humans have to be attentive, intelligent, reasonable, responsible and loving—despite the myriad ways people stray from that drive. The drive towards authenticity should lead to affirming reasoned "positions" and to reversing false "counterpositions"[118] in one's search for truth in *any* intellectual endeavor—not just in theology.

On the other hand,

> Inasmuch as one accepts the counterpositions, one thinks of the real as a subdivision in the 'already out there now real,' of objectivity as extroversion, and of knowing as taking a good look; similarly, on the counterpositions, the good is identified with objects of desire while the intelligible good of order and the rational good of value are regarded as so much ideological superstructure that can claim to be good only inasmuch as it furthers the attainment of objects of desire.[119]

The normative, universal nature of human intentionality that Lonergan explored led to his linking continuity with renewal in theology. For

---

117. *Second Collection*, 52, 268.

118. *Insight*, 413. Lonergan develops "positions" from the experience of being "attentive, intelligent, rational and responsible." He argues that 1) the real is the concrete universe of being: 2) the thinking person knows self as the consequence of affirming self as intelligent and self-critical, and 3) that objectivity is considered in that light and not as a "property of vital anticipation, extroversion and satisfaction." Counterpositions contradict one or more of these points. For Lonergan, the position implies experiential objectivity that is "the given as given. It is the field of materials about which one inquires, in which one finds the fulfilment of conditions for the unconditioned, to which cognitional process repeatedly returns to generate the series of inquiries and reflections that yield the contextual manifold of judgements." *Insight*, 405–06.

119. *Insight*, 647. This is the antithesis of Milton Friedman's insistence that a firm's only responsibility to society is to maximize its profits. One might ask whether the 0's and 1's and the *concept* of empty set as foundation of the universe introduced by George Boole are a threat to the good of humanity in that pragmatic digitalization now drives humans to make money. The empty set may be one form of the "already-*out-there-now-real*" (*Insight*, 276) that neglects or downplays the notion of a thing which exists as an intelligible whole.

example, genuine continuity is achieved when theologians realize that people of different times and places operate under the same normative structure of their conscious intentional operations. One seeks for continuity not in concepts, but in the common cognitional operations possessed by people of different times and places. One discovers that intentional consciousness can build upon past achievements. While this implies development, it also means that contemporary work is linked to and continuous with the past, albeit critically. Lonergan argues that it is human minds who do theology (anthropology, economics, physics, etc.). He intended his method to be a specific application of the general transcendental method (intentionality analysis) developed in *Insight*—which is why it applies to all who seek to understand something. Both *Insight* and *MiT* help readers discover the dynamic structure of their own conscious intentional operations. In both books, Lonergan assumes his readers are cognitive, moral and affective beings. It is crucial to realize that what he sought is, in fact, *the* method of all human attempts to know. His is *not* just another resource for solving particular problems, or for addressing theological content.

By making explicit the conscious, intentional operations of theologians, and by extension, of all thinkers, Lonergan adds clarity, intelligibility[120] and precision to the searcher's task. He does so by outlining what human authenticity is in relation to theological activity. *MiT* evaluates the degree to which a theologian *operates* in authentic human fashion. The word "operates" is crucial because Lonergan's lifework was dedicated to understanding how our minds operate. He defines method

---

120. In *Insight*, 101–02, in the section on the canon of relevance, Lonergan asks whether there should be introduced a technical term to denote "the intelligibility immanent in the immediate data of sense" that resides in the relations of things, not our senses, but to one another. He answers: "The trouble is that the appropriate technical term has long existed but also has long been misunderstood. For the intelligibility that is neither final nor material nor instrumental nor efficient causality is . . . formal causality. But some people misinterpret the latter, assuming that one means something connected with formal logic; others are bound to assume that one means merely the heuristic notion of 'the nature of . . . ', the 'such as to . . . '. If both these misinterpretations are excluded, what we have called the intelligibility immanent in sensible data and residing in the relations of things to one another . . . might be named a species of formal causality."

as a "normative pattern of recurrent and related operations yielding cumulative and progressive results."[121] A method implies distinct operations; each operation is related to others; the relation forms a pattern which is verified as the *correct* way of performing the task; the pattern's operations may be repeated indefinitely.[122] Lonergan does not impose his method upon readers as if it were a procedure deduced from supposed first principles. Nor does he expect his readers to unintelligently follow a set of prescribed operations. Rather, he invites them to attend to their *own conscious activities* and to find *within* themselves the relevant intentional conscious operations he describes. His method explores the set of operations[123] that can help one think authentically and collaboratively. A reader will have to discover in his/her own experience the dynamic relationships leading from one operation to the next. This is in a nutshell the long process of self-appropriation outlined in *Insight*. Were a reader to fail to understand Lonergan's invitation to self-appropriate

---

121. *MiT*, 4. *CWL* 14, 8.

122. *MiT*, 22; *CWL* 14, 24. Implied here is the heuristic process of intending.

123. David Oyler writes that the FS, as associated with different general contexts of operations, are metaphorical in the sense that there is a correlation between the results of the full set of operations for each specialization in each field and the context of consciousness that provides the potentiality for the field of its achievement. The relation between the general contexts of the FS and the operations is analogical, not metaphorical; but if the relation is thought of in terms of levels, then it is metaphorical." http://www.davidoyler.org. The only element in our consciousnesses that is radically a priori, innate, naturally given, is our threefold transcendental intending (see *A Third Collection*, 28). The interaction of that "radical upper blade" with data that we encounter (the "radical lower blade") unfolds in the pattern that is proper to an embodied, spiritual subject, namely, the four "levels" of experiencing, understanding, judging, and deciding. That four-level structure is the pattern of our activities in a wide diversity of areas. Insofar as we perform those activities attentively, intelligently, reasonably, and responsibly, we make valid achievements in the various areas and we develop skills enabling us to make similar achievements more easily in the future. The *pattern*s of those particular achievements and skills can themselves be objectified, articulated, spelled out, so as to enhance their usefulness as guidelines, organizing principles, heuristic structures in relation to future achievements. This is the pattern of the eight FS, which a community of thinkers follows in investigating objects of thought embodying meaning. However, the pattern of the FS is *not* a radically *a priori*, innate, naturally-given pattern of human subjects as such. Rather, it is a pattern of the differentiations of our transcendental intentions interacting with information that can, indeed, should arise as we experience, understand, judge, and decide together.

one's *own* conscious activities, one would find his reflections on method "about as illuminating as a blind man finds a lecture on color."[124]

For Lonergan, method is not a prescribed set of operations that can be blindly followed. "Neither discovery nor synthesis is at the beck and call of any set of rules." Method is not to be followed by a dolt, rather it is a framework of collaborative creativity; it is cumulative and progressive. Lonergan's invitation to be authentically creative helps bring theology in line with, and attuned to, the standards of modern science. Lonergan never rejects logic; he places it within a wider context in his account of human intentional operations.[125] GEM-FS is not dictated by the objects of its investigations. Being concerned with a subject's conscious intentional operations, it is an open structure for various types of inquiries.[126]

The discovery of mind marks the transition from the first stage of meaning to the second. In the first stage the world mediated by meaning is just the world of common sense. In the second stage, the world mediated by meaning splits into the realm of common sense and the realm of theory. Corresponding to this division and grounding it, there is a differentiation of consciousness.[127]

For Lonergan, "philosophy finds its proper data in intentional consciousness." It should seek to promote the self-appropriation "that cuts to the root of philosophic differences." Its secondary functions are to distinguish, relate and ground the several realms of meaning, and to ground the methods of the sciences so as to foster their unification. Lonergan wants to show that what in the third stage of meaning are differentiated, specialized moving towards an integration, were in the second stage

124. *MiT*, 7. *CWL* 14, 11.

125. "One is constantly tempted to mistake the rules of logic for the laws of thought." *Insight*, 596.

126. *MiT*, 4. *CWL* 14, 8. And read the chapter on functional specialties, *MiT* 120–138, *CWL* 14, 121–37, and for the word "theology," substitute the name of your discipline.

127. *MiT*, 90. *CWL* 14, 87. Robert Doran, "Primary Process and the Spiritual Unconscious" Lonergan Workshop, Vol. V, Scholars Press, 29, writes that "In the third stage of meaning, intellectual and psychic conversion refer both to the integrity of cognitional and psychic conversion (primary process) and to *the self-appropriation* of cognitional and psychic process (secondary process).

still "more of less undifferentiated."[128] GEM-FS follows upon the three stages of meaning and the discovery of mind based on differentiations of consciousness. GEM-FS is not bound to deductive logic; it is based on recurrent sets of operations which form a progressive cycle of investigative activity. Research uncovers new data, provides new observations and generates new insights that may verify or challenge a given hypothesis.

> The wheel of method . . . rolls along. The field of observed data keeps broadening. New discoveries are added to old. New . . . theories express not only the new insights, but also all that was valid in the old, to give method its cumulative character and to engender the conviction that, however, remote may still be the goal of the complete explanation of all phenomena, at least we are now nearer to it than we were.[129]

Rationale for MiT's Eight FS Being Treated within Two Phases

We have indicated, in summary fashion, *MiT*'s division into two phases whereby the mediating phase treats the first four FS: research, interpretation, history and dialectic. The second mediated phase then treats the remaining four FS: foundations, doctrines, systematic, communications. Lonergan argues that contemporary theology, like other disciplines, has ·become so specialized to the point that it can no longer be *one set of operations*; rather, it is a series of independent sets of operations. We can better appreciate this point by first alluding to Lonergan's outline of three distinct forms of specialization.

---

128. *MiT*, 95; *CWL* 14, 92. There follows a three-page summary of how intentionality analysis arose.

129. *MiT*, 5. *CWL* 14, 9. In *Topics in Education*, 50–51, Lonergan adds that the dynamic process of consciousness "functions as a wheel: situation, insight, counsel, policy, common consent, action, new situation, new insight, new counsel, new policy . . . The wheel can turn indefinitely. Such an analysis of process is mainly in terms of experience and insight, and also choice." Since our cognitional activities occur within the universe, and since cognitional theory and the economy intermingle, it follows that the economy falls within the law of emergent probability.

1) Field specialization which divides and subdivides the field of data so that one narrows the field of data with which one is concerned.

2) "Subject" or "department" specialization. It arranges and divides the results of its investigations.

3) Lonergan's own discovery of functional specialization which divides neither data nor results; instead, it "distinguishes and separates successive stages in the process from data to results."[130] Field and subject specializations have resulted in a proliferation of specializations of subjects and fields in human studies; they have produced a problematic fragmentation of efforts which undermine the effectiveness both of universities and of scholars.

For present purposes, we shall radically curtail the first three FS; we shall explore them in more detail later. Suffice it to say that FS 1 can be that of textual criticism which determines what is written. In this book, FS 1 is mostly concerned with the data of economics. Our FS 2, "Interpretation or commentary," focuses on what was meant in the writings of various economists. Our FS 3, history, attempts to get at what Adam Smith, Karl Marx and others meant. An important point is that Lonergan's FS are *not* disparate operations; they are successive *stages of a holistic, united process* of which they form a part. The eight FS involve many types of mental operations—dynamically, intrinsically and functionally related to one another. Each FS needs and complements the others. Later FS presuppose and complement the earlier ones. We are concerned with

---

130. *MiT*, 126. *CWL* 14, 122. The first FS, research, is straightforward: it makes available relevant data. Research gathers data that can be used in the later FS. Lonergan distinguishes general research from special research. General research (the activity that locates and retrieves previously unknown data) is unspecified in its goals. A possible outcome of general research could be a complete information retrieval system. For Lonergan, special research is an activity concerned with collecting data on a specific issue (e. g. global warming). In *Making Progress in Housing: A Framework for Collaborative Research*, (Routledge, 2014), Sean McNelis argues that science is constituted by a complete set of eight inter-related questions. Descriptively, they are an empirical question, a theoretical question, a historical question, a critical/evaluative question, a visionary/transformative question, a policy question, a strategic question and a practical question. In a broad way, we adhere to such a collaborative procedure.

the strategies and policies[131] that might best relate and apply Lonergan's original method to his two volumes on economics so as to draw out the complementary aspects of his writings on method, philosophy, theology and economics. With this in mind, we now briefly touch on the final five FS; we shall develop them in more detail when we give a fuller account of the eight FS in Part III (FS 1–4) and in Part IV (FS 5–8).

FS 4, Dialectic. While history judges as to what was going forward within a religion or a discipline, it is a fact that there have been a multiplicity of movements featuring dynamic, concrete and often contradictory aspects. Dialectic calls us to responsibly decide as to the movements' authenticity and values. Lonergan notes that dialectic takes material from the conflicts between historical accounts and theological interpretations of different movements.[132] Dialectic's function is to seek a "comprehensive viewpoint of different conflicts." Lonergan proposes that such a viewpoint can be attained by understanding the character, oppositions and relations involved in contradictory historical movements. Dialectic thus critically compares conflicts. It seeks to clarify what given differences are irreducible, but also what the proponents of different positions do share. It aims to reconcile the differences where possible. It does so by stressing that conflicts may be seen as *stages*[133] *in a united process of development.*

Dialectic corresponds to the transcendental precept, "be responsible." Based on this approach, dialectic decides which movements are worthwhile and coherent—and which movements are not; it adds to history by *evaluating* achievements; it discerns within them good or evil.

---

131. Policy is the sphere within which subordinates can make decisions within an organization; strategy has the larger task of defining how an organization's goals are to be achieved. This book focuses first on Lonergan's life-long strategies which include a universal viewpoint but also seeks to coordinate policies in given instances.

132. *MiT*, 129; *CWL* 14, 124–25. In times of relentlessly ongoing changes, a GEM-FS process approach is a reliable way to restore and coordinate stability. This requires deep human commitments (as we suggest in Part I and develop more fully in Parts II-IV).

133. "Stages" loom large in Lonergan's exposition of the stages of meaning in general and in his transposition of productive and exchange processes in the economy—e. g., in *CWL* 15, 28–35, *CWL* 21, 238–42, 246–50, 278.

(This is precisely what we attempt to do later when we evaluate various proposals that recognize or not *the need to act justly*.) Dialectic seeks to correct views based on unsound reasons, *ad hoc* explanations, suspicions or malice. It would do this by helping resolve conflicts—not by adding new data—but by adapting a sounder, transformational *horizon*.[134] In short, dialectic's function is to arrive at a comprehensive viewpoint which acknowledges meaningful, as opposed to merely contingent, differences. It determines the grounds for such differences and seeks to eliminate unnecessary conflicts.

FS 5. The result of dialectic is a commitment to the new horizon revealed in the process. "Foundations objectifies conversion. They bring to light the opposite poles of a conflict in personal history."[135] Conversion, "a transformation of the subject and his world," changes a person's mind and heart: one's life takes on a new direction with new values, new concerns, new interests. Normally, it is an ongoing, lasting process, best discerned on the basis of its pivotal moments of judging and deciding. Foundations objectifies what flows from a person's depths—whether of an "average person," an ethicist, a social critic, an economist. Conversion, as an authentic, ongoing movement from one viewpoint by a new conscious *decision*, opens one to a new horizon. Within such a new horizon, one will judge, evaluate one's world in new, more meaningful ways. In the case of a theologian, one's conversions will determine one's stance

---

134. For Lonergan, the term horizon has a technical meaning: "Horizons are the sweep of our interests and of our knowledge; they are the fertile source of further knowledge and care; but they are also the boundaries that limit our capacity for assimilating more than what we have already attained." *MiT*, 223; *CWL* 14, 208.

135. *MiT*, 126. *CWL* 14, 122. We cannot remain with the givens of our *operations*; we have to get into the givens of applied *operators* in various fields and their operational processes. This was one of Lonergan's key discoveries which involve the data of consciousness as well as the data of sense. Lonergan stresses that in "the realm of interiority language speaks of the subject and his/her operations as objects. This rests upon a self-appropriation that has verified in personal experience the operator, the operations, and the processes referred to in the basic terms and relations of the language employed." *MiT*, 257; *CWL*, 14, 241. It is due to such a verification process that one can then move on to authentic foundations—to GEM-FS' second transformative healing phase anchored in the various conversions. In the second healing phase of *Healing and Creating in History*, Lonergan defines the role of grace in his evaluation of B. F. Skinner and Karl Marx.

toward ecclesial teachings. For Lonergan, a person should operate know-ingly, morally and lovingly in an ongoing process of seeking to be liber-ated from counterpositions so as to reach a self transcendent horizon of truth, goodness and value.[136]

Conversion is a movement from one world of meaning to another. It is an existential, very personal occurrence, but it can be shared with others—yielding communities with transformed horizons. When this happens, a community forms which holds in common a new horizon affecting that community's members' conscious and intentional opera-tions.[137] On the personal level, conversion is existential, utterly intimate. But it is not so private as to be solitary. It can happen to many, and they can form a community to sustain one another in their self-transformation and to help one another in working out the implications and fulfill-ing the promise of their new perspectives.[138] Such conversions deepen understanding, affect judgments and influence personal and community decisions.[139] When addressing such conversions—making it the object of deliberation—one is operating within FS 5, foundations. Foundations pivots on responsible decisions about what is valuable and meaningful and what is not. FS 4 and 5 define the horizons by which beliefs can be evaluated. This approach evaluates the horizons which enable or impede the needed decisions that have to be made when communities, be they political or business entities, address economics. We shall speak of needed horizonal transformations in evaluating economics. How

---

136. For Lonergan, "The World Mediated by Meaning," *Philosophical and Theological Papers 1965–1980, CWL* 17, 115; "Science is an ongoing process."

137. Environmental and economics turnarounds can only occur within such a socie-tal perspective. They are integral GEM-FS elements of science as an ongoing process.

138. *MiT*, 115. *CWL* 14, 112. With Lonergan, we seek a *radical new* approach to eco-nomics rooted in ethics and values that includes an "intensely personal" commitment to needed transformations in a new age. Radical was first an adjective, borrowed in the 14th century from the Latin *radicalis*, itself from Latin radic-, *radix*, meaning "root."

139. For Catholics and Anglicans, "reconciliation" is at the heart of the process of conversion. Being forgiven, one can give comfort to those experiencing sorrow or pain. This process needs a source deeper than mere natural impulses; it can glocally be found in GEM-FS process. By integrating Lonergan's economics within his larger opus, we seek to glocally reconcile the social teachings of the Church and the strivings of liberation theolo-gians in *mutually broadening* horizons for the good of all.

discern and implement ways of bringing about such transformations? In theology, FS 5 *lets one latch on to, commit oneself to the horizons* within which religious teachings have meaning. This is why we postulate a need for a turnaround in societal views on economics that has to be complemented by an *environmental turnaround*[140] perspicaciously called for by Rachel Carson in 1962.

FS 6, Doctrines. FS 6 is concerned with "doctrines," but our text addresses FS 6 in terms of the policies needed to implement universal values in economics in the light of our overall approach to decision-making explained in FS 4 and FS 5. In FS 6, one concretizes ways that the transcendental precept, "be reasonable" applies to church doctrines—or, in our case, in economic policies. Lonergan argues that doctrines express judgments of both fact and value. His notion of doctrines does not rest on arbitrary truths divinely revealed; rather it envisages doctrines as resulting from a determinate method.[141] FS 4, dialectic, manifests the various options between attained truths and troubling errors of the past. FS 5 decides between truth and fallacy by considering the options dialectic has uncovered. On the basis of what horizon is a policy meaningful or meaningless? Doctrines, e.g., economic policies, stand within the horizon of foundations, without which they would lack meaning. Policies are judgments within a determinate horizon through which are selected and affirmed certain of the options presented in dialectic. Such judgments must be compatible with and intelligible within foundational horizons. In economics, they are viable policies that achieve the betterment of the standard of living.

FS 7, Systematics. For Lonergan, doctrines are not theology's terminal function[142] because the facts and values affirmed in doctrines give rise to further questions of meaning. FS 7 seeks to establish what

---

140. Alyssa Corkery's dictum, "Individual actions are good but systemic change can save the planet," *Earth Beat*, Jan. 22, 2021, anticipates what an environmental conversion is.

141. Specific to theology is the development of doctrines, "that obscure, analogical and imperfect understanding that throws some light upon the truth *known from elsewhere* and enables us to possess it more fully." Lonergan, *The Triune God: Systematics, CWL*, vol. 12: eds. Robert Doran and H. Daniel Monsour, trans. Michael Shields (Toronto: Univ. of Toronto Press, 2017), 107. Emphasis added.

142. Lonergan, *MiT*, 324–25. *CWL* 14, 301–03.

doctrines actually mean,[143] and why this is so. As regards our investigations on practicing justice both personally and in corporate policies, FS7 is important as we shall see when we evaluate the main scenarios guiding the policies of persons, firms and nations. For now, we merely recall Lonergan's notion of systematics' aim which, in theology, is to systematically conceptualize doctrines so as to solve apparent inconsistencies in an effort to come to some grasp of the mysteries affirmed in doctrines. Systematics corresponds to the transcendental precept, "be intelligent," because FS 7 searches for the meaning doctrines seek to uncover and explain. In the discipline of economics, FS7 is where one explains and defends principles underlying policies.

FS 8, Communications. In this eighth FS, the first seven FS come to fruition; it is concerned with theology in its external relations. Those relations may be with practitioners of the arts, sciences, or other religions. FS 8 is concerned with the relations that come from the transpositions that theology must make so that a religion can retain its integrity, while also appealing to the minds and hearts of people. Credibly communicating with different people means that the theologian must find common meaning and understanding with those whom one is addressing. It is on such basis of common understanding that one can transmit one's acquired knowledge to others. Because effective communication requires common understanding, crass forms of ideologies whereby the hearers simply repeat dogmatic concepts are ruled out. Communications resumes, completes the transcendental precept "be attentive" by providing the fresh new theology to those willing to hear it.

A community of economists can also apply GEM-FS to common goals[144] since the eight FS are different but related stages in a process:

---

143. In speaking of the constitutive function of meaning, Lonergan writes. "The family, the state, the law, the economy are not fixed and immutable entities. They adapt to changing circumstances: they can be reconceived in the light of new ideas; they can be subjected to revolutionary change." *MiT*, 78. *CWL* 14, 76.

144. GEM-FS is an ideal method for scholars to interrelate the sciences, economics and the humanities. It can help promote dialogue *and* cooperation. GEM is the general method, whereas the sciences are special methods. One extrapolates into the "isomorphism" of ethical reflection as does Lonergan in *Insight* and in his section on values in *MiT*,

they distinguish and relate the successive stages of scientific and human disciplines on the basis of the processes they use in evaluating data and arriving at results. GEM- FS seeks the good divulged in any discipline, in religion or ethics so as to help bring about a living wage and a fair distribution of goods. Recognizing the fact that our world is now largely guided by secularist thought, coordinating the efforts of persons of faith and of ethicists—religious *and* secularist—in favor of a just distribution of goods and services is crucial. Religion differs from spirituality. Believers in religion are often divided or persecuted. Many now realize that all religious traditions share certain common spiritual impulses. GEM-FS, a deep form of "dialogue," recognizes a transcendent, unifying spirituality. Spiritual life is not just about "us": it is about *all* life on the planet. Personal experience, spirituality,[145] ethics and the various sciences are all vital elements in developing and deploying strategies for social justice. GEM-FS strategies call for a global ethics which will help people become more aware of the overall implications of our lives and the ways life itself is now threatened.

In *MiT*'s first phase, one learns from the past; in the second phase, one addresses contemporary problems so as to help guide the future.

34–4, *CWL* 14, 35–37. Phil McShane addresses this issue in *Futurology Express*, noting that it is a difficult climb for both physicists and philosophers to get to grips with the cycle of functional collaboration as essential to all human inquiry. The issues raised in *Insight* and in *MiT* on the human good and on values can only be solved effectively in the full GEM-FS cyclic structure. This is clearly implied in an oft-quoted passage: "Generalized empirical method operates on a combination of both the data of sense and the data of consciousness: it does not treat of objects without taking into account the corresponding operations of the subject; it does not treat of the subject's operations without taking into account the corresponding objects." Lonergan, *A Third Collection*, 38.

145. Humans are endowed with spiritual capacities as they seek universal values. This is a fact testified to by the founders of all the world religions as well as by sages and philosophers throughout history. With Shalom Schwartz, we recognize that human values may seem like an abstract concept to some and that cultures may differ in their value priorities. But we also argue that values are fundamentally important in a person's identity and can bind multifaceted quests. We argue that a global ethics and the Universal Declaration of Human Rights are based on such values as peace, freedom, social progress, equal rights and human dignity, enshrined in e.g., the Charter of the United Nations. https://www. un.org/News/ Press/docs/ 2003/sgsm9076.doc.htm

This is in keeping with how Lonergan distinguished the four levels in each person's conscious and intentional operations: experiencing, understanding, judging and deciding. We stress GEM-FS' ability to help humans address the many transformations now affecting life on our planet. It is a process method grounded in the transformed metaphysics Lonergan developed in *Insight*, chapters 14–17.[146] A reduplicative feedback process method based on humans' four levels of conscious intentionality serves as criterion to deploy the eight FS—be it in theology or in any other academic or scientific field (with due consideration of these fields' own specialized criteria). Let us first situate our effort within the vast perspective of emergent probability.

Emergent Probability

Insight develops a worldview based on emergent probability, that is, "the successive realization in accord with successive schedules of probability of a conditioned series of schemes of recurrence."[147] This worldview along with Lonergan's revision of metaphysics potentially enables us to intelligently discuss the relationships among academic disciplines and the worlds they explore—including the question of the

---

146. In Parts III and IV, we argue that Lonergan's stress on the dynamic functions of human knowing influenced his presentation in *CWL 15* on the functional aspects of an economy. This is reinforced by Jim Kanaris' *In Deference to the Other, Lonergan and Contemporary Continental Thought* (SUNY, 2004). For Kanaris, "the presence we have of ourselves is a constitutive presence because, not despite, the fact that it is a decentering presence. Our presence to ourselves as subjects is a constitutive presence of human subjectivity . . . in the sense "that it brings us closer to ourselves as engaged in a process which can provide us with access to the intelligible universe." (28). Kanaris rebuts claims of Continental thinkers that our presence to ourselves is another instance of the metaphysics of presence. Instead, Lonergan enables us to "willingly surrender all of ourselves to the radically decentering of ourselves whereby we participate in the transcendent sources of meaning and values." This book challenges modern societies to distribute goods more justly in accordance with authentic notions of the good or values.

147. *Insight*, 148. Schemes of recurrence point to the diverging series of conditions for events that coil around in a circle; the fulfilment of conditions for one scheme leads to the occurrence of other schemes denoted by a series of conditionals. *Insight*, 141.

finality of the universe and its directed dynamism.[148] The universe is upwardly but indeterminately directed. If the universe is intelligible, if it responds to our questioning–as science presupposes–where is all this heading? The natural sciences such as physics, chemistry, biology, investigate the empirically ascertainable world. The humanities such as philosophy, psychology, sociology and ethics are more likely to ask about human understanding, judgment and decision-making. How do we link all these disciplines together in such a way as to gain an adequate understanding of the issues involved in the practice of ethically sound, effective economics?[149] Lonergan's view of a dynamic finality in the world involves schemes of recurrence considered as series of events or of operations.

Schemes of Recurrence as a Series of Events or Operations: An Effort to Relate these to Universal Values and Emergent Probability[150]

For Lonergan, a "scheme of recurrence" means a series of events or operations intelligibly linked together by the natural laws of physics,

---

148. For Lonergan, finality refers to a theorem of the same generality as the notion of being. It affirms 1) a parallelism between the dynamism of the mind and the dynamism of proportionate being; 2) that the objective universe is not static, not fixed in the present, but in process, in tension; 3) as regards present reality in its dynamic aspect, the dynamism is open. Lonergan works out various characteristics of finality as the dynamism of the real. "Men are apt to judge the universe by anthropomorphic standards. They look for the efficiency of their machines, the economy of their use of materials and power, the security of their . . . plans, the absence of disease and death, of violence and pain, of abuse and repression that reflects the desires and the aspirations of their hearts. But human utopias are paper schemes. They postulate in the universe more perfect materials than those with which it builds. They suppose that the building can be some extrinsic activity apart from the universe itself. They forget that they themselves, (and) their great achievements are by-products of the universe . . . in accord with its proper intelligibility," that includes "an ever fuller realization of being." *Insight*, 470–77.

149. *Investopia*, Dec. 2020, notes that a basic standard of living that allows all to reach their full potential is a required aspect of a just economy.

150. "The fundamental element in emergent probability is the conditioned series of things and schemes; that series is realized cumulatively in accord with successive schedules of probabilities; but a species is not conceived as an accumulated aggregate of theoretically

chemistry, biology, etc.[151] His analysis of classical and statistical scientific methods and their interrelationships[152] leads to his insisting that the laws of science are subject to conditions. The combination of classical and statistical methods yields an understanding of the universe as "emergent probability." This notion which he originated is now widely applied across several disciplines.[153] Our universe is a conditioned series of schemes of recurrence which may or may not happen. Lonergan reminds readers that

> The notion of scheme of recurrence arose in *Insight* when it was noted that the diverging series of positive conditions for an event might coil around in a circle. In that case, a series of events A, B, C . . . would be so related that the fulfilment of the conditions for each would be the occurrence of the others. Schematically, then, the scheme might be represented by the series of conditionals: If A occurs, B will occur; if B occurs, C will occur; if C occurs [...] A will occur. Such a circular arrangement may involve any number of terms, the possibility of alternative routes, and in general any degree of complexity.[154]

---

observable variations; on the contrary, it is an intelligible solution to a problem of living in a given environment, where the living is a higher systematization of a controlled aggregation of aggregates of aggregates of aggregates, and the environment tends to be constituted more and more by other living things." *Insight*, 290.

151. Lonergan, *Insight*, 143.

152. Lonergan begins *Insight* with the dramatic instance of insight by Archimedes He often appeals to Descartes on "understanding extremely simple things" (60). With an illustration from algebra, he compares the differences between classical and statistical laws—the latter of which touch on frequencies and inverse insights (70, 76). At present, "the profound significance of statistical laws is coming to light. But if this . . . is not to degenerate into the old talk about what commonly happens, it must retain its contact with the empirically established precision of classical formulations." (135). Inverse insights suppose a positive object of inquiry; they deny intelligibility to the object. This runs counter to the spontaneous anticipations of intelligence (78).

153. Mathew Lamb, "Emergent Probability as Open Synthesis of Sciences" (1965), argues that Lonergan's world view of emergent probability provides an open and ongoing method for correlating the sciences. See also Michael Bretz,: "Emergent Probability: A Directed Scale-Free Network Approach to Lonergan's Generic Model of Development." https://arxiv.org/abs/cond-mat/0207241

154. See Elizabeth and Mark Morelli, editors, *The Lonergan Reader*, 87.

Patrick Byrne puts Lonergan's schemes of recurrence in perspective: "In Lonergan's explanation of emergence certain kinds of schemes of recurrence *themselves* form the prior conditions for other subsequent schemes.[155] Byrne argues that a biological species is an intelligible solution to a problem of living in a given environment.

> Later species are solutions that . . . rise upon previous solutions. A solution is the sort of thing that human insight hits upon. Simply put, the intelligibility of strictly natural emergent probability is compatible with the termination and even extinction of particular schemes of recurrence.[156]

Science seeks to correct the understanding of how events are intelligibly connected within a scheme of recurrence. When new schemes begin to function, genuinely new intelligibilities emerge; scientists seek to correctly understand those newly emergent intelligibilities. Universal

---

155. Patrick Byrne, *Worldviews: Global Religions, Cultures and Ecology* Vol. 7, No. 1/2 (2003), 22, referring to *Insight*, 145. Philip McShane's *Randomness, Statistics, and Emergence*, 1970, notes that Lonergan has four distinct goals in mind: (i) inaugurate dialogue between various schools of philosophy; (ii) orient the philosophy of science away from general considerations; (iii) provide a detailed account of various points treated in Lonergan's works; (iv) establish on a wider basis of contemporary mathematics and science the position of Lonergan on the nature of randomness, statistics, and emergence. To arrive at a principle of emergence, McShane focuses on actual procedures of empirical investigators and the type of explanation they seek. Those doing the relevant sciences—biophysics and biochemistry can verify objective randomness and emergence by attending to their performance. McShane concludes that emergence and evolution are explained in terms of probabilities of emergence and probabilities of survival of recurrence-schemes.

156. In "Ecology, Economy and Redemption as Dynamic: The Contributions of Jane Jacobs and Bernard Lonergan," *Worldviews*, 1. Byrne adds that for Lonergan schemes of recurrence are quite complex, involving intricate sub-loops and alternative pathways. He situates the conflict 'of development within the larger context of evolutionary emergent probability. This raises an important issue. On the one hand, emergence depends on the continued functioning of prior recurrent schemes that constitute ecosystems. If these are violently destroyed, they and the subsequent emergent forms that depend upon them are lost. On the other hand, development cannot proceed without the transformation of prior schemes by later ones. In nature, emergent probability "respects" its underlying conditions, and yet it does not leave prior schemes untouched. We need to learn to respect the delicate interplays, (Byrne, 11), while reaching "group agreements and decisions ever more fairly and effectively." (*Insight*, 233–34). See https://www.degruyter.com/document/doi/10.3138/9781442676794-022/pdf for linking economics with emergent probability.

values, expressed in ethics[157] and in the world religions, inform but also *sublate* mere systemic schemes of recurrence.[158] Rather than simply accept types of "recurrent schemes" that have *institutionalized* forms of injustice in the world polity, ethical principles must transform them.[159] Some schemes must be sublated or transposed with an ethics based on the common good.[160]

The process of environmental science, advocacy and long painful revisions of public policy illustrates the need and possibility of self-correcting *human* schemes of recurrence.[161] Such self-correcting schemes

---

157. The Council for Global Education (CGE) seeks to create a world where universal values such as peace, reverence for all forms of life, and responsibility are the norm. Its global education model is founded upon: Universal Values, Global Understanding, and Service to Humanity. CGE's values education goes beyond critical analysis and intellectual appreciation by connecting it to volition and the desire for improvement. CGE's goal complements our own stance on universal values. Mere knowledge of ideals and principles is not enough. We need to translate the ideals into action. CGE would implement the good and a high level of intellectual and moral developmental: it could benefit from a self-corrective GEM-FS analysis. The basic GEM structure's developmental patterns are at work in human societies despite bias and downright evil.

158. "Sublating" is a notion made famous by Hegel. Following Karl Rahner, Lonergan transposed Hegel's notion of *Aufhebung* (sublation): what sublates goes beyond what is sublated; it puts all things on a new basis; far from interfering with the sublated or harming it, it includes, preserves "all its proper features . . . and carries them forward to a fuller realization within a richer context." *MiT*, 241. *CWL* 14, 227.

159. "Proponents of world-polity theory argue that rationality, purposes, and interests are profoundly cultural constructs bound up in . . . an underlying foundation that endows actors with properties, identity, meaning, interests, and guides to action." The theory recognizes the key role played by international nongovernmental organizations" in forming and propagating world culture. John Boli, Selina Gallo-Cruz, and Matt Mathias, "World Society, World-Polity Theory, and International Relations," *Oxford Research Encyclopedia of International Studies*: https://oxfordre.com/ international studies/ view/10.1093/ acrefore/9780190846626.001.0001/acrefore-9780190846626-e-495

160. Margaret Benefie in *The Leadership Quarterly*, Vol. 16, 5, Oct. 2005, pp. 723–47 writes on a Lonerganian approach to the "Spiritual leadership for organization transformation." She points to two challenges unaddressed in the current theories of spiritual leadership: 1) the growing epistemological critique of the existing empirical studies of organizational spirituality and 2) the need for a more sophisticated understanding of spiritual leadership. She draws on Burrell and Morgan's organizational paradigms as extending Lonergan's work on spiritual transformations.

161. There are many fine NGOs who advocate for various values, for instance, the Southern Poverty Law Center: https://www.splcenter.org

show that the notions of universal values and the common good underpinning human efforts are not empty slogans but are essential to correct present-day distorted economic priorities and goals.[162]

In FS 4–6, we explore how Lonergan helps us do so by working toward effectively changing national and global policies so as to help implement needed changes in the world order. Eileen de Neeve's notion of "decoding" the facts and "recoding" them ethically is very much appropriate.

"Decoding-Recoding" the Global Economy with a GEM-FS Ethics

Having examined the implications of Covid-19, Zeynep Tufecki concludes that in the face of mutual recriminations, lies, and denials,

> A better path forward is one of true global cooperation based on mutual benefit and reciprocity. Despite the current dissembling, we should assume that the Chinese government also doesn't want to go through this again—especially given that SARS, too, started there. This means putting the public interest before personal ambitions and acknowledging that despite the wonders of its power, biomedical research also holds dangers.[163]

In a similar vein, we hold with Lonergan and Eileen de Neeve that cooperation based on the productive process's transformational roles should prevail. De Neeve's *Decoding the Economy: Understanding Change with Bernard Lonergan*[164] paves a way. With her and Lonergan, we

---

162. The route towards progress requires the recognition that if intelligence and responsibility contain their own immanent norms, then progress can be cultivated only through the growth of the whole human person. "Human progress can never be realized merely through the transformation of social or economic life conditions or through the imposition of the rule of force. The condition of possibility for this emergence is a sufficient randomness. See https://lonerganresource.com/pdf/ books/6/ Melchin,_Kenneth-History,_Ethics,_and_Emergent_Probability.pdf

163. *The New York Times*, June 26, 2021.

164. De Neeve, *Decoding the Economy* (Thomas More Institute Papers, 2008).

attempt to "recode" macroeconomics within the framework of *MiT*'s last four FS. Our GEM-FS "recoding-or-discerning" approach parallels the Indian economist Amartya Sen's "capability approach" that focuses upon the moral significance of individuals' capability of achieving the kind of lives they have reason to value.[165] This distinguishes it from utilitarianism which focuses exclusively on subjective well-being. For Sen, a person's capability to live a good life is defined in terms of the set of valuable qualities such as having loving relationships with others. Both Lonergan and Sen focused on the subjective and objective aspects of reality to foster the human good—generally and in economic terms. They show how one can maintain the schemes of human living while working to bring about new schemes.[166] The ongoing emergence of human schemes of cooperation normally follows a self-correcting criticality for pursuing better courses of action, although irrationality often interferes.[167] These, in turn, provoke further questions and insights enabling us to

---

165. Sen won the Nobel Prize for Economics 200 years after Malthus predicted starvation. Spiro Gangas' *Sociological Theory and the Capability Approach* (Routledge, 2020) is another perceptive attempt to mediate between the approaches of Adam Smith and Karl Marx. As we do, Gangas focuses on rebuilding social ethics through capable institutions, but he does so by appealing to the capability approaches of Amartya Sen and Martha Nussbaum. They, too, build upon an explanatory and normative method which, unlike Rawl's, appeals to a *theory of justice that is empirical and can be operationalized*. See also *Stanford Encyclopedia of Philosophy*, "The Capability Approach," 2011.

166. Louis Navellier, in *Investor Place Media*, 2021, notes that new industries are springing up at an ever-increasing pace, while old industries are being disrupted. "Family businesses and portfolios have been ruined." As Uber and Lyft soared to billion-dollar valuations, the taxi industry was devastated—losing millions of dollars in revenue.

167. Human practical intelligence devises arrangements for human living, that is patterns of cooperation based upon understanding and expectations of other persons (*Insight*, 239, 248). Our insights maintain the schemes of human living but constantly transform them so as to bring about new schemes—for better and for worse. (Byrne, *Worldviews*, 11). Hannah Bowman in her review of Marc Lamont Hill's *We Still Here: Pandemic, Policing, Protest, and Possibility* (Haymarket, 2020) in the *National Catholic Reporter*, May 2021, notes that Hill analyzes systemic forms of oppression in the USA. He seeks to identify the interconnected structures of oppression that have marked the US as well as "the settler colonialism of Israel and the pandemic response that prioritized economic activity over people." These are all signs of "a racialized 'politics of disposability' that structures the institutions of our society to deprioritize and devalue Black lives and other marginalized people."

re-examine situations as needed. Lonergan's GEM-FS provides a series of important bridges to help us cope with many human problems. GEM-FS is a foundational method that guides operations indwelling in all humans, namely, how we humans arrive at knowledge and make decisions in all facets of life. All humans of whatever culture come to know through the fourfold, reduplicative feedback process Lonergan has identified and developed in the FS. On the basis of this reduplicative fourfold process, the various human disciplines can engage in building transcultural-transformative bridges—powerful helps in our age of constant, mindboggling changes. Ideally, their effectiveness derives from humans' ability to appropriate their own knowing-doing operations and to act justly in an all too unjust world.

Towards Discerning Emerging Schemes of Human Cooperation

GEM-FS' holistic viewpoint distinguishes human schemes of recurrence from natural ones—both of whose emergence and survival may depend in their own fashion, as we saw, *upon acts of human intelligence and choice*. We refer to these as schemes of human cooperation which were prefigured in *Insight* and then systematically implemented in *MiT's* FS. As noted, *MiT's* eight FS are based on the four reduplicative levels of human intentional consciousness. All persons use these operations in their daily lives; thinkers use them in coming to explanatory knowledge in the sciences and in various other disciplines.[168] Still, our lives are not sufficiently guided by the values needed to cope with issues of justice. We need a "logic of the heart,"[169] which fosters repentance, a resolve to

---

168. "Our goal is not any scientific object, any universal and necessary truth, any primary propositions. Our goal is the concrete, individual, existing subject that intelligently generates and critically evaluates and progressively revises every scientific object, every incautious statement, every rigorously logical resting place that offers prematurely a home for the restless dynamism of human understanding." *Insight*, 91.This quote indicates the general context of chapter 2, "Heuristic Structures of Empirical Method."

169. See John Raymaker, A Buddhist-Christian Logic of the Heart: Nishida's Kyoto School and Lonergan's "Spiritual Genome" as World Bridge (Lanham MD: UCA Press, 2002).

do better. GEM-FS, *if* it be a logic of the heart, can help motivate people to "pay the price." We keep in mind the various levels of and multifarious approaches to ethics in which virtues and values[170] play critical roles. An inclusive GEM-FS addresses human limitations which, in fact, require self-transcending horizonal transformations.[171]

The Greek term used in the New Testament for a heart-felt conversion is *metanoia*; it points to a new state of mind cleansed of self-centered pursuits. Buddhists, for their part, speak of *samadhi*, the highest stage of mental concentration; it helps one overcome the

---

170. In *The National Catholic Reporter* April, 2021, Eugene McCarraher writes against today's myth of "meritocracy." Unlike the previous hierarchies of divine right, nepotism, and riches, "meritocracy apportions power, status, and income on the basis of 'merit' (technical knowledge), money and power.'" Whereas traditional democracy rooted legitimacy in social and political equality, meritocracy redefines democratic promise as "equality of opportunity," as a course of competition, "open to all, through which positions in schools, industry, and government are allocated." McCarraher counters: "Meritocracy produces the most insufferable ruling class in history." Because they think they've received what they truly deserve, the meritocratic elite is "no longer weakened by . . . self-criticism." Defining moral, political, and ideological issues as problems of technical or managerial know-how, meritocratic politicians abandon the notion of justice. . . . In this "providentialism without God," everyone gets what they deserve." The less intelligent should be excluded from political life. For McCarraher, the meritocratic ethic discards the idea that chance or contingency or grace have any role in human affairs. He counters that the admission of grace into the heart of "our moral universe, far from rendering us lazy or amoral, would make us less self-satisfied and more magnanimous and open-hearted." In his assessment of three authors writing on meritocracy, he notes that no matter how bourgeois-bohemian they may seem, meritocrats remain more bourgeois than bohemian: they believe that their power and wealth are deserved.

171. One reaches cognitional self-transcendence when one attends, inquires, reaches direct and reflective understanding (judges). One reaches moral and religious self-transcendence by deciding for the truly good and loving the truly lovable. To the extent that one achieves cognitional, moral and religious self-transcendence, one is authentic. One is unauthentic to the extent that one is not open to all data, scoffs at understanding, refuses to reflect and judge, rejects the love of the truly lovable. When facing the complexity that arises in investigating human subjects, the data may be a mixture of authenticity and inauthenticity. The investigation of the data may be skewed due to a lack of authenticity in the investigator. Unlike some modern philosophies, one must presume neither a speculative intellect, nor a pure reason drawing necessary truths from self-evident principles. For Lonergan, philosophers' analytic propositions must be submitted to a critical verification related to how one comes to know.

blockages that prevent one from attaining an enlightened awareness that all is interconnected. The processes at the heart of both *metanoia* and *samadhi* open wide the pathways of the mind to the larger picture of the quasi-unlimited Universe in which every point of view can be understood as part of the unfolding Cosmos. Since the Universe is so magnificently complex, it cannot be fully grasped by the limited perspectives of philosophy, science, or theology. Taking hints from the world religions and the insights of ethicists from various traditions, after our brief examination of the history of economics in Part II, in Parts III and IV, we shall suggest dialectical-foundational ways through which humanity may fulfill its spiritual and social responsibilities. Following Lonergan, we seek ways to holistically develop the foundations (FS 5) of the common good and of universal values to be practically (FS 6) and systematically (FS 7) integrated and duly communicated (FS 8).

How may goods and services be effectively distributed so as to overcome poverty?[172] Steven Greer writes of the danger[173] that "our technology has marched ahead of our spiritual and social evolution, making us, frankly, a dangerous people."[174] A difficulty we face is that while many writers on religion and philosophy speak of foundations as we do, philosophers such as Richard Rorty reject such foundations.[175] We shall argue with Philip McShane in Part IV that in dealing with economics, GEM-FS foundations are best approached from a viewpoint

---

172. Geoff Mann, "Poverty in the Midst of Plenty: Unemployment, Liquidity, and Keynes Scarcity Theory of Capital," (Univ. of Chicago, Critical Historical Studies, 2, no. 1) writes that Keynesian ideas are rooted in a theory not of capitalism per se, but of the ongoing threat capitalism poses to civilization. A due consideration of effective demand, liquidity, unemployment, and scarcity shows the ways in which they contribute to what Keynes once called a scarcity theory of capital, according to which scarcity is socially-produced in capitalism. Mann helps us understand the tragic paradox of poverty in the richest societies in history, and the irrepressible anxieties that tragedy elicits.

173. Modern technologies such as genetic engineering and cloud seeding present us with moral issues. Technology shapes our lives. FS-5 provides ways to address the issues.

174. Stephen M. Greer, "Evolution." See www.goodreads.com/author/quotes 23515

175. Richard Rorty does not reject the liberal tradition; rather, he seeks to offset abuses caused by the market. See "Progressive Utopias, Marcuse, Rorty, and Wright," *Administrative Theory and Praxis*, 34, March, 2011, 60–84.

of "discernment,"[176] one that can lead to needed horizonal transformations on the part of individuals, groups and communities. We shall first examine some of the relevant aspects explored in theories on the economy in past centuries.

---

176. Philip McShane, *Pastkeynes: Pastmodern Economics, A Fresh Pragmatism* (Halifax, Nova Scotia, 1982), 62–65, 130–31. In *One-Dimensional Man*, (Boston: Beacon Press, 1964), xii, Herbert Marcuse argued that our industrial society can start in a new direction to let the productive process benefit all. He urged that we abandon the capitalist market so as to protect the environment. He foresaw the need of what we name "socio-communal conversions."

PART II

A Brief Annotated History
of Economics

Originally, Westerners understood that the purpose of economic activity is to provide the material goods needed to attain ends more important than material goods. In his *Politics*, Aristotle distinguishes between making money and managing to focus on things more important than money. With the rise of capitalism, allied with individualism and materialism, a main goal of economic activity began to center on material wealth. The result is that economics was divorced from ethics—a catastrophic development. Marx focused on those aspects, but, due to his being a materialist, his diagnosis was incomplete. He did understand that a capitalism that encourages greed is a mistake, but he failed to understand that materialism is also a mistake. In fact he accepted too many of the capitalist premises of his time.[1]

In his chapter on Malthus and Ricardo in *The Worldly Philosophers*, Robert Heilbroner makes only a passing allusion to James Townsend's *Dissertation on the Poor Laws*, 1786, which as Floyd Matson in *The Broken Image*, argues "presented an account of economic balance independent of human effort and intervention—a balance arising wholly from natural forces and biological conditions."[2] Heilbroner and Matson remind us of the purpose and the limits of economics. In terms of our GEM-FS strategy, Heilbroner and Matson offer analyses similar to ours: they analyze the imprisoning philosophical dimensions of the economic plight in which humans have been caught since the Industrial Revolution. But they offer no liberating strategy of the type Lonergan provides. In Part II, we first comment on Adam Smith's influence,

---

1. See for example, David G. Dick, "What Money Is and Ought To Be," *Journal of Social Ontology*, vol. 6, no. 2, 2020, pp. 293–313. *https://doi.org/10.1515/jso-2020-0033*. Although capitalism and communism are viewed as polar opposites, they, in fact, agree more than they disagree; they are both materialist, quibbling about how to distribute wealth. With Dick, we focus on ethical implications, relying more on an Aristotelian teleology than on Locke's. Lonergan's views on an emancipative cosmopolis helped him promote a teleology sounder than Locke's. Locke and Lonergan agreed on God's benevolence; but Locke's teleology conforms with capitalist, money-making goals. GEM-FS seeks to reconcile Greek notions of teleology as perfecting human nature with modern notions that define right conduct as promoting the glocal good of all.

2. Floyd W. Matson, *The Broken Image, Man, Science and Society*. (New York: Anchor, 1964), 19.

then elaborate on the writings and influence of other noted economists with the aim of re-evaluating and re-interpreting these writers' views in Parts III and IV.

One of our concerns is that today's increasingly "scientific" economics is overlooking fundamental social and political issues that are central to a needed theory of a valid and authentically liberating economics. With Lonergan, we inquire into the historical problems that have distorted thinking on economics while calling for needed, effective, countervailing policies. Affirming notions of value and justice in human affairs is essential to sound macroeconomic theory. We shall argue that Adam Smith launched a process which led to versions of rudderless theoretical accounts in which the *entrapment* of human beings became a reality due to questionable theory-praxis approaches. We view it as imperative to reverse various unethical approaches to economics in ways Lonergan's GEM-FS approach pioneered.

ADAM SMITH'S NOTION OF AN "INVISIBLE HAND" THAT LED TO "LAISSEZ-FAIRE,"[3] NEOLIBERALISM, AND SOCIALIST REACTIONS

It was in his *The Theory of Moral Sentiments*, (1759)[4] that Adam Smith (1723–1790) introduced his "Invisible Hand" to describe the unintended social benefits brought about by individuals acting in their own self-interest. Smith's theoretical work is viewed as having been a scientific breakthrough inasmuch as it shows that our moral ideas and actions are a product of our nature as social creatures. It argues that a social psychology is a better guide to moral action than is reason. It identifies basic rules needed for society to survive; it seeks to explain what enables a

---

3. Tradition has it that "*laissez-faire*" is derived from the answer Jean-Baptiste Colbert, comptroller of finance under King Louis XIV, received when he asked industrialists what the government could do to help business: "Leave us alone." That liberal attitude leading to a predatory "freedom" is reflected in Jean-Jacques Rousseau's first sentence in his *Social Contract*: "Man is born free but is everywhere in chains." We seek true freedom.

4. *Moral Sentiments* provided the ethical, psychological and methodological underpinnings for Smith's later works.

society to flourish.[5] Smith referred to *an* invisible hand (not of *the* invisible hand). In *The Wealth of Nations*, "invisible hand" appears only once. Yet, this so-called invisible hand is now linked to the liberalism[6] of a *laissez-faire* underpinning what is today known as a "trickle-down" economic theory—a concept often taken for granted in classical theory such as is the phrase "The gluttony of the rich serves to feed the poor."[7] Jonathan Schlefer has argued that "There is no Invisible Hand."[8] Smith himself often noted situations where "natural liberty" does not work. If, for example, banks charge too much interest they will wind up lending to prodigals and precipitate crashes. Smith argued that when people of the same trade meet, "they wind up talking about ways to raise prices . . . Let market competition continue to drive the division of labor, and it produces workers as 'stupid and ignorant as it is possible for a human creature to become.'"[9]

The imprecise term "neoclassical economics" is used in different ways. It was coined by Thorstein Veblen,[10] who sought to describe the synthesis of the subjective and objective theory of value by way of

---

5. See the Online Adam Smith Institute: www.adamsmith.org/

6. Politically, liberals in Europe support a broad tradition of individual liberties and a constitutionally-limited form of government. In America, liberals might be confused with social-democrats who call for a larger government, and a form of protectionism. GEM-FS can help us rediscover and deploy the core radicalism of an authentic, just liberalism.

7. Adam Smith, *The Theory of Moral Sentiments*, vol. 1, 184 in The Glasgow Edition of the Works and Correspondence of Adam Smith, 7 vol., Oxford Univ. (1984).

8. Jonathan Schlefer, "There is no Invisible Hand," *Harvard Business Review*, April, 10, 2012. Roger Farmer, *How the Economy Works*, 30–31, alludes to Pareto's important first theorem of welfare economics which says that there is a connection between Pareto's notion of a better allocation of commodities and the way that commodities are allocated in market economies. Farmer concludes "that the first welfare theorem does not apply to real economies" due to the fact that, unlike the general equilibrium theory would have us believe, people are subject to losing their job as happens in a time of recession. For Farmer, Pareto efficiency is another version of the invisible hand.

9. Smith, *Wealth of Nations*, Part I, Chapter 10, quoted by Schlefer in "No Invisible Hand."

10. By neoclassical, Veblen stressed that there was more continuity than discontinuity between classical economics and the school of marginalism. For him, neoclassical theory had been outpaced by the society it sought to explain. It had closed itself off from sociology and history at the very time when interdisciplinary studies were needed to understand the evolution of society's institutions. See www.veblen-institute.org/Have-read-Veblen.html.

a diagram of supply and demand, first developed by Alfred Marshall. Marshall had combined the classical understanding that the value of a commodity results from the costs of production with the new findings of marginalism which argued that the value is determined by individual utility. Marginalism was the dividing line between classical and modern economics. Up until the present time, the "market diagram"—used to illustrate how the forces of supply and demand interact to determine prices and quantities sold, and representing the intersection of objective supply and subjective demand—has been a central element of neoclassical economics.[11] The paradigmatic core of neoclassical theory now dominates economics education and research. It argues that the central economic problem is the organization and allocation of scarce resources. This implies that efficiency—optimally using available resources in order to maximize individual utility and a nation's welfare—is the most relevant evaluation-criterion. The central research domains of neoclassical economics are: microeconomics, (analyzing the behavior of households and firms); macroeconomics, (examining economic aggregates and the interaction of markets); and its analytic tool of econometrics. Today, various mathematical models are used in the analysis of the economic system. For neoclassical economists, these models are best suited to uncover causal relationships.[12] But Lonergan, as a general principle,

---

While classical economic theory assumed that a product's value derives from the cost of materials plus the cost of labor, neoclassical economists say that consumer perceptions of the value of a product also affect its price and demand.

11. Its main proponents are Robert Solow and Trevor Swan. The theory states that economic growth results from labor, capital, and technology. While an economy has limited resources as to the first two, contribution from technology to growth is boundless. Lonergan focused "on the need to pay special attention to the concrete intelligibility of specifically *economic* events" that had led to "the permanent gap between the earnings of (fully employed) workers and the cost of a minimally adequate standard of living." *CWL* 15, xxix. He stressed the need to find a foundation for accurate analyses.

12. Benjamin M. Friedman's *Religion and The Rise of Capitalism*, 2021, borrows its title from a famous 1926 work by R. H. Tawney—a historian and a crusader for social justice—who lamented the loss of moral criteria in humanity's rush to increase the GDP. Tawney and Friedman anticipated some of our arguments on Smith as to how morality can be reinstated into the causal relations affecting today's secular societies. Lonergan avoided extensive use of the word "causal" in favor of "classical" due to his wanting to concentrate on the significance of heuristically anticipating the intelligibility immanent in data. In the

insisted that "If we want a comprehensive grasp of everything in a unified whole, we . . . have to construct a diagram in which are symbolically represented all the various elements of the question along with all the connections between them."[13] The diagrams in our Fig. 4–5 illustrate this. Early on, Lonergan had an all-important insight, namely that

> The moral precept of a just wage . . . is or should be a principle of justice—as well as of charity. The gap between well-intentioned moral demands and economic exigencies led Lonergan to inquire into how economic moral precepts could be based in the economy itself.[14]

Lonergan's Theory of the Two Distinct Phases of Expansion

For Lonergan, economic growth is not uniform.

> It requires first understanding that there are . . . two distinct phases of expansion. Normatively, a surplus expansion is to be followed by a basic expansion, which the surplus expansion makes possible. A surplus expansion involves major investment in production of the means of production, (that is . . . in surplus goods and services.[15]

---

statistical heuristic structure, such an intelligibility is denied. We believe that Friedman, https://international.la-croix.com/news/ culture/theologys-invisible-hand/14869 in fact reinforces our GEM-FS argument on heuristics.

13. Lonergan, The Ontological and Psychological Constitution of Christ, *CWL 7*, Univ. of Toronto Press, 2002, 151.

14. *CWL* 15, Editors' Introduction, p. xxviii.

15. Paul St. Amour, "An Introduction to Lonergan's Macroeconomic Theory," Marquette University Colloquium, Feb. 28, 2013, 3. "Insofar as there occurs an increase in the rate of production of surplus goods and services, there is facilitated a subsequent increase in the rate of production of goods and services that enter directly into a community's standard of living (which Lonergan terms basic goods and services). Ideally executed, economic history becomes not a sequence of boom and busts, but a successive sequence of surplus and basic expansions, through which humanity's standard of living mounts to successively higher plateaus. Hence the purpose of capital formation and surplus expansion is to set conditions necessary for a subsequent basic expansion." The word *surplus* has no negative connotation of "too much"; the term "surplus product" denotes the precise analytical definition of a point-to-line item; "surplus income" is to be spent for the purchase of capital for repair and maintenance or expansionary investment rather than for a standard of living.

"Surplus" goods and services make production more efficient but do not directly enter into people's standard of living, that is, the measure of the "basic" economy. Eileen de Neeve argued that, in contrast to Lonergan's stress on the two phases at the heart of economic growth, neoclassical economists take equilibrium growth as empirically evident. They assume that people behave rationally when choosing their level of employment, consumption and investment. But for Lonergan, *medium-term processes* are central to understanding capitalism. It is in the period of economic growth after World War II that "economists' interest turned to economic growth rather than cycles."[16] Due to this, Lonergan cautioned that

> Misunderstandings can sidetrack both the surplus and basic expansions. If rising consumer prices in the surplus expansion are misunderstood, they can lead to protests for higher wages or price controls. As well, falling consumer prices in the basic expansion can lead producers to restrict their output in an effort to keep prices and profits steady. What needs to be understood is that the extraordinary profits of the surplus expansion or boom are temporary, to be saved and invested in capital goods to extend the production of consumer goods. However, instead of being reinvested, profits can disappear into the excessive salaries of managers or speculative returns to shareholders.[17]

---

16. Eileen de Neeve, "Economic Dynamics: Does It Complete Hayek, Keynes and Schumpeter?" *Journal of Macrodynamic Analysis* 5 (2010), 109. Let us note that neoliberalism can hardly hide its predatory nature, including its demands for huge public subsidies for private projects benefitting them. It is exploitation through which the global elites with the help of rightist politicians get their way.

17. Eileen de Neeve, "Economic Dynamics," 111. She notes, p. 94, that for Lonergan, although markets define what is bought and sold in an exchange economy, "production decisions are more fundamental. These decisions are choices about the direction of development, . . . and variations in the distribution of wealth . . . They depend on market constraints, as production is for sale." For Lonergan, the proper functioning of an economic expansion includes the implementation of its basic expansion phase.

The Failure of General Equilibrium Theories[18]

In "There is no Invisible Hand," Jonathan Schlefer notes that

> In the 1870s, academic economists first began to seriously attempt to build 'general equilibrium' models to prove the existence of the invisible hand. They hoped to show that market trading among individuals, pursuing self-interest, and firms, maximizing profit, would lead an economy to a stable and optimal equilibrium.[19]

Schlefer, noting some economists' confident assertions in the media, asks why are their explanations often at odds with equally confident assertions from other economists? Why are economic predictions rarely borne out? Due to his frustration with these contradictions, Schlefer set out to investigate how economists arrive at their opinions. While they cloak their views in the aura of science, "what they actually do is make assumptions about the world, use those assumptions" to build imaginary "models," which they use to generate conclusions. "Their models can be useful or dangerous; it is . . . difficult to tell which is which.[20] Schlefer helps us understand the assumptions of various models stretching from Adam Smith to cutting-edge theorists today. Although abstract mathematical thinking now tends to dominate economists' work, Schlefer stresses that economists are unavoidably human. They fall prey to fads and subscribe to problematic ideologies. Schlefer addresses current controversies such as income inequality and financial crises, for which he holds economists

---

18. The general equilibrium theory for an economy at rest calls for people to maximize profit and utility. While efficiency is one criterion, dynamic theory is not well served by economic behavior that only maximizes profit and utility. For Lonergan the behavior of participants in the economy depends on their understanding the operations of the economy's production phases and on a shared willingness to act in ways that move the production of both surplus and basic goods toward benefiting society as a whole.

19. Schlefer, "There is no Invisible Hand," *Harvard Business Review*, April, 2012, 2. For Eduardo Pol, "Reconciling the Invisible Hand and Innovation," July 2013, *Economics of Innovation and New Technology*, 22 (5), the "failure to distinguish the Invisible Hand Theorem from the Invisible Hand *Doctrine* distorts thinking about Smith's message." It creates the misconception that the Invisible Hand "excludes business innovation."

20. Schlefer, *The Assumptions Economists Make*, Harvard Univ. Press, "Overview," p. 2, https://www.degruyter.com/ document/doi/ 10.4159/harvard.9780674065529/html?lang=e

accountable. Although theorists have won international acclaim for creating models that demonstrate the inherent instability of markets, many economists have ignored these, relying instead on their faith in unregulated enterprise. Schlefer makes "the behavior of economists much more comprehensible, if not less irrational;"[21] he notes that the Swiss economist, Léon Walras, in his *Elements of Pure Economics*, (1874), was the first to claim that he had succeeded in finding the so-called invisible hand, but Schlefer argues that "he had fallen far short."[22]

In 1954, Kenneth Arrow and Gerard Debreu developed the canonical "general equilibrium model" for which they won a Nobel Prize. "Making assumptions to characterize competitive markets, they supposedly 'proved that there exists some set of prices that would balance supply and demand for all goods.' However, no one has ever shown 'that some invisible hand would actually move markets toward that level. It is just a situation that might balance supply and demand if by happenstance it occurred. In 1960, Herbert Scarf of Yale showed that an Arrow-Debreu economy can cycle unstably. "The picture steadily darkened. One paper in the 1970's authored by Debreu eliminated "any last forlorn hope of proving that markets would move an economy toward equilibrium."[23]

As for Lonergan, he approaches equilibrium theories by first commenting on the attempted renewal of economic method that began around 1870 "and gradually transformed basic concepts." An understanding of these issues is necessary to clarify the views of earlier and later economists, the innovations of the multinational corporations,

---

21. Quoting a review of Schlefer's *The Assumptions Economists Make*, Harvard University, 2012, p. 2, https://www.hup.harvard.edu/catalog.php?isbn=9780674975408

22. Schlefer, "There is no Invisible Hand," 2012, 2, adds: "Milton Friedman once told Franklin Fisher he saw no point in studying the stability of general equilibrium because the economy is obviously stable—and if it isn't, "we are all wasting our time." Fisher retorted that "the point about economies being stable was not perceptive."

23. Schlefer, "There is no Invisible Hand," April, 10, 2012, p. 2. While post-Keynesian and Kaleckian economists rely on disequilibrium in their theories, orthodox proponents of market equilibrium have assumed that conflicts over rights and cycles *can be reconciled* inasmuch as they are caused by exogenous shocks. See Marie Constance Morley, "Economic Disequilibrium: a Philosophical Analysis of Economic Inequality, Property Rights and the Future of Democracy," St. Paul University, Ottawa, Sept 15, 2019.

and his own "exposition of circulation analysis."[24] Having distinguished between methodologically static and dynamic analyses, on the one hand, and between stationary and evolutionary states, on the other, Lonergan notes that, for Schumpeter, these distinctions were gradually worked out between 1870 and 1914 but not quickly enough or rigorously enough to take effect before 1914. During this period, the common viewpoint that affected the notion of competition "was that of John Stuart Mill and even of Adam Smith."[25] Lonergan concludes that "In pure competition the seller has no alternative strategy; in pure monopoly he has no competitors; and so neither gives rise to the necessity of doing things better . . . than the fellow next door."[26]

The Key Problem Affecting the Modern Economy

In *CWL* 15, Lonergan writes that in the ideal pure cycle, the long-term expansion proceeds from a static phase through a proportionate-expansion phase, then through a surplus-expansion phase, then through a basic-expansion phase, and finally into a higher static phase of greater abundance, yielding a higher standard of living. He notes that at the beginning, there arises a basic expansion:

> An economic system is confronted with an intrinsic test. Its success will be established if it can complete the major basic expansion and— without mishap, without inflation, without unemployment, without a break in confidence—make its way serenely into the haven of the stationary state. I mean, of course, not the stationary state of mere

---

24. *CWL* 15, 86. Free entry is an assumption of general equilibrium theory needed to ensure that "the law of cost" applies: prices are equal to the marginal cost of production.

25. *CWL* 15, 87. Lonergan quotes Schumpeter, *History*, 892: "No conceptual creation of the period points toward a new fact or a new slant. . . . They continued to look upon the competitive case . . . as the normal case of reality."

26. *CWL* 15, 89. Schumpeter's theoretic achievement was published as *The Theory of Economic Development* (New York and London: McGraw-Hill) in 1911. This "beautifully thought out piece of work," as Lonergan describes it, provided a theoretical basis for Schumpeter's two volume masterwork *Business Cycles* (McGraw-Hill, 1939). https://en.wikipedia.org/wiki/Heterodox_economics lists Lonergan among heterodox economists.

backwardness, not the stationary state of stagnation when a disastrous crash follows on an earlier apparent triumph, but the stationary state that preserves all the gains of the preceding major expansions. It is content to reproduce their gains at a constant rate. Its duration may be short or long, for in each case it must wait until such time as further new developments are grasped by human intelligence and eventually become practically conceived possibilities.[27]

After noting some mistaken expectations in the transitions from the major surplus expansion which may lead to a recession or worse, and the resulting problems of financing, Lonergan goes on to say that the basic expansion should be directed to raising the standard of living—but it often does not do so. The reason for that is not the reason

> On which simple-minded moralists insist. They blame greed. But the prime cause is ignorance. The dynamics of surplus and basic production, surplus and basic expansion, surplus and basic incomes are not understood, not formulated, not taught. . . . When intelligence is a blank, the first law of nature takes over: self-preservation. It is not primarily greed but frantic efforts at self-preservation that turn the recession into a depression, and the depression into a crash.[28]

The equilibria of a properly functioning economy are not understood. Over and above the static equilibria of supply and demand treated in microeconomics there are superseding dynamic macroeconomic equilibria that are not grasped. Lonergan notes that Schumpeter acknowledged that a dynamic analysis was needed to shed a new light on equilibrium.[29]

---

27. *CWL* 15, 80. When profits are reinvested, the basic expansion in the production of consumer goods and services can also be completed.

28. *CWL* 15, 82. Greed and ignorance work in tandem; fossil fuel giants have sought billions of euros from European countries in the global-fossil-fuel-phasing-out process. *New York Times*, Feb. 22, 2022. Such greed points to the need for the six turnarounds or conversions we advocate.

29. *CWL* 15, 92. Phil McShane, *CWL* 21, xxv, notes that Lonergan wrote that "Schumpeter takes his start from the dynamics of a stable economy and moves to a consideration of the 'destabilizing' effect of entrepreneurial activity. Lonergan, however, focuses

New light arises when, over and above the equilibria of supply and demand with respect to goods and services, there are recognized further macro-equilibria that that have to be maintained if an economy chooses to remain in a stationary stage . . . (to eventually arrive at) a more affluent state. Such macro-equilibria are more fundamental than the micro-equilibria assembled by Walras. The former are the conditions of a properly functioning economy. In the measure such conditions are met, there result aggregates acceptable to the economic society in its entirety, while the Walrasian equilibria are confined to the distribution of receipts among producers and income among householders.[30]

Lonergan on the Proper Functioning of an Economy

Lonergan argued that prices cannot be regarded as ultimate norms guiding economic decisions. "The function of prices is merely to provide a mechanism for overcoming the divergence of strategically indifferent decisions. . . . Since not all decisions possess this indifference, the exchange economy is confronted with the dilemma either of eliminating itself by suppressing the freedom of exchange . . . or of augmenting the enlightenment of the enlightened self-interest that guides

---

immediately on such activity, particularly in its occurrence on the massive scale associated with economic cycles, revolutions and surges. He approaches that focus armed with precise analytic distinctions between basic and surplus activities, outlays, incomes, etc. It is extremely important to note that these distinctions are equally relevant to the understanding and control of an economy without major surges. . . . There is no sidetracking into some labor theory of value." McShane adds: "The perspective towards which Lonergan leads is concretely heuristic, especially opposed to the abstract model-building, mathematical or not, that is currently fashionable That perspective, in its fulness, involves cultural shifts that require some attention." With Schumpeter, (*History, of Economic Analysis*, 1106), Lonergan wanted to address "the fundamental need for economic theory to 'cross the Rubicon', to leave the main body of economic theory on the static bank of the river (and) replace it by a system of general economic dynamics." In *CWL* 15, 237, Lonergan rejects the "indeterminacy of the relation between certain products and the ultimate products that enter into the standard of living," on the basis of his point-to-line and higher correspondences.

30. *CWL* 15, 92.

exchanges."[31] For Lonergan, the proper functioning of an economic expansion includes implementing its basic-expansion phase. The ideal pure cycle suffers no contractions nor layoffs. In this pure cycle the basic expansion succeeds the surplus expansion in an orderly fashion.[32] So, if unfortunate events are not inevitable, why do they occur so often? What do we fail to understand? Is the problem "the cut-off of the basic expansion?" Does the basic expansion get truncated rather than fully implemented? Can this problem be explained as an increase in the flow of basic products without a proportionate increase in the flow of incomes to purchase these products? Is there a lack of concomitance of one flow with another?[33] Philip McShane argued that the key problem of the modern economy is the cutting-off of the basic expansion due primarily to discouraging basic businesses' experience of shrinking prices. "Basic outlay, basic income, basic receipts should keep pace, a climbing pace, with climbing basic production. But that keeping-pace has conditions which are impossible to fulfill given the present mindset of businessmen and economists."[34] Changing the mindset would involve a massive cultural shift:

> The present mindset mistakenly calls for the continual growth of surplus-stage incomes, when in fact the economic process is not generating these incomes. The present mindset fails to understand that pure surplus income may increase geometrically in the initial stage

31. *CWL* 15, 5–6. Anthony M. Annett, *Cathonomics: How Catholic Tradition Can Create a More Just Economy* (Georgetown Univ., 2022) centers his book on Pope Pius XI's dictum in *Quadragesimo Ano*, sec. 88, that "The right ordering of economic life cannot be left to the free competition of forces. For from this source, as from a poisoned spring, have originated and spread all the errors of individualistic economic teaching."

32. Tad Dunne, "A Purely Relational Foundations for Economics: Explanatory Systematics and a New Standard Model of the Objective Economic Process" https://functionalmacroeconomics.com/table-of-contents/why-and-how-the-basic-expansion-fails-to-be-implemented/

33. For McShane, the *principle of concomitance* of money and product flows (whereby continuity and equilibrium are achieved, enabling an orderly process of circulation) is the *key word* in Lonergan's economic thinking (see *CWL 21*, 326, 329). Dictators' undue self-interest, not the glocal, subverts the principles of exchange used in free economies.

34. McShane, *Economics for Everyone: Das Jus Kapital*, (Axial, 2017), 69. One must differentiate capital from capitalism. Pure surplus income is capital; investing it in the surplus stage and then in the basic stage is "capital-ism" in the good sense. Investing it only in the surplus stage is a social evil we are decrying. This is a key point!

of a long-term expansion, but must give way to the basic expansion, systematically decline, and finally revert to zero as the expansion is completed. . . . Figuring out the details of this massive cultural shift regarding wages is not going to be easy, and implementing it in this century is to be a psychic climate-change.[35]

After having insisted that a condition of circuit acceleration is the underlying need for the concomitance of income with outlay and expenditures and that these be "identical with the adjustments to the rate of saving to the requirements of the productive process," Lonergan continues: "It follows that one may legitimately project a division of expenditure into a division of income, and it is in this manner that we arrive at the concept of a pure surplus income."[36] He insists on not misinterpreting pure surplus income:

> At the root of the depression lies a misinterpretation of the significance of pure surplus income (as the monetary correlative of a surplus expansion). In fact, it is the monetary equivalent of the new fixed investment of an expansion . . . Our culture cannot be accused of mistaken ideas on pure surplus income as it has been defined, for on that precise topic it has no ideas whatever. However, the phenomena referred to by 'pure surplus income' are well known. Entrepreneurs know that there are times of prosperity in which even a fool can make a profit and other mysterious times in which the brilliant and the prudent may be driven to the wall . . . Pure surplus income may be identified best of all by calling it net aggregate savings and viewing them as functionally related to the rate of new fixed investment[37]

---

35. McShane, *Economics for Everyone*, iii. We further discuss pure surplus income, a notion crucial to Lonergan's model, in Appendices D, E and in fig. 4 and 5. Lonergan has given us a general background as to how ethics should modify greed and exploitation. The problem is that it is not easy to change human nature for the better. At first, we were not conscious of the need for six conversions or turnarounds—four on the part of individuals and two on the part of economists and socio-communal entities. Logically they follow suit. Since bringing about the six conversions would involve extremely demanding GEM-FS processes, we appeal to a prophetic vision based on a "realistic hope."

36. *CWL* 15, 144.

37. *CWL* 15, 152–53. Income includes wages and salaries, depreciation allowances narrowly defined, interest and dividends: "Depending on income size, different proportions

Lonergan stresses that we must realize that a greater abundance of basic goods is made possible by the invention, production, installation and operation of new skills and techniques. If for once people were content to function on the basis of their inheritance,

> There may come a time when innovations and developments once more occur. This may happen in a variety of manners, but the simplest assumption is that it begins in the basic circuit. It consists in a greater abundance of consumer goods and services, and it is achieved by taking up slack; the unemployed become employed, and there is put to use capital plant and equipment that had been functioning under capacity.[38]

> It is to be noted that the monetary correlate of any expansion is pure surplus income, but it is unaccounted for when it is buried and undetected as a component of wages and salaries and dividends. Pure surplus income would systematically rise as the surplus expansion tapers off; and when surplus income systematically begins its inevitable decline as the surplus expansion tapers and the process to a basic expansion begins, then increasing basic income is required for recipients to purchase the increasing abundance made possible by the new capital equipment. People who would consume more must be paid more. The flow of basic incomes must keep pace with the flow of a greater abundance of basic products. Yet ignorance leads managers, seeking to satisfy the conventional criterion of ever-increasing profits, to reduce basic incomes by layoffs and contractions following the mirage of greater real profit that the economy is not producing. Managers do the opposite of what the science of functional macroeconomic dynamics calls for. By

---

are consumed and saved. Basic income is income that is consumed or becomes part of one's standard of living however large. Surplus income is income that is saved and invested. The proportions of total income consumed and invested—not their proprietary sources— are significant for the macroeconomy. Lonergan's functional distinctions can be tracked statistically: In a surplus expansion, "If the pure surplus income is captured by the higher income brackets alone, the anti-egalitarian shift in the distribution of income is being achieved and savings will be sufficient." *CWL* 15, 151.

38. *CWL* 15, 76.

layoffs and contractions they violate the precepts implicit in a normative scientific macroeconomics.[39]

When selling prices and profits fall, there follows a vicious cycle of contractions, layoffs, reduced demand, reduced profits, contractions, layoffs, reduced demand, reduced profits, etc. until the position of even the least vulnerable is undermined. Entrepreneurs know that there are times in which it is difficult to continue to grow the company, increase corporate income, and enjoy higher stock valuation. "The brilliant and the prudent may be driven to the wall."[40] Basic income is best identified by calling it the basis (monetary correlate) of basic demand and viewing it as the functional monetary element required for the implementation of the phase of a long-term expansion and for the avoidance of a painful downward spiral. We may ask why has Lonergan's perceptive argument on the vicious cycle not found general approbation by economists. McShane is forthright:

> The first difficulty is psychological. The basic and static phases are a somber world for men brought up on the strong drink of expansion. They have to be cured of their appetite for making more and more money so that they may have more money to invest. They have to be fitted out with a mentality that will aim at and be content with a stable going concern and a stable standard of living. It is not so easy to effect this change, for as the Wise Man said, the number of fools is infinite.[41]

---

39. https://functionalmacroenonomics.com/table-of-why-and-how-the-basic-expansion-fails-to-be-implemented/ The site gives a good mathematical explanation of Lonergan's reasoning, relating his argument to schemes of recurrence and to the good of order. Functional macroeconomic dynamics "is a set of intelligible relations linking what is implicitly defined by the relations themselves. It is a set of relational forms. The form of any element is known through its relations to all other elements." See *CWL* 10, 154.

40. *CWL* 15, 153.

41. Quoted from http://www.philipmcshane.org/wp-content/themes/philip/online_publications/series/joistings/joist-10.pdf Part Three of *CWL* 15 centers on "Measuring Change in the Productive Process." As part of "measuring," Lonergan lists possibilities based upon the relation between basic and surplus acceleration and the cycle of the productive process; 113–28.

Notions of Value to Offset Equilibrium Theories' Myopia

The notions of value expressed by Adam Smith and Lonergan differ in many ways. For Smith,

> The rich . . . consume little more than the poor, and in spite of their natural selfishness and rapacity, though they mean only their own convenience, though the sole end which they propose from the labors of all the thousands whom they employ, be the gratification of their own vain and insatiable desires, they divide with the poor the produce of all their improvements. They are led by an invisible hand to make nearly the same distribution of the necessaries of life, which would have been made, had the earth been divided into equal portions among all its inhabitants, and thus without intending it, without knowing it, advance the interest of the society, and afford means to the multiplication of the species.[42]

The most important principle in Smith's moral psychology is that of sympathy, of fellow feeling, "placing of ourselves in the situation of another." For Aristotle, whom Lonergan follows here, what counted most was to make humans care and love (*philein*) their being lovable (*agapeton*).[43]

How Townsend Corrupted Smith's Core Notions

In his two volumes on economics, Lonergan makes surprisingly few references to Adam Smith's vast influence among his peers and on

---

42. *The Theory Of Moral Sentiments*, Part IV, Chapter I, 184–5, para. 10. Smith's interest in value was restricted to "value in use" of objects and their value in exchange" (*Wealth of Nations*, 28). His "theory of sympathy is mainly a formative concept lacking in moral substance." See Ayman Reda, *Prophecy, Piety and Profits: a Conceptual and Comparative History of Islamic Economic Thought*, Dearborn, MI, 2018, 283. For Lonergan, values imply being motivated by self-transcendence. He includes particular goods within an economic system. This implies the need to consider the value a system as a whole. It is within such a perspective that economics can best exert its influence. It is not bureaucrats, but economists motivated by authentic values who can help us in this endeavor. Further, the need of personal and communal transformations is fundamental.

43. *Politics*, 1262b22-3. See also Laurence Berns, "Aristotle and Adam Smith on Justice," *The Review of Metaphysics* Vol. 48.1 (Sept. 1994), 71–90.

future generations. Heilbroner makes only a passing allusion to James Townsend (1739–1816) who in many ways distorted Smith's core notions in economics. Sandra Ujpétery, for her part, argues that Townsend was the first one to have claimed that

> Letting markets operate freely . . . should involve letting people fend for themselves even in case of destitution and starvation. He also claimed that poverty and hunger must always exist (and freely operating market mechanisms would make sure they affect those people who deserve it most), whereas Smith had stated that mass misery is incompatible with progress. Townsend did not advocate the workhouse test, however—on the contrary, he strongly condemned workhouses and other deterrent measures, realizing that they would deter many 'deserving' applicants while attracting a very problematic mix of the most shameless . . . people. In Townsend's view abolishing any right to relief was the only solution, the alternatives being either draconian deterrent measures or . . . encouraging overpopulation.[44]

Ujpétery adds that although Townsend's ideas were perceived as *extreme* by most contemporaries, his ideas later became very influential

---

44. Sandra Ujpétery, "A corrective to common views of Smith's ideas of Laissez-Faire—Smith, Townsend, and the Workhouse Act," 1, https://victorianweb.org/misc/whatsnew. Html. Recent research has shown that Smith was not opposed to poor relief. On the contrary, he was sympathetic to the laboring poor. It was only after his death that classical Political Economy became decidedly inimical to poor relief and social security. This happened mainly in the 1790's. The blame for this shift belongs to Townsend, Malthus, Bentham, and Edmund Burke, not to Smith. Burke in his *Thoughts and Details on Scarcity* advocated that governments should not 'meddle with people's subsistence' even during famines, but this came to be seen as 'Smith's view on famine policy'; this interpretation of Smith is dubious at best. Meanwhile even Malthus did in fact allow for government aid to famine victims; in later editions of his *An Essay on the Principle of Population*, he admitted that the Poor Laws may be less disastrous than he originally thought, but "Malthusianism" vigorously spread the belief that all poor relief and famine relief is dangerous and should cease. In the end, the Benthamite idea of less-eligibility and deterrent workhouses came to be enshrined as a sort of compromise for those who wanted to retain a right to relief for the poorest but were afraid that over-generosity would lead to near-universal idleness and reckless early marriages among the poor.

due to their being adopted by Thomas Malthus. Smith himself had criticized only one aspect of England's Poor Laws, namely the Settlement regulations. He argued for their abolition because he wanted freedom of movement even for poor workers. But he "never stated that poor relief as such violates market freedom, nor did he advocate that it should be administered in a more deterrent way." He pointed out how other government interference in the labor market almost always favored the employers. Some of his statements might even be read as an endorsement of intelligent labor market regulation in the interest of workers. Smith argued that higher wages would be advantageous and spoke out against the "utility-of-poverty" beliefs that low wages are better for discipline and competitiveness. In Ujpétery's view, Emma Rothschild has convincingly demonstrated how Smith's ideas were seen by contemporaries as a subversive "critique of the *status quo* in England and even more so in France." They helped inspire the French Revolution. In fact, all the aristocratic and corporate monopolies, and other restrictions on market freedom prevailing as part of the *Ancien Régime* were even more severe than those existing in England. Most if not all of them "benefited the privileged few at the expense of the poor, and the not-so-privileged many."[45] Thus

> It is easy to see that, on the Continent even more so than in England, Smith and his contemporaries had good reasons to believe that more market freedom would not only increase prosperity but lead to more equality and less poverty as well. Considering the status quo at the time, there was in many respects no trade-off but complementarity between free markets, egalitarianism, and poverty alleviation . . . (making it) all the more . . . tragic that the science that helped bring down the Paris Bastille would become the science in whose name the New Poor Law "bastilles" were erected.[46]

---

45. Ujpetery. "The Victorian Web https://victorianweb.org/misc/whatsnew.html 2
46. Ujpétery, "Victorian Economics," 3.

The Roles of Money and Labor Value in Various Authors

Philosophers and scholars since the days of Plato and Aristotle have debated the relation between money and labor—summed up in the phrase, "labor-value." Money arises due to the need of holding advanced societies together. For Michael Eldred:

> Money enables a complex, intermeshing unity of the manifold usages in which things are used. This is the sense in which money has to be understood . . . As *related to usages*, the use of money is in itself a usage unifying the multifarious uses by enabling and facilitating the exchange of what is needed for these uses. Since it is incorporated into the usage of exchange, and this is its *raison d'être*, money itself can be changed or taken out of use. This does not mean, of course, that the necessity for *some* kind of money as a substitute unifying all the various uses could be done away with. Thus money is both customary and necessary.[47]

Remarkably, Smith, Ricardo and Marx agreed on the central role of labor-value.[48] In the following sections we shall briefly examine how

---

47. Michael Eldred, "The notions of exchange, value, justice in Aristotle, Adam Smith and Karl Marx." www.arte-fact.org/untpltcl/exchvljs.html. Eldred concludes, 5, that money "is not merely a self-evident thing whose being does not pose subtle philosophical problems" demanding well-thought solutions as to ways of exchange.

48. Eileen de Neeve, "Interpreting Bernard Lonergan's General Theory of Economic Dynamics. Does it Complete Hayek, Keynes and Schumpeter? *Journal of Macrodynamic Analysis*, (2010) 93–94, writes that for Marx, "Man as worker has to appropriate the means of production which stands at the center of Lonergan's economic theory. Both men argue that economic conditions drive history—but their views of history differ. Lonergan sets the economy within the social context of the good of order to include the states of production, exchange, finance and consumption. "The structure of the productive process is a series of stages, where each stage is an aggregate of rates of production, and each lower stage receives from the next higher stage the means of long-term acceleration of its rates." He qualifies this, noting that 'productive process' is to be used broadly. It denotes not merely 'making things' but the extraction or cultivation of raw materials, their . . . assembly, the planning and designing of products. . . . It includes not only activities upon material objects but also services of all kinds, not only labor but also management. . . . In brief, it is the totality of activities bridging the gap between the potentialities of nature, whether physical, chemical, vegetable, animal, or human nature, and, on the other hand, the actuality of a standard of living.

this played out among their followers and those they inspired. Part of our interest is to examine some of the repercussions this has had on the dehumanization-mechanization[49] of humans and the need to rehumanize society in ways Lonergan can help us do.

Neoliberalism:[50] Ricardo and his Followers

In Part I, we argued that GEM-FS can help counter today's *de facto* mechanization of humanity. How did this mechanization arise? Floyd Matson has shown[51] that it began with Adam Smith's notion of an "Invisible Hand" guiding exchanges. Smith argued that the sources of a nation's riches are neither those of mercantilist theory nor of the 18th century Physiocrats who constituted the first scientific school of economists. Francois Quesnay, known for his 1758 *Tableau Économique* and as the Physiocrats' founder, acknowledged three economic classes in France: the proprietary class consisting only of land owners, the productive class of agricultural workers, and the "sterile class" of merchants.[52]

---

49. Dehumanization may include what is called "neo-feudalism or new feudalism—a "theorized contemporary rebirth of policies of governance, economy, and public life reminiscent of those present in many feudal societies, such as unequal rights and legal protections for common people and for nobility. The concept of neo-feudalism often focuses on economics." https://en.wikipedia.org /wiki/Neo-feudalism; also https://lareviewofbooks.org/article/neofeudalism-the-end-of-capitalism/

50. The term neoliberalism originates from a small academic conference held in Paris in 1938 where Mises, Hayek, and others hailing from the classical liberal political tradition. Marxists and Critical Theorists attack this "neoliberalism." In his *A Brief History of Neoliberalism* (Oxford Scholarship, 2005), David Harvey argues that for neoliberal proponents, market exchange is an ethic in itself, capable of acting as a guide for all human action. It has become dominant in both thought and practice. Claude-Frédéric Bastiat (1801–1850), known for his criticism of protectionism, developed the economic concept of opportunity cost and used a journal he published to advance his anti-protectionist views.

51. Floyd W. Matson, *The Broken Image*, 19.

52. https://sites.google.com/site//macroeconomics/quesnay. Toni Vogel Carey, *Journal of Scottish Philosophy*, 18 1, March, 2020, argues that Smith's *Wealth of Nations* is "concerned with two rival economic theories, Mercantilism and Physiocracy." Smith initially dismissed Quesnay, but later praised "his theory to the skies. . . . That cries out for explanation. Like Mercantilism, Smith's system emphasizes commerce, whereas Quesnay's is confined to agriculture. But, as with the Physiocrats, "Smith's system is built on individual

The Physiocrats had reacted against mercantilist views that national strength and security are due to a country's manufacturing capabilities and trade rather than on the products of the soil. They insisted that agriculture is the primary source of a nation's wealth, arguing that producers merely turn agricultural products into consumable products. For Smith, however, it was the effective contributions of laborers that matters most. On this point, Smith agreed with the mercantilist view that the price of goods is determined by the amount of labor that goes into their production. The market adjudicates the price based on balancing costs and profits. Prices reflect the need to provide for the maintenance of those who produce goods. Quesnay's views were implemented by Turgot, the minister of finance under Louis XV. But his policies were soon rejected.

European liberalism attempted to do away with the injustices of mercantilism.[53] Smith sounded mercantilism's death-knell. Let us trace the processes that led from the rejection of mercantilism[54] to the adoption of liberalism followed by the Marxist reaction to liberalism. Government

---

liberty, whereas Mercantilism is one of government control." Our sandwich approach takes historical developments such as have occurred since the 18th century very seriously. This leads us to urge Lonergan scholars to sufficiently develop economic and environmental policies that amount to two crucially needed turnarounds.

53. Liberalism was not concerned whether a state gains more or less than another, but only whether a state's wealth is increasing in absolute terms. Mercantilism, which began in Europe in the 16th century, on the other hand, insisted that each state should protect its own interests at the expense of others.

54. Lonergan, *CWL* 21, 9–10, writes: "In an appendix to his *General Theory*, Keynes presents as a corollary a new interpretation of mercantilist thought: for the facts of the mercantilist period, he is content to go to a standard work of research." As to interpreting those facts, "he pays no attention to the laborious research workers who . . . merely reechoed classical views; on the contrary, he brings his own *General Theory* into play to show that, after all, the mercantilists might not have been the fools that classical theory makes them. The legitimacy of the procedure is evident, for, if research is necessary to determine in detail what the mercantilists thought and did, it cannot claim any competence in judging whether the mercantilists were wise or foolish. That question is answered only by economic theory, and each theory will give its own answer." The classicists, the Marxists have their own. "Keynes has given us a third; nor is the cause of the divergence a difference in the factual data but a difference in the principles accepted by the judging mind. Accordingly, if we succeed in working out a generalization of economic science, we cannot fail to create simultaneously a new approach to economic history. Such an approach . . . is already a historical synthesis."

control had become more subtle over the centuries. Smith and his fellow "liberals" advocated the freedom that popular control of government might bring. It was a radical idea. They wanted to introduce a new era of free-market capitalism, but they had not anticipated that business wealth would eventually concentrate in entities stronger than governments able to bring governments under their control. Capitalism today is not the kind of capitalism that Smith would have recognized. Capitalism was supposed to deliver a world of small businesses in free and fair competition, overseen by honest men. Governments were not supposed to "rule": they were to ensure that contracts were honored and to prevent foreign invasions. People were deemed to be responsible free citizens. Constitutional checks and balances were initiated to ensure that government knew its place. But, in fact, no such checks and balances were used to prevent companies from dominating the global economy.[55] Adam Smith himself was a very moral man who argued that control of the market should be in the hands of responsible citizens. One should not interpret Smith's system of political economy merely in terms of mere self-interest. Smith's analyses should be restored within the moral perspective which he himself espoused—a perspective that has been distorted over the course of the past two centuries, but which is evident in his conclusion to his chapter "On the Profit of Stock":

> Our merchants and masters complain much of the bad effects of high wages in raising the price and lessening the sale of goods. They say nothing concerning the bad effects of high profits. They are silent with regard to the pernicious effects of their own gains.[56]

For Smith, morality stems from our social nature. Though we are self-interested, we have to work out how to live alongside others without doing them harm. Smith saw this as an essential minimum for the survival of society. "If people go further and do positive good. . . . we welcome it but cannot demand such action as we demand justice."[57]

---

55. Dave Darby, www.lowimpact.org/why-adam-smith-father-of-capitalism-would-have-hated-neoliberalism/

56. Smith, *Wealth of Nations*, 98.

57. See www.adamsmith.org/the-theory-of-moral-sentiments.

Chris Hedges on "Neoliberalist Absurdity"

In general, neoliberalism refers to market-oriented policies such as "eliminating price controls, deregulating capital markets, lowering trade barriers" and reducing the influence of government in the economy through forms of privatization. In its more extreme form it claims that market exchange is an ethic in itself, capable of acting as a guide for all human action. It has become dominant in both thought and practice throughout much of the world since the 1970's. The worst side of neoliberalism has been analyzed in an article by Chris Hedges who contends that neoliberalism as economic theory is absurd, having as much validity as past ruling ideologies such as the divine right of kings or a fascist belief in the *Übermensch*. None of their vaunted promises were remotely possible. Concentrating wealth in the hands of a global oligarchic elite, while demolishing government controls, creates massive income inequality. Monopoly power fuels political extremism and destroys democracy. One need not need slog through Thomas Piketty's *Capital in the Twenty-First Century* to figure this out. But economic rationality was never the point; the point was restoring class power.[58] Hedges notes that neoliberalism's role as a ruling ideology led, in the 1970s, to the ousting of its Keynesian mainstream critics from academia and from many state institutions. Even financial organizations such as the International Monetary Fund (IMF) and the World Bank tended to be shut out of the media.

> Intellectual poseurs such as Milton Friedman were groomed in places such as the University of Chicago and given . . . lavish corporate funding. They disseminated the official mantra of fringe, discredited economic theories popularized by Friedrich Hayek and Ayn Rand. Once we knelt before the dictates of the marketplace and lifted government regulations, slashed taxes for the rich, permitted the flow of

---

58. See Chris Hedges, "Neoliberalism's Dark Path to Fascism," October 25, 2020, a reprint from *Truthdig*, Nov. 26, 2018. It took the Great Depression to convert Keynes from tolerating *laissez-faire* to advocating deficit spending. Keynesian economics is based on two main ideas: (1) aggregate demand is more likely than aggregate supply to be the primary cause of a short-run economic event such as a recession; (2) wages and prices can be sticky; in an economic downturn, unemployment can result.

money across borders, destroyed unions and signed trade deals that sent jobs to sweatshops in China, the world would be a happier, freer and wealthier place. It was a con. But it worked.[59]

As would a ruling class, proponents of neoliberalism needed ideas which they fabricated under the labels of freedom of the market, privatization, individual liberty, etc. Their ideas became the basis of a new social order implemented in the 1980s and 1990s.[60] "As a political project, it was very savvy. It got a great deal of popular consent because it was talking about individual liberty and freedom, freedom of choice. In fact, "when they talked about freedom, it was freedom of the market." The neoliberal project said to the '68 generation, "OK, you want liberty and freedom? That's what the student movement was about. We're going to give it to you, but it's going to be freedom of the market. The other thing you're after is social justice—forget it. So, we'll give you individual liberty, but you forget the social justice. Don't organize." This was the beginning of efforts to dismantle "the collective institutions of the working class such as the unions, then bit by bit the political parties advocating the well-being of the masses." Hedges argues further that while the idea about the *market is that it seems to be egalitarian, it is very unequal.* It promises equality of treatment, but it really means is that the rich get richer. "If you're very poor, you're

---

59. Hedges, "Dark Path to Fascism," 2018, 1. For Hedges, "The con of neoliberalism is now widely understood across the political spectrum. It is harder and harder to hide its predatory nature, including its demands for huge public subsidies. Amazon, for example, recently sought and received multibillion-dollar tax breaks from New York and Virginia to set up distribution centers in those states. The ruling elites are forced to make alliances with right-wing demagogues who use the crude tactics of racism, Islamophobia, and misogyny to channel the public's growing rage away from the elites and toward the vulnerable." Donald Trump's administration abolished numerous greenhouse gas regulations. It slashed taxes for wealthy individuals and corporations, wiping out $1.5 trillion in government revenue, while embracing authoritarian forms of control..

60. Naomi Klein's *The Shock Doctrine* (Knopf, 2007) argues that neoliberal free market policies rose to prominence because of a deliberate strategy of "shock therapy." She shows how, from Chile in 1973 to the invasion of Iraq in 2003, Milton Friedman and his followers repeatedly spoke of terrible violence as a pretext to implement their radical policies. Klein has updated her views to explain the way that force, stealth and crisis are used in implementing neoliberal economic policies https://youtu.be/B3B5qt6gsxY

more likely to get poorer. What Marx showed brilliantly in volume one of *Das Kapital* is that freedom of the market produces greater and greater levels of social inequality."[61] Even health care, housing, and education become essentially exchangeable "commodities," not necessities:

> Students have to borrow in order to get the education which will get them a job in the future. That's the scam of the thing. It basically says if you're an entrepreneur, if you go out there and train yourself, you will get your just rewards. If you don't get your just rewards, it's because you didn't train yourself right. You took the wrong kind of courses (such as) philosophy or classics instead of taking it in management skills of how to exploit labor.[62]

A Lonerganian Alternative in the Form of a Motorcar Analogy

According to Hugh Williams, Phil McShane held that Lonergan began by focusing on the massive scale of historically-recorded economic cycles and revolutions—relying on precise analytic distinctions between basic and surplus activities, outlays, and incomes. For Lonergan, understanding the value of labor, how to measure capital, and the propensies of consumers are all determined by a strictly defined analytic context and a normative context that transpose the meaning of rational expectations. Williams uses a motor car metaphor to heuristically help us grasp the theoretical-practical essentials guiding economic systems. Without some grasp of the meta-theoretic significance of a metaphor, one is unlikely to get what Lonergan's economic theory implies. Williams argues that Lonergan's distinctions are relevant for understanding a stable economy without major surges as well as such familiar economic notions as labor value, capital, and the propensities of consumers. Lonergan's re-orientation is informed by the theory's novel analytical and normative contexts, which, in turn will require

---

61. Hedges, "Dark Path to Fascism," *Canadian Dimension,* Nov. 27, 2018.

62. Hedges, *Truthdig*, "Neoliberalism's Dark Path to Fascism," Nov. 2018, 3.

what McShane calls a massive reorientation of statistical analysis[63] as to economic actualities, probabilities, and possibilities.

A helpful analogy for this theory's normative novelty for economic thought is that of a motor vehicle. It is as if the central focus of even advanced economic analysts tends to be preoccupied with the optimal behavior of drivers and the rules of the road while ignoring the motor's drive train mechanism. Lonergan draws attention to the dynamic functioning of what is a two-circuited, credit-based economy. One must properly understand what is required of economic agents just as one must understand how a motor's drivetrain functions, how it helps deliver power to the drive wheels. However, conventional common-sense economics keeps missing the point. It persists in purveying a massive disorienting overreach—being obsessed with driver behavior and the rules of the road while ignoring motor and drive-train mechanics.[64] The stochastic educational reorientation required today is an issue that affects both the future of the earth's ecology and of democracy.[65] This has glocal implications due to the linkage of what is a very complex global system requiring functional collaboration to be properly guided in the right direction. It is with this in mind, that we develop a GEM-FS approach to complex systems.

---

63. Lonergan is not offering a definitive foundation for statistical science. He seeks the pre-conceptual insights and heuristic anticipations informing such investigations.

64. Hugh Williams, "Reinterpreting the Motor Car Analogy Lonergan's economic ideas track a different line of thought from that taken by contemporary economists," *Journal of Macrodynamic Analysis*, Vol. 12, 2020.

65. The most important part of Lonergan's economic theory is the values underlying it. This makes it hard to explore all GEM-FS constructive ramifications. Of course, the oligarchs will oppose GEM-FS economics. They have a lot to lose if economic process comes under democratic control. Education is crucial to getting there. Lonergan's economic ideas track a different line of thought from that taken by contemporary economists. For him, an educated class united by a common language, common loyalties, "may affect many of the uneducated" in positive ways, but, in general, "the uneducated find themselves in a tradition beyond their means." Still, for people who are economically interdependent, the culture of the educated does affect the uneducated, much as theory affects pre-theoretical common sense. "By successive adaptations the innovations of theory can penetrate . . . through all layers of a society to give it some approximation to the homogeneity necessary for mutual comprehension." *MiT*, 99. *CWL* 14, 95.

The Danger of Simplifying Assumptions in Economic Theories

Due to Adam Smith's influence economists today are obsessed with simplifying assumptions.[66] Smith was interested in market efficiency, which he argued is best achieved by a division of labor. In a famous image of the "very trifling manufacture" of pins Smith demonstrates a 4,800-percent productivity increase when the process is broken into 18 specialized tasks.[67]

In contrast to Smith's writing about the inevitability of collusive relationships between business interests and politics,[68] (such as their contrivance in raising prices), in Part I we sought to coordinate such underlying notions as how an operating subject operates upon objects in GEM-FS' two phases. We aim to show in Parts III and Parts IV how this two-phase process can be applied in ways that retrieve and respect *just* exchange processes in optimal fashion.[69] Of course, Smith, neoliberals and Marxists could not have been aware of how a GEM-FS process approach can work in this fashion. Smith was instrumental in refashioning Aristotle's traditional political notions of justice into considerations of an exchange system. We are interested in how such notions of justice and values, all too often ignored by market economists, can be retrieved. This is the explicit aim of Parts III and IV where we investigate how best coordinate Lonergan's various achievements in the fields of theology, philosophy, morality, and interreligious dialogue with an ethical economics.[70] In so

---

66. For Ayman Reda, *Prophecy, Piety and Profits*, 287, "Smith promotes a one-dimensional moral framework" focusing on the means rather than motivations or ends.

67. See Jean-Louis Peaucelle. "Adam Smith's use of multiple references for his pin-making example." European Journal of the History of Economic thought." Routledge, 2006, 13 (4) 489–512.

68. "Filibuster" from French *"flibustier"* (pirate) from the Dutch *"vrijbuiter."* In English, a "freebooter" is one who freely enriches himself by theft of booty—from Dutch *beuten*, (booty, spoils.) Our text argues for the need to end free-booting (pirating) legislation so as to let free speech and democracy prevail rather than be obstructed by free-booting techniques. Parts II and III are concrete efforts and proposals on how to do so. As to Smith on collusive relationships, *Wealth of Nations*, p. 52 of 1797 edition.

69. We seek to coordinate the phases of GEM-FS cognitional process and of economics.

70. Here, it is well to refer to the social teaching of the Catholic Church that began with Leo XIII. Pope Francis has vigorously promoted this teaching at the risk of splitting

doing, we shall compare and integrate the two phases of both GEM-FS and economics.

Excursus on Exchange Value, Labor-Value and Justice

This excursus is based mostly on articles by Michael Eldred on the notions of exchange value and justice.[71] Eldred argues that for Marx, money is not merely a self-evident entity whose being does not pose subtle philosophical problems demanding well-thought concepts of human association through exchange. In addition, for Marx, the value of useful things in daily life comes about through a process of reciprocal social recognition in exchange that can be attributed to any intrinsic measure "such as the labor-time embodied in those useful things . . . Given that such a thing as 'value creation' cannot be attributed to spent labor power measured by time, there is no injustice *per se* involved in workers hiring their labor power to an employer who directs the exercise of that labor power.[72]

Eldred contends that nevertheless for Marx, "hired labor-power is directed by another, namely the employer." It is therefore "'alienated' in a literal sense."[73] This means "that association through the interplay of money-mediated exchange goes *essentially* hand in hand with the socio-ontological possibility of existence of the free individual who is the hallmark of Western liberal society." Eldred recalls that it was Aristotle who, in his *Nicomachean Ethics*,[74] first

> dealt with the notion of reciprocity in relation to justice. For both
> Plato and Aristotle, social life in the polis is based on a division of

---

the Church. See, for example, George Weigel's *The Next Pope: the Office of Peter and a Church in Mission* (Ignatius Books, 2020). Like his namesake in the Middle Ages, Pope Francis has lived the life of a reformed reformer and promoted ways of so doing.

71. Michael Eldred, "The notions of exchange, value, justice in Aristotle, Adam Smith and Karl Marx," www.arte-fact.org/untpltcl/exchvljs.html

72. Eldred, quoted at https://users.wfu.edu/cottrell/OPE/archive/0602/0120.html referring to Karl Marx's 1847 speech "Introduction to Wage, Labor and Capital."

73. Eldred, "Notions of exchange, value," 3.

74. Book V, Chapter on "Justice," on money, exchange involving voluntary actions.

labor and the exchange of the products of labor for the satisfaction of need and provision of the 'conveniences of life.' In fact, Aristotle stressed that in exchange transactions, justice should prevail because it is justice which holds them together. He calls this 'reciprocal justice on the basis of proportionality and not on the basis of equality', and a proportional reciprocity, namely that of the polity.[75]

Eldred adds that for Aristotle, money is the solution in daily life for how various things—suitable for different uses—can be measured, "thus forming the basis for a just, proportional exchange of everything in which one value is exchanged for another, equal value. The justness is apparent in the mutual satisfaction of the exchangers themselves who have struck a deal on the proportions to be exchanged."[76] Money is the universal representative for useful things in the broadest sense; it is the medium or middle term which mediates their exchange with one another and thus the give and take of daily social intercourse. It arises as a practical solution from the context of the practice of exchange itself, enabling fair and just association in dealings with one another. "Thus, like a measure, money makes things measurable and creates an equality, for without exchange no community would be possible and without

---

75. This is reflected, according to Eldred's "Notions," in the Greek word *koinonia*, whose semantic field stretches from "sociability" to "community." Aristotle uses the example of the exchange of a physician's services for a farmer's products" which have to be equalized. For both Aristotle and Lonergan, there is a link between the practice of exchange and the constitution of a community.

76. Eldred, "Notions of exchange, values." 4. Only the abstracting from all concrete, useful qualities to pure quantities "allows a just exchange of goods because, according to Aristotle's treatment of exchange, a kind of proportionate equality has to be achieved in the exchange relation." The context for considering exchange as a paradigmatic form of reciprocal justice is found in Book V 1133b13 of the *Nicomachean Ethics* on "social life in its habitual usages." Such usage for the sake of living well is what Aristotle has in view when "considering money as a kind of "substitute" for use. It mediates the procurement of what is used habitually in the usages of daily life. Money represents these uses and substitutes for them as a thing which can be used now or in the future to supply what is needed for use in the practices of daily living. For Aristotle, money as a conventional substitute exists not by nature but by customary usage . . . and can be changed and made useless by us" (1133a31). This passage is usually taken to mean that Aristotle is a proponent of a "conventional theory of money."

equality there would be no exchange, and without commensurability there would be no equality."[77] While Aristotle taught that money is an abstract social thing mediating the exchanges among all the various use-values—enabling society to be "held together" in a practical, every-day way—in the 18th century the Aristotelean understanding of money and exchange-value was modified by Adam Smith's notion of labor-value which "obscures the nature of exchange-value as abstract use-value."[78]

Adam Smith's Notion of Labor-Value

For Smith, labor, (the effort required to acquire a thing), is the "real measure" of value; it is not simply measured in time. He adds:

> The real price of everything, what every thing really costs to the man who wants to acquire it, is the toil and trouble of acquiring it. What every thing is really worth to the man who has acquired it, and who wants to dispose of it or exchange it for something else, is the toil and trouble which it can save to himself, and which it can impose upon other people. What is bought with money or with goods is purchased by labor, as much as what we acquire by the toil of our own body. That money or those goods indeed save us this toil. They contain the value of a certain quantity of labor which we exchange for what is supposed at the time to contain the value of an equal quantity. Labor was the first price, the original purchase-money that was paid for all things. It was not by gold or by silver, but by labor, that all the wealth of the world was originally purchased; and its value, to those who possess it, and who want to exchange it for some new productions, is precisely equal to the quantity of labor which it can enable them to purchase or command.[79]

The common-sense notion of labor-value, (what it is worth), is based on a qualitative insight into social exchange. It does not aim primarily

---

77. Eldred, "Notions of exchange, values," 4.

78. Eldred, "Notions of exchange, values," 5.

79. Smith, *The Wealth of Nations*, edited by Edwin Cannan, Modern Library. 30–31.

at erecting an empirically applicable, quantitative theory of exchange relations, i.e. a labor theory of value. Rather, the insight consists in grasping that the exchange-value of a thing stems from "the quantity of labor which it can . . . purchase or command."[80] This amounts to saying that in an exchange, it is the finished goods as reified entities that are the most important. What counts most is the *services* of providing those goods that are paid for in exchange. The exchange relation of purchasing a commodity is basically a relation of *recognition* of the labor required to provide that commodity.[81] What is directly purchased is the finished product, but more or less indirectly, one pays for the provision of a labor-service. Money is valuable, because it can "command" the labor of others. Eldred comments that "the kernel of truth disclosed in a distorted way by the so-called labor theory of value is a recognition of labor providing services to the marked when hired. The productivity of those abilities depends on an individual's knowledge and other factors of production such as land, capital, entrepreneurial management." This knowledge is a "shared social good" which has to be "individually appropriated."[82]

Smith did qualify his insight into labor-value in terms of hardship and ingenuity which refer to the dimensions of the intensity and productivity of labor, respectively. A more intense labor is a compression of time, and a more highly skilled labor produces a qualitatively better product than unskilled labor could do or more in a given time.[83] "The upshot of these qualitative considerations is that one cannot posit a quantitative law of labor-value that regulates exchange."[84] Smith concedes that what he calls "real price" is measured by labor expenditure but it diverges from "nominal price." His intention is to establish a qualitative insight into

---

80. Stefano Fenoaltea, "Reconstructing The Past: The Measurement of Aggregate Product," Munich RePEc Archive https://mpra.ub.uni-muenchen.de/97042/1/MPRA_paper_97042.pdf

81. A commodity, for Marx, *Das Kapital*, 125, is an external object, a thing, which through its qualities satisfies needs of any kind, and is then exchanged for something else.

82. Eldred, "Notions of exchange, values," 5

83. Adam Smith, *The Wealth of Nations*, Bk. 1, Chapter 5, 34.

84. Eldred, "Exchange, Value, Justice—Aristotle, Adam Smith, Karl Marx," 3

"exchangeable value" and not to erect a quantitative theory. Labor-value for Smith is thus a measure of "rough equality which, though not exact, is sufficient for carrying on the business of common life."[85] This is in line with the Aristotelean insight that a search for knowledge demands that one adapt one's method to the phenomena being investigated.[86]

Smith's insight into labor-value is not divorced from his notions of use-value and abstract value. Whereas Aristotle argued that it is use value that holds everything together,[87] in that exchange practically equates all the different use-values by dealing with them as abstractly useful in quantities of money, for Smith, exchange brings the labor-services of providing exchangeable use-values into an equivalence relation with one another, thus constituting an ongoing process of abstract, reciprocal social recognition of labor performed by diverse individuals, which could also be said to 'hold everything together'. But the drive toward a quantitative 'labor theory of value' became unstoppable for the theory lends itself to obscuring the practical abstraction from use-value and concrete, useful labor performed by generalized commodity exchange in favor of taking it to be merely a quantitative price theory. On its way to becoming the social science of economics, political economy emulated the natural sciences in proclaiming a "law of value." As we shall see, Karl Marx, the trenchant critic of bourgeois political economy, contended that this so-called "law of value" is the basis of class exploitation, thus providing a would-be "scientific proof" of the injustice of the capitalist form of economic life.

David Ricardo and the Quantity Theory of Money

Ricardo espoused the quantity theory of money that emerged in the 16th–17th centuries. It states that the general price level of goods and

---

85. Smith, *The Wealth of Nations*, Bk 1, Chapter 5, 31.

86. Aristotle, *Nicomachean Ethics*, Chapter 12, iii. It is also in line with Lonergan's *CWL* 15, 21 both of which, we argue, search for a middle-way approach to economics.

87. For Aristotle, the use value (the utility of a good or service) depends upon fostering a person's good. The use value of a given article can vary among individuals. The demand for an item is a function of its use value.

services is directly proportional to the amount of money in circulation, or money supply. It affirms that prices increase if the amount of money increases, but "money has no impact on the economic activities and is just a veil."[88] The theory is expressed in the following equation:

$$money \text{ supply} \times velocity \text{ of money} = price \text{ level} \times real \text{ GDP}^{89}$$

In Ricardo's time there was no generally accepted alternative theory. He assumed that gold backed money. He further erroneously assumed that the amount of money follows the increase of the national income. Actually, it is the other way around. Fifty years earlier, Adam Smith and David Hume had realized that an increase in the amount of money tends to "have an impact on the national income."[90]

The quantity theory of money can be conceived in two different ways, that is, *whether or not* paper money is backed by gold. Ricardo argued in the affirmative that "only something scarce by nature, something that cannot be multiplied arbitrarily, like gold, could serve as money.[91] No explanation is given for Ricardo's sentence: "A circulation can never be so abundant as to overflow; for by diminishing its value, in the same proportion you will increase its quantity, and by increasing

---

88. *"The Veil of Money. Real-World Economics Review Blog.* 2016-04-26. Retrieved 2017-04-08.

89. GDP (gross domestic product) is the value of a nation's finished domestic goods and services during a specific time period.

90. "Theory of Money," https://www.economics-reloaded.com/1_classical_theory/David _Ricardo/1_2_4_money_theory.htm The article adds "Nowadays, (in 2013), it is easy to see that the quantity theory of money doesn't fit very well with reality." For example, central banks now often flood the market with money without any noticeable impact on prices. However, deflation causes the nominal costs of capital, labor, goods, and services to fall which, in turn, causes a decrease in prices and induces bubbles on the stock market. The inevitable collapse of asset bubbles wipes out the net worth of investors and causes exposed businesses to fail. This can lead to a cascade of debt deflation, even a financial panic that can spread to other parts of the economy resulting in a period of higher unemployment and lower production.

91. "Theory of Money." Perhaps the most well-known history of money is John Kenneth Galbraith's *Money: Whence It Came, Where It Went* (New York: Penguin Books, 1977). More recently Niall Ferguson published a darker version: *Ascent of Money: Financial History of the World* (Penguin, 2009).

its value, diminish its quantity."[92] According to this theory, an increase in the amount of money will lead to an increase in prices, to inflation; conversely, a decrease in the amount of money leads to falling prices. This view has been disputed by those who argue that money does have an impact on the real economy; with money idle, resources can be activated.[93] Nor was this scenario the one Adam Smith presented. In Smith's view, the national income shrinks but *not* the amount of money. Therefore, part of the money is superfluous for transactional purposes and can be used, if foreign countries have the same currency, to import commodities. Susumu Takenaga has argued that Ricardo didn't understand that. In fact, gold or silver is the means of payment or, at least, the anchor of paper money.[94]

The quantity theory of money is much more complicated than Ricardo argued, however. Ricardo could have known this had he observed the facts. Fifty years earlier, in *Of Money and Other Economic Essays*, Hume had argued that as net exports *increased and more gold* flowed into a country to pay for them, the prices of goods in that country would rise.[95] Ricardo argued that "If the increase in the amount of money leads to a higher demand that cannot be satisfied, it will lead to inflation."[96] Takenaga rejects Ricardo's view on the ground that "it is empirically wrong and theoretically not plausible . . . Ricardo's basic error is his assumption that capital or money is backed by things produced in the past, but actually, money is backed by the things produced in the future."[97]

---

92. Ricardo, *On The Principles of Political Economy and Taxation*, Chapter 27."

93. See, Sayre P. Schatz, "Underutilized Resources," www.jstor.org/stable/1884308? seq=1

94. Susumu Takenaga, "Theory of Money of David Ricardo: Quantity Theory and Theory of Value," July, 2003, *Lecturas de Economia* (59) 73–126.

95. The Library of Money and Liberty, "David Hume." www.econlib.org/library/ Enc/ bios/Hume.html

96. https://www.economics-reloaded.com/1_classical_theory/David_Ricardo/1_2_4_ money_theory.htm

97. https://www.economics-reloaded.com/1_classical_theory/David_Ricardo/1 _2_4_money_theory.htm Smith also erred in saying that "a reduction in the amount of money will reduce the amount of money for investment purposes. The percentage of money needed for transaction purposes will be higher and the percentage of money for

Although it is true that the actual production of goods does depend on machines used, on raw materials, capital to pay the workers, etc., "this capital will be disinvested, reconverted into money. However, only if the 'capitalist' can substitute his machines, buy new raw materials and employ the workmen once again" can the money he earns be of any use. This means that accumulating must be understood in real terms. Saving leads to the production of capital goods instead of consumption goods. In this sense, and only in this sense, does it follow that savings lead to a reduction of consumption.[98] However, this only applies in the case of full-employment. In the event of high unemployment, if there are idle productive resources, both capital goods and consumption goods can be produced.[99] Any other definition of saving leads to countless errors in thinking. In case of unemployment, money is needed but savings can be a problem for they reduce still more the already insufficient demand. We see that as well if we take a closer

---

investment purposes lower. This will lead to an increase in the interest rate. Investments will decrease and unemployment increase. This will lead to a lack of demand . . . , although not proportionally." The problem is that Smith "assumed that prices, wages, prices of commodities, interest rates etc. will fall proportionally." Nicholas A. Curott, "Adam Smith's Theory of Money and Banking," SAE/No. 47, Feb. 2016, argues that Smith presented a (chemical-like) reflux theory based upon the premise that the demand for money is fixed at a particular nominal quantity. Smith's theory denies that an excess supply of money can . . . influence prices or employment."

98. www.caixabankresearch.com/en/perspectives-household-consumption-and-savings

99. Michael Eldred, argues in *Social Ontology: Recasting Political Philosophy through a Phenomenology of Whoness* (de Gruyter, 2008), 202, that "All modern economic theory, since it measures itself against the paradigm of mathematical physics ushered in by Newton, is fixated upon quantitative laws and derides metaphysical consideration of the simple phenomena themselves which . . . are the most 'obvious' and apparently 'self-evident'. It is precisely that "obviousness" that has to be questioned. For Schumpeter, Marx's labor theory of value stemmed from Ricardo. "His theory of value is the Ricardian one. . . . Marx's arguments are merely less polite, more prolix and more 'philosophical.'" Schumpeter favored an empirical social scientific analysis," that requires "a philosophical consideration of the simple phenomena themselves that can provide the way forward for liberating Marx's' philosophy from "the constrictions of a Ricardian labor theory of value in particular and from the self-evident standard quantitative, pre-calculative concerns of economic theory in general, "in order to gain insight into the essence of money and exchange relations and ultimately into the enabling dimension of human association itself and the nature of human interchange." [https://doi.org/10.1515/9783110617504]

look at the quantity theory of money,[100] which held that the amount of money can only be increased if there is a demand for money. Only when some people want to invest is there a demand for money. The banking system can offer as much money as it wants, but if there is no demand, they can't lend. It is obvious that banks want to lend because they live from such a practice. The money lent out should meet the needs of borrowers. It is the demand for money that determines the offer of money and not the supply.[101]

Re-Imagining Money as Legal Tender to Pay for Debts, and Some Causal Relationships

Let us give a specific example. We often think of money in terms of coins, notes, or perhaps a number in a bank account. But when one looks on the face of a US dollar bill, it says, "This note is legal tender for all debts, public and private." In other words, if there were no debts, it would be worthless. Who needs money to pay for debts if there is no debt? So we need to reimagine money, not just as a hard asset, but as a legal tender to pay for debts because it encompasses all global transactions. However, there are also historical debts that transcend monetary transactions.[102]

---

100. Real national income is the national income fixed on an arbitrarily chosen price level. Price level is the difference, in a percentage, at the original price level and the actual price level. This must correspond to the amount of money multiplied by the circulation velocity (how many times a coin goes from one hand to another). The higher the circulation velocity, the less money is needed. Note that the equation does not distinguish between situations of full and partial employment.

101. The Austrian school argued that low-interest rates present a risk in that low-interest rates change the expectations concerning profits. They are higher if interest rates are low which leads to more demand for capital goods, that the supply can't satisfy. This, in turn, leads to an increase in capital goods. See, e.g., Fred Foldvary, "The Austrian Theory of the Business Cycle." *The American Journal of Economics and Sociology* 74, no. 2 (2015): 278–97. https://www.jstor.org/stable/43818666. See also Chris Seabury. "How Interest Rates Affect the U. S. Markets" in *Investopia*, Dec. 17, 2020.

102. These include historical debts of injustice and inequality that still need to be paid—recall the international slave trade. The fact that there is no currency to pay for these debts does not mean that they do not exist. Thomas Harding's White Debt: The Demerara Uprising and Britain's Legacy of Slavery (Orion, 2022), for example, shows the magnitude of dishonesty of education in Britain that fails to teach the truth about how much of

The quantity theory of money is not really a monetary theory. It just describes an equilibrium. However, if we want to move from one equilibrium to another, we need to know the causal relationships. When the amount of money is increased, given a determined national income, the money disposable for investment purposes increases, interest rates fall. This will lead to higher investments because the hurdle to overcome for investing is lower. The argument is that low-interest rates change the expectations concerning profits. (They are higher, if interest rates are low.) This will lead to a significant demand in capital goods, that the supply can't satisfy. The prices of capital goods will increase again. This would be no problem if other investors would be prevented through higher prices of capital goods from investing. Such is the assumption of the Austrian school, due to the fact that all invest at the same time; once started, the process can't be stopped, the investments won't be profitable, and many companies go bankrupt. The argument is not very logical, because if we take this argument seriously, the only way to prevent people from buying things they can't afford is through raising prices. Following this logic, high prices are always good, the higher, the better.[103]

People who possess money are interested in high interest rates; they want money to be kept scarce. The complaints against (recently-abandoned) monetary policies[104] of the central banks such as the European Central Bank and the US Federal Reserve, come mostly from

England's 'greatness' is due to exploiting enslaved people and plundering their land. For a perceptive analysis of government debts, see https://sdyearwood.medium.com/paradigm-shift-ad6c2253d3aa

103. Daniel Kahneman, recipient of the 2002 Nobel Prize for Economics, warns against inconsiderate judgments and decisions when conducting transactions affecting investments in general—a precept GEM-FS strongly endorses. Kahneman, contrary to the expected utility theory (which models the decision that "perfectly rational agents" would make), aims to describe the actual behavior of people.

104. *A Monetary History of the United States, 1867–1960* was written in 1963 by Milton Friedman and Anna J. Schwartz. It uses historical time series and economic analysis to argue the then-novel proposition that changes in the money supply profoundly influence the U.S. economy and the behavior of economic fluctuations. The book implies that changes in the money supply had unintended adverse effects, and that sound monetary policy is necessary for economic stability; it is considered as one of the most influential economics books of the century. See Wikipedia, "Monetary History of the United States."

pension funds and insurance companies. Their business is to collect money from savers and invest it, but this becomes more difficult the more money is printed by the central banks. Higher interest rates paid to savers are not compatible with the interests of the economy as a whole. That means that pensions funds, insurance companies and banks would never say that low-interest rates militate against their interests.[105] Rather, they argue that low-interest rates are risky, but this is pure ideology. From today's perspective, the gold standard is a strange kind of monetary system, but in the context of the 18th/19th centuries, it made sense.[106] If the national income was simply unknown, there was no way to find out how much money was actually needed. Therefore, in such a situation a monetary system is needed which adapts itself automatically to the national income.

Marxist Critiques of Capitalist Social Relations as Being Unjust

In the move from Adam Smith to David Ricardo, one can detect a gradual shift to a more quantitative view of economic phenomena. Ricardo's name is associated with the "law of labor-value" inasmuch as he proposed that there was indeed a measure for the fairness of the exchange of goods apart from fair price and that this measure resided in the amount of labor embodied in the things exchanged. He argued for a labor theory of value: the value of a commodity, or the quantity of any other

---

When recently asked about contemporary massive amounts of government stimulus amidst today's economic experiments, Warren Buffett answered: "It's a fascinating time. We've never really seen what shoveling money in on a [fiscal] basis [like] we're doing it, following a monetary policy of something close to zero percent interest rates. It is enormously pleasant. But in economics, you can never do only one thing. You always have to say 'and then what?' There are consequences to everything in economics."

105. Current monetary policy is primarily concerned with the management of interest rates.

106. The "rules of the game" is a phrase Keynes used in the 1920s. While the "rules" were not explicitly set out, governments and central banks were implicitly expected to behave in a certain manner during the period of the classical Gold Standard. See www.gold.org/about-gold/history-of-gold/the-gold-standard

commodity for which it will exchange, depends on the relative quantity of labor which is necessary for its production, and not on the greater or less compensation which is paid for that labor.[107] Ricardo believed that landlords tended to squander their wealth on luxuries, rather than invest and that the Corn Laws were leading to England's economic stagnation.

Eldred argues that "the untenability of the labor theory of value as a theory of just exchange" masks exploitation."[108] For him, even with the move from Smith to Ricardo one can detect a shift to a more quantitative view of economic phenomena. Ricardo is firmly associated with the law of labor-value. For him, there was indeed a measure for the fairness of the exchange of goods apart from fair price; it resided in the amount of labor embodied in the things exchanged.

The labor theory of value was adopted by Karl Marx who went further than his predecessors in investigating how "abstract labor" whose magnitude purportedly determined exchange-value ultimately assumed the form of price and money under generalized commodity production and exchange.[109] He offered an ontology of that unique social thing, money, thus echoing Aristotle's deep insights in his *Nicomachean Ethics*, Book V, into the nature of money. For Marx, following Ricardo, the equitable exchange of goods was based on the exchange of equal labor-times embodied in those goods. Marx not only viewed the phenomenon

---

107. Ricardo, (1817) *On the Principles of Political Economy and Taxation.* See Piero Sraffa (Ed.) *Works and Correspondence of David Ricardo*, Volume I, Cambridge Univ. 1951, 11. The editors of *CWL*, 15, lxii, note that "Sraffa does not use his sophisticated explanation of the 'Ricardo effect' . . . or 'concertina-like phenomena associated with it in the way Lonergan does." Only Lonergan *uses this difference in economic activities to specify* "the significant variables in his dynamic analysis . . . no one else considers the functional distinctions between different kinds of productive rhythms prior to, *and* more fundamental than, wealth, value, supply and demand, price levels and patterns, capital and labor, interest and profits, wages, and so forth. . . . Only Lonergan analyzes booms and slumps in terms of how their (explanatory) velocities, accelerations, and decelerations are or are not equilibrated in relation to the events, movements, and changes in two distinct monetary circuits of production and exchange as considered both in themselves (with circulatory, sequential dependence) and in relation to each other by means of crossover payments."

108. Eldred, "Exchange Value, Justice," 3. See also Kehinde Andrews, *The New Age of Empire: How Racism and Colonialism Still Rule the World* New York: Penguin, 2021.

109. Eldred, "The notions of exchange, values," 3.

that the practice of the generalized exchange of the products of labor as commodities practically effects a kind of equalization[110] of diverse kinds of concrete labor and thus the constitution of what can be termed "abstract labor," but he went further. He affirmed abstract labor to be the "value-building substance" which both constitutes exchange-value and quantitatively determines its magnitude. To take this additional step and obtain a value-substance, "Marx had to introduce an ambiguity . . . , a polysemy, into the concept of abstract labor. It cannot be i) simply commodity-producing labor in its quality as being universally practically equated on the market with all other kinds of labor, but it must have ii) an intrinsic existence *independent* of the practice of commodity exchange (which is a *relation*) if it is to serve as a 'value-substance' and measure capable of quantitative determination of the magnitude of value.[111]

It is on the basis of such an understanding of abstract labor as value-substance that the peculiar commodity, labor power, has the characteristic of creating in the production process more labor-value than it is itself worth on the market. Labor power is the potential to labor residing in the laborer. It is not simply a congealed objectification of labor, but it is embodied in a living human. Its value, according to Marx, must therefore be determined q*ualitatively* and *quantitatively* by the exchange-value of the goods consumed in maintaining and reproducing that labor

---

110. Marx-Engels *Werke Band* 23 S. 65, *Das Kapital* Band I (1867), Dietz Verlag, Berlin 1962/1975 cf. Aristotle *Eth. Nic.* V 1133a13

111. Eldred, "The notions of exchange, value," 5, adds that one of Marx's most clear-sighted critics took the so-called "law of value" to task as the theoretical foundation of *Das Kapital* "shortly after Engels . . . published the third volume of this momentous work in 1894. In his *Karl Marx and the Close of his System*, (1896) Eugen von Böhm-Bawerk criticized the labor theory of value. He sought to show the contradiction between the 'law of value' and the theory of prices of production at which capitalists sell their commodity products. . . . This has to do with the "transformation problem" that arose in the 1880's, (finding a rule by which to indicate the "values" of commodities based on their socially necessary labor content) into the "competitive prices" of the marketplace. "Yet, the transformation problem is confronted with the contradiction of two different quantitative determinations of commodity prices, namely, the quantities of abstract labor time, on the one hand, and the costs plus average profit, on the other. This transformation problem can be formulated as a system of simultaneous equations, which many economists have since done over the last century in various ways."

power. On the basis of assuming that both the fair and factual exchange of goods are determined by magnitudes of socially necessary labor-time (measuring abstract labor as value), whilst excluding the possibility that entrepreneurial labor plays a part in determining the value of the commodity product, Marx developed the concept of surplus value[112] which would demonstrate that laborers give more value to the capitalists than they receive in wages and are thus quantitatively deprived of a portion of the exchange-value they produce through the expenditure of their labor power during working hours.

Eldred insists that "without postulating a quantitatively determinate value-substance residing in a kind of abstract labor, Marx would not have been able to develop the theory of surplus value as a quantitative theory of class exploitation" as the foundation of so-called "scientific socialism" from which Marxism has drawn much of its persuasive strength due to its "purported proof of capitalism's essential social injustice. The *essentially* unfair exchange between a wage-laborer and the capitalist entrepreneur . . . , serves to expand into a critique of the entire 'capitalist system' as socially unjust *in toto* (due to the distributive injustice suffered by the working class)."[113] Marx adds "The genius of Aristotle shines precisely in the fact that he discovers a relation of equality in the value expression of commodities. Only the historical barrier of the society in which he lived prevented him"[114] from discovering what this equality relationship is, namely that all labor is of equal worth.[115] Aristotle could

---

112. Yan Shi, "The Formation of Marxist Theory of Surplus Value," *Frontier of Higher Education*. (2020). 1.10. https://doi.org/10.36012/fhe.v1i2.1433

113. Marx, *Das Kapital*, Vol. 1. In his *Critique of the Gotha Program*, Marx wrote: "Any distribution of the means of consumption is only a consequence of the distribution of the conditions of production themselves. The latter distribution, however, is a feature of the mode of production itself." www.marxists.org/archive/marx/works/1875/gotha/ch01.htm

114. Marx, *Das Kapital*, Vol. 1, 23. Some left-leaning commentators are frustrated because few are willing to follow what to them seems obvious to promote a more just distribution of goods. We need much mediation to reconcile extremes. Such mediation is this book's main goal.

115. For Christians, the Social Justice perspective is based on the gospel values of Jesus; it should be the way of life of Christians. That means that the motivating concern for the poor must be translated at all levels—including, national and international governments—into concrete actions. Promoting true development of peoples requires the desire and

not discern this because Greek society was based on slave labor and therefore had as its natural basis the inequality of people and their labor powers, which he supported as "natural."[116] The secret of the expression of value as the equal worth of all labors lies in the fact that human labor in general can only be deciphered once the concept of human equality is well understood. This, however, is only possible in a society in which the notion of commodity is the general form of the product of labor as well as the basis of human relations.[117]

An Excursus on Lonergan and Socialism: Implications for Two Further GEM-FS Turnarounds

President Harry Truman remarked on October 10, 1952 that

> Socialism is a scare word they have hurled at every advance the people have made in the last 20 years.
>
> Socialism is what they called public power. Socialism is what they called social security.
>
> Socialism is what they called farm price supports.
>
> Socialism is what they called bank deposit insurance.
>
> Socialism is what they called the growth of free and independent labor organizations.
>
> Socialism is their name for all that helps all the people.[118]

---

the responsibility to ensure justice for all people, especially the poor. Woke is a political term of African American origin that refers to a perceived awareness of issues concerning social justice and racial justice. It is derived from the African American Vernacular English expression "stay woke," whose grammatical aspect refers to a continuing awareness of these issues." Woke capitalism opposes capitalist, profit-driven approach of corporations—capitalizing on the stir and popularity of social movements to achieve their ends.

116. See e.g., Malcolm Heath, "Aristotle on Natural Slavery." *Phronesis* 53, no. 3 (2008): 243–70. http://www.jstor.org/stable/40387959

117. Marx, *Das Kapital*, Part I, Chapter I, "Commodities and Money."

118. Moderate forms of socialism should not be "scare words" as Truman stressed. This is so because needed radical changes in environmental policies can only occur to the extent that enough industrialists and policymakers, duly aware of the environmental crises

Truman respected the socialism that helps all people. While Lonergan had his reservations about socialism, he did have a notion of a social dividend to help ensure that future goods and services will be produced for the good of all. We stress the need for a socio-ethical guidance in today's economics. We argue that besides GEM-FS's generally recognized four conversions—psychic, intellectual, moral and religious—which focus primarily on personal dynamics—there is a need for two other GEM-FS turnarounds or conversions of a socio-communal nature, that is, turnarounds in economics and environmental policies[119] to round out, complement the personal aspects of intellectual, moral, religious and psychic conversions. Lonergan's work implies a need for an environmental, socially-conscious turnaround that would radically change policies to counter climate change for the good of all. This is the major point made in John Raymaker and Ijaz Durrani's *Empowering Climate-Change Strategies with Bernard Lonergan's Method*,[120] which makes an implicit claim for the need of a turnaround in environmental policies to counteract environmental problems.[121] Raymaker and Durrani argue with Lonergan that an eye of love is needed to resolve some of the conflicting issues clouding present climate change debates. "An important point is that Lonergan tended to focus on the processes of thinking within individual persons, how they arrive at insights, how they are converted. We locate individuals within the goals of society in general."[122] Let us cite some problematic examples in need of rectification:

---

our planet is now undergoing, begin to take action. This could be helped by an eco-spirituality which connects the science of ecology with spirituality. In his message for the Season of Creation, Pope Francis noted that an environ conversion must occur not only among individuals but within "the community of nations," with particular attention to United Nations conferences focused on addressing climate change and biodiversity loss.

119. A nagging question as to the need of two actually-pursued-and sometimes-achieved social-communal conversions or turnarounds is whether and how legal systems fail to represent the intrinsic value of nature: lawmakers typically consider only economic or human interests.

120. Raymaker, Durrani, University Press of America, 2015, 57, 61.

121. Such conversions would principally apply to entrepreneurs and governments.

122. Raymaker, Durrani, 2, 68.

§ Nitrogen alters the chemistry of the atmosphere and of aquatic eco-systems. It contributes to overgrowths of the biosphere; it also has sub-stantial regional effects on biological diversity in the most affected areas. Human land use has transformed one third to one half of Earth's ice-free surface. In and of itself, this is a critical component of global cli-mate change for the present and foreseeable future: it has had profound effects on biological diversity on land and on ecosystems downwind and downstream from affected areas. Such adverse degradations of the global environmental are the primary causes of climate changes and of ongo-ing losses of biological diversity. There is an emerging consensus about the components of climate change and its causes—though that reality is denied by some. We need to shift the focus of public discussion on what can be done about global environmental changes.[123]

§ Although 71% of US citizens believe in the science of climate change,[124] corporations let fossil fuel billionaires such as David and Bill Koch who bankroll climate deniers sit on the boards of prestigious educational institutions.

Robert K. Musil has recognized Rachel Carson's work in shaping the environmental movement in the U. S,[125] with her 1962 bestseller Silent Spring. It wasn't until the use of synthetic chemical pesticides became widespread, that Carson began to make the connection between these chemicals—particularly DDT ("Elixirs of Death")—and their harmful impact on the welfare of animals. Sadly, the problems she documented have, to a large extent, gotten worse, more acute. This makes it impera-tive for ethicists to take the initiative.

---

123. Raymaker, Durrani, 27. In 2022, the National Oceanic and Atmospheric Admin-istration predicted a one-foot sea-level rise by 2050, This makes the need of environmental conversions on the part of many ever more urgent.

124. Raymaker, Durrani, 34.

125. Robert K. Musil, *Rachel Carson and Her Sisters: Extraordinary Women Who Have Shaped America's Environment* (Rutgers Univ. Press, 2014).

The Need for GEM-FS Turnarounds in Economic Policies

Pessimism and despair differ. One can be intellectually pessimistic but temperamentally optimistic and spiritually hopeful.[126] Our middle-ground approach to a GEM-FS economics explicitly focuses on the need for a turnaround in economic policies. Such a turnaround, we argue, is a precondition for implementing Lonergan's macroeconomics. Economic democracy is a socioeconomic philosophy that proposes to shift decision-making power from corporate managers and corporate shareholders[127] to a larger group of public stakeholders that includes workers, customers, suppliers, and the broader public.[128] In line with an economic democracy, our middle-ground approach to economics advocates the need for experimental, cooperative movements such as 1) the Antigonish movement that Lonergan supported early in his career or 2) another experimental movement such as the Mondragon corporation launched in Spain's Basque Region in 1956. The latter is the outcome of a cooperative business project, meant to promote fair corporate values: inter-cooperation, grassroots management, corporate social responsibility, democratic organization, and social transformation. The group bills itself as being "a dedicated group of people with a cooperative identity forming a business group that is profitable, competitive and enterprising—capable of successfully operating in global markets." Mondragon uses democratic methods in its corporate organization. Its aims "are employment, the personal and professional advancement of its workers, and the

---

126. A NOAA report has shown that 310 climate-linked disasters have cost the US over $2 trillion since 1980. It is dishonest to refuse to face up to the scientific facts about climate change and to the imbalance between population and resources, pollution, and financial inequities due to corporate power. (In fact, Pope Francis has explicitly declared it a sin in his encyclical *Laudato Sì*.) We focus on the need for an economics conversion to complement and help "undergird" the environmental conversion.

127. For Noam Chomsky, "It's ridiculous to talk about freedom in a society dominated by huge corporations. What kind of freedom is there inside a corporation? They're totalitarian institutions - you take orders from above and maybe give them to people below you. There's about as much freedom as under Stalinism." www.goodreads.com/quotes/777491

128. https://artsandculture.google.com/entity/economic-democracy/m08cyy4?hl=en

development of its community."[129] We cite this as an example of a corporation guided by self-transcending cooperative judgments.[130] Fostering such community-motivated ethical entities that safeguard nature is essential if humanity is to flourish. These forms of ethically-motivated communities embody what we name "group economics turnarounds," which are to be complemented with changes in environmental policies—both of which an ethical GEM-FS calls for.

Lonergan's Alternative: An Inherently Dynamic Theory of the Productive Process

Paul Hoyt-O'Connor and colleagues have written that for Lonergan an economy is a good of order[131] which, when properly disposed, makes possible the regular provision of the material conditions for the fuller flourishing of humans. For example, Lonergan insisted that

> The good of order is not some design for utopia, some theoretic ideal, some set of ethical precepts, some code of laws, or some super-institution. It is quite concrete. It is the actually functioning or malfunctioning set of "if-then" relationships guiding operators and coordinating operations. It is the ground whence recur or fail to recur whatever instances of the particular good are recurring or failing to recur. It has a basis in institutions but it is a product of much more, of all the skill and know-how, all the industry and resourcefulness, all the ambition and fellow-feeling of a whole people, adapting to each change of circumstance, meeting each new emergency, struggling against every tendency to disorder.[132]

---

129. See https://en.wikipedia.org/wiki/Mondragon_Corporation

130. Cooperative judgments are implemented on a self-transcendent, ethical basis.

131. Hoyt-O'Connor, P., Cermelli, M. & Calvo-Sotomayor, I. "The Basque socio-economic model (BSEM): a Lonergan perspective." *Int Rev Econ* (2021). https://doi.org/10.1007/s12232-021-00380-2

132. *MiT*, 49–50. *CWL* 14, 49, Although we call attention to problems inherent in a capitalist doctrine advocating only profit, we believe that capitalism can co-exist with counterbalancing forces to redress the causes of injustice, as suggested in *Insight*, 619–20: "Besides the good that is simply object of desire, there is the good of order. Such is the

For Lonergan, the economy is related to a society's civic institutions, political orders, and cultural traditions. He explained the normative rhythms of economic development[133] and the conditions of its dynamic equilibrium; his analysis presents an alternative to conventional accounts of economic progress. His alternative can be compared to the kind of economic progress the Basque Country has enjoyed in past decades—in ways that resonate with the Basque emphasis on the centrality of the productive process and the values of its people. We cite this account as evidence of Lonergan's middle-ground approach to unfettered capitalism and Marxism. Our GEM-FS ethical critique of modern society is partly based on notions of prophetic transformational process such as those of Pope Francis who urges people not to let themselves be motivated only by profit-seeking. Lonergan's awareness of the need for an economy of scale helped him lay a middle ground between the extremes of capitalism and socialism.

HOW LONERGAN'S GEM-FS LAYS AN ETHICAL MIDDLE GROUND BETWEEN CAPITALISM AND COERCIVE FORMS OF SOCIALISM

We noted above how Adam Smith's "Invisible Hand" led to opposing views on the nature of the productive process and the distribution of

---

polity, the economy, the family as an institution. It is not the object of any single desire, for it stands to single desires as system to systematized, as universal condition to particulars that are conditioned, as scheme of recurrence that supervenes upon the materials of desires and the efforts to meet them and, at the price of limited restrictions, through the fertility of intelligent control, secures" an otherwise unattainable abundance of satisfactions.

133. On economic development that de-emphasizes instrumental reason, see Ronald Inglehart, *Modernization and Postmodernism* (Princeton Univ., 1977). Such a de-emphasis is necessary to promote environmental and economic conversions. Ours is in a way an exercise in re-humanization that confronts violence and injustice in a topsy-turvy world. Frederick Douglass, MLK, and Fred Hampton of the Black Panther Party were prophets; the "dynamics" of prophetic voices tend to replicate what happened to the prophets of old, to Socrates, to Jesus. There is an urgent need to explore the dynamics of the six GEM-FS conversions and of ethical discernment by economists. Hopefully, humanity would try *to maximize profit for all*. Our aim is to analyze what this latter phrase might mean: what processes would be involved therein. This does not call for the shedding of blood as has occurred in much of history, but for changes of heart needed to underly the search for effective, just economic policies.

goods. In preparation for Parts III and IV, we want to establish adequate ethical notions of value and justice needed to lay the foundations for a middle-ground approach to economics that respects legitimate profit as well as the rights of workers. For Phil McShane, Lonergan's shift in economic thinking was based on a conviction that there was a need for something more fundamental than the pricing system. Lonergan was convinced that economics went astray when Adam Smith in the fourth chapter of Vol. I of *The Wealth of Nations*, after discussing the need for money in a social economy, gets fascinated by the distinction between money price, real price, and exchange value and from then on . . . his interest gets bogged down in the question of how values and prices for products are determined. One can trace a more or less continuous development of price theory from the subsequent chapters of Smith through Ricardo, Walras, Marshall, right up to Debreu and the most sophisticated "Americans";[134] referring to Kaldor, "The Irrelevance of Equilibrium Economics."

We have argued that in both neoliberalism and Marxism, humans have been subjected to processes that debase their humanity: people tend to become mere tools used in the productive process. The capitalist-socialist divides result in conflicting government priorities. Elites enjoy privileges denied the average citizen. Polarization of many types set in. As a transition to Part III, we now allude to four examples of how Lonerganian commentators have suggested ways to undo the unethical patterns in which societies across the world are organized.

First, Michael Gibbons argues that unlike the long line of equilibrium theorists,[135] Lonergan's *Circulation Analysis* (*CWL* 15) is an

---

134. Phil McShane, "Features of Generalized Empirical Method and the Actual Context of Economics," in *Creativity and Method*, (Marquette Univ. Press, 1981), 559.

135. Eileen de Neeve, *Journal of Macrodynamic Analysis*, Vol. 4, 2004, 181, argues that "Lonergan proposes the pure cycle as a normative model of macro-dynamics. It differs from the static Walrasian equilibrium model, first because it is about the dynamics of production and sale and, second, because it does not make prior assumptions about human behavior. Walrasian equilibrium is automatic because individuals are assumed to act to maximize their utility or profit, which is regarded as rational behavior. She adds that perhaps Hayek was right: the discussion of dynamics is unclear because economists have been reluctant to use the term "profit" in macroeconomics after Marx. Lonergan's theory can contribute a new generalization to the study of innovative growth and cycles; but his pure

inherently dynamic theory, concerned with the rates and volume of change in the different parts of the production process. Lonergan addresses processes in motion, the flows of goods and services through the production process and the parallel flows of payments as they move from investments to consumption, with "systems on the move."[136] Gibbons adds that *CWL* 15 is "a theory within a concrete heuristic." It "is abstract only in the sense that it omits the inessential." Lonergan is trying "To get us to understand the functionally normative and heuristic relationships which connect flows of goods to the circulations of payments made and received. It is in respect to the theoretical development of these functional interdependencies that . . . Lonergan has moved beyond contemporary thinking."[137]

A second example touches on the confusion of insight and would-be systematic unifications based on visual imagination as attempted by Freud. The confusion of insight and visual imagination has been at the root of countless problems in the modern age affecting science and economics. Insight is not mere visual imagination. The development of modern classical and statistical approaches in the past several centuries demands this distinction. Lonergan points out the world of difference between a systematic unification of physical laws and an imaginative synthesis:

> As systematic unification does not include imaginative synthesis, so it does not even guarantee its possibility. It is true enough that images

---

cycle economic choices needs to take into account changes in production and their price effects. Economic behavior needs to be based on an understanding of production lags, as well as a willingness to reinvest excess profits as widely as possible to maintain output and employment and avoid a downturn in the economy. The decline of excess profits at the end of the surplus expansion does not mean the end of the normally higher incomes of management. It does suggest that incomes will become less unequal than in the boom. As Keynes also understood, Lonergan sees that raising interest rates to stabilize the economy's high prices in a boom can influence savings and investment, but does so by adjusting the rate of production to the rate of saving rather than vice versa.

136. Michael Gibbons, "Insight and Emergence: an Introduction to Lonergan's *Circulation Analysis*," *Creativity and Method*, (Marquette Univ. Press, 1981), 532–33.

137. Gibbons, "Insight and Emergence," 533.

are necessary for the emergence of insights, but the images may be not representative but symbolic, not pictures of the visible universe but mathematical notations on pieces of paper.[138]

The point is that we cannot reach a representative image of what scientific reality is. Scientific explanation in its very essence transcends imaginative representation. It relates things to one another in their systematic correlations—not to our visual imagination. Paul Symington instances the disastrous confusion in the work of Freud which is based on imaginative synthesis rather than on psycho-organic functions integrated in human functionality according to probabilistic schemes of recurrence:

> Lonergan offers a theory of the psychological problems of repression and inhibition not primarily as functions of subverted organic desires, but more properly according to the functioning of intellectual bias. Lonergan thereby provides a more comprehensive understanding of the unity of the human self at the psychical level.[139]

Lonergan compares Freud's imaginative approach to psychical unity with his own explanation that avoids Freud's psycho-biological presuppositions.

A third example[140] comes from Catherine King. It illustrates GEM-FS' healing-creating vectors. Our own approach is in tune with hers inasmuch as we strive to relate people's transformative operations from a GEM-FS healing-creating viewpoint. Although King does not go into economics, her depiction of how people can use the two healing-creating vectors a la *MiT*'s eight-step functional approach is helpful:

---

138. *Insight*, 116. We acknowledge David Bibby's help on this topic.

139. Paul Symington, "The Unconscious and Conscious Self: The Nature of Psychical Unity in Freud and Lonergan," *American Catholic Philosophical Quarterly*, Vol. 80, 4, Fall 2006, 563.

140. This example is in keeping with our general argument that GEM-FS is a transformational-unifying framework that can interrelate many fields of studies.

Vector 1	Vector 2	Concrete Subject
Creating ⇑	Healing ⇓	Vector 1 Begins Again ⇑
From Below Up⇑	From Above Down⇓	
Differentiation⇒	Interrelation⇒	⇐Integration (A State) ⇒
Dialectic (critique)	Foundations (change of mind)	
⇑	⇓	
History	Doctrine (from Foundations)	
⇑	⇓	
Interpretation	Systematics (understanding doctrines)	
⇑	⇓	
⇐Research (from)	Communications⇒(with others)	

The above should be read as the overlapping movement of questioning, thought, states of mind, and communications in the concrete continuum that is human history. What is first *heard* and processed in and through the activities of Vector 1 becomes a *state of mind communicated* through Vector 2, even if only to oneself in one's interior dialogue in the life of our albeit-limited self-creation and development.[141]

Fourth example: We noted above Karl Rahner's view that Lonergan's method leads to the abnegation of what is specific to Catholic theology. In fact, we argue that Lonergan's method is a "Third Way" as explained in John Raymaker's *Third Way*.[142] The Lonerganian Third Way, we argue, is more in line with Foucault's view of neoliberalism rather than the

---

141. Catherine Blanche King/10-04-2020, reproduced with permission and based on Emile Piscitelli, "The Fundamental Attitudes of the Liberally Educated Person: Foundational Dialectics," *The Lonergan Workshop 5.* (1985): 289–342. We add that to become effective, a GEM-FS approach to economics should be read by economists as well as by liberation theologians, political theologians, and others inside and outside of religious organizations interested in justice and alternative approaches to economics.

142. In *Bernard Lonergan's Third Way of the Heart and Mind: Bridging some Buddhist-Christian-Muslim-Secularist Misunderstandings with a Global Secularity Ethics*, John Raymaker seeks to extend GEM-FS's bridging-reforming ability to the global stage. In reality, head and heart cannot be separated; they are mutually interdependent. As is the case with the *Third Way*, this book focuses on a "global secularity"—an approach fitted to the present world's vast complexities—one parallel to Foucault's view of neoliberalism.

traditional view of it. The latter, as we have seen is a market-oriented, profit-seeking ideology. Our Third-Way approach offers an alternative to current views of neoliberalism.

In Part III and IV, we study possible ways to bring about structural economic transformations. Such transformations are essential if we are to live in a just world. How can this be done without using coercion? Lonergan has set a new precedent, on which we rely in our pursuit of truth, the good and loving care—all of which are essential if societies are to redress the injustices plaguing humanity. A basic question is how can the privileged elite in the world be persuaded to engage in economic activities and governmental policies that will redress injustices? In the light of the GEM-FS approach we outlined in Part I, we argue that Lonergan offers us a theory of dynamic equilibrium rather than a static one. We do so with a view to re-humanize the often dehumanized roles people play in the productive process.[143]

---

143. In "Healing and Creating in History," *Third Collection*, 102, Lonergan accuses multinational corporations of making life for most people "hopelessly worse off than they otherwise would be." Because the discipline of economics is seriously flawed, a radical criticism is needed. We agree with Michael Shute, "Preparing to Read Economic History Functionally," *Journal of Macrodynamic Analysis*, Volume 10: 80–104, and the editors of *CWL* 15, 12–55, that Lonergan's account of economic circuits and the pure cycle are an instance of elements of a standard model generating the special categories for a standard model in economics that can correct many of the flaws in present approaches to economics. The first four FS are a search for reformed reformers of economics; the last four FS seek ways to implement their reforms discerned in the first four FS.

PART III

———◆———

Towards Correcting Inadequate Approaches to Economics:[1]

The Mediating-Creative Phase of Lonergan's Method—the First Four Functional Specialties

---

1. Eileen de Neeve, www.eileendeneeve.com/122.pdf, wrote that "Lonergan sought to explain how key variables interact and change over time"; he argued that "how the circular flows operate depends on how people function in their economic activities and the failure to understand the changes in the economic system during innovative growth, or to adapt to their requirements, explains the occurrence of booms and slumps in the economy. His economics proposes an ideal of . . . economic development and growth that offers the potential" to avoid crises in business cycles. Lonergan's interest in economic issues prepared him for the writing of *Insight*. His distinction between basic and surplus products is functional. "It depends not on who owns the goods but on how they affect the economy."

121

I n *CWL* 15, 21, Lonergan's goals were firstly, to help us grasp that the economy is relatively autonomous from but nonetheless related to a society's civic institutions, political orders, and cultural traditions; secondly, to explain the normative rhythms of economic development and the conditions of its dynamic equilibrium.[2] Both goals are related to the issue of economic sustainability that avoids exploitation.[3]

Our discussion of the ethical foundations of economics contrasts the notion of sustainability with the vicious types of exploitation that have sullied the ways rich nations have dealt with developing ones. Sustainable development has the goal of eradicating poverty and hunger and guaranteeing a healthy life.[4] It would universalize access to basic services such as water, sanitation and sustainable energy as well as support the generation of development opportunities through inclusive education and decent work. The reality is that many developing countries have had their natural resources such as gold and other precious metals exploited by corrupt politicians[5] in league with Western companies and China. An enthusiasm for sustainability calls for caution. On the other hand, "Our Common Future," also known as the Brundtland Report, published in October 1987 by the United Nations, promotes a broad ethical principle with two key components:

2. O'Connor, P., Cermelli, M. & Calvo-Sotomayor, The Basque socioeconomic model: a Lonergan perspective. *Int Rev Econ* (2021). https://doi.org/10.1007/s12232-021-00380-2

3. Jason Hickel, *The Divide: Global Inequality from Conquest to Free Markets* (Norton: 2018) amply details the intentional predation which has caused poverty in the Global South since the late 15th century. His later *Less is More: How Degrowth Will Save the World* (London: Cornerstone, 2021) seeks to show how we can bring our economy back into balance with the living world while building a thriving society for all. He warns us that this is our last chance to do so. He proposes ways to renovate the global economy to mitigate climate breakdown while providing for the needs of all humans.

4. Thomas Hartmann, *Common Dreams*, Nov. 19, 2021, reports on "The Corporate Plan to Murder Medicare," a plan "getting closer everyday." Hartmann, *Common Dreams,* Sep. 9, 2022 prognosticated that in the current year, despite Russia's war on Ukraine, Wall Street giants have made huge profit off global hunger and the energy crisis.

5. *The New York Times*, Oct. 30, 2021, on how a self-dealing elite's corrupted misrule in Lebanon led to a deadly port blast, a triple-digit inflation and energy shortages

First, it frames the goals of development in terms of meeting people's needs. In this respect it differs from some theories of development that use less value-laden terms, especially those relying on GDP or general economic expansion.

Second, it makes an explicit commitment to future generations. It adopts a philosophical approach in environmental ethics[6]—often associated with anthropocentrism, or the view that protection of the environment should be based primarily "on benefits that humans derive from utilizing natural resources."

Some ethicists see problems in the Brundtland commitment to the future. Derek Parfit introduced a number of philosophical paradoxes deriving from the ways we affect both the people that are yet to be born, as well as the formation of their preferences.[7] Thus, commitments to future generations can be tricky to implement.

In a way, Lonergan's economics foreshadows what is now known as Unified Growth Theory. This theory was developed due to the failure of endogenous growth theory to capture key empirical regularities in the growth process and how these led to a momentous rise in inequality among nations in the past two centuries. The Unified Growth Theory was fueled by the conviction that the understanding of the contemporary growth process would be limited and distorted unless growth theory would be based on micro-foundations that would reflect the qualitative aspects of the growth process in its entirety. In particular, the hurdles faced by less developed economies in reaching a state of *sustained economic growth would remain obscured* unless the origin of the transition of the currently developed economies into a state of sustained economic growth *would be identified*, and its implications

---

6. Environmental ethics is the discipline that studies the moral relationship of human beings to the environment and to non-human life. We here argue for the pressing need of environmental conversion-turnarounds.

7. Derek Parfit, *Philosophy and Public Affairs* 45 (2) 118–57 (2017). See also 1) P. B. Thompson, "Sustainability: Ethical Foundations," *Nature Education Knowledge* 3 2021 (10),11, which argues that sustainability may be the most important concern faced by environmental ethics today; 2) "Common Declaration on environmental ethics by John Paul II and the Ecumenical Patriarch his Holiness Bartholomew on June 10, 2002.

modified[8] to account for the additional economic forces faced by less developed economies in an interdependent world.[9] Our account of the eight FS in Parts III and IV addresses the key empirical regularities[10] in the growth process; it presents the ethical core of GEM-FS relevant to freeing people from the traps they face in life.

FIRST FUNCTIONAL SPECIALTY: GATHERING RELEVANT DATA IN ECONOMICS

As noted earlier, Lonergan insisted that "What is needed is a new political economy that is free from the mistakes of the old, a democratic economics that can issue practical imperatives to plain men."[11] He went on to say that instead of the old political economy which was all too often

---

8. JD Hamilton and J. Monteaguto, "Mankiw, Romer, and Weil's augmented Solow model," *Quarterly Journal of Economics* 107, 407–37 (1992), argue that the marginal product of human capital accrues to three factors of production: directly to human capital, and as an external effect to physical capital and labor. They estimate national stocks of human capital in 1990 created from prior investment in schooling and show that for 36 countries the (macro) marginal product of human capital accruing to workers in 1990 was consistent with estimates of the (micro) marginal return on investment in schooling in workers' earnings studies. They give empirical evidence for the augmented Solow model which would explain long-run economic growth by looking at capital accumulation, labor growth and increases in productivity through technological progress.

9. See, for example, "The Least Developed Countries Report, 2019."

10. We keep in mind, in agreement with Jane Jacobs, that all economies are before everything else, local. Lonergan's economic theory starts there as well. Global finance-dominated capitalism is still dependent on the functioning of smaller units of economic activity, down to the local. Another point to keep in mind is that worker-owned corporations function as capitalist enterprises. The label "socialist" attributed to them is misapplied, since the means of production in the entire economy are still in the hands of private corporations, democratic and otherwise.

11. *CWL* 21, 5. How best address the evils of both coercion and irresponsible profit-taking is a challenge. Terry Quinn and John Benton, *Economics Actually Today and Tomorrow. Sustainable and Inclusive* (Island House Press, 2019) introduce a Lonerganian structure for economic science that has yet to be picked up by professional economists. It begins with facts and data to reveal key functions and relations by which to understand any economy and any economic event. As we also argue, the Lonergan structure is operative in firms of all sizes, from the smallest roadside business to global corporations and world stock markets. It is a much-needed basis from which to address today's unprecedented social, economic and ecological crises in need of turnarounds.

based on power politics, a new political economy is needed, a truly scientific one. He begins by noting that dynamically speaking,

> A science is the interplay of two factors: there are data revealed by experience, observation, experiment, measurement. And on the other hand, there is the constructive activity of the mind. By themselves the data are objective, but they are also disparate, without significance, without correlation, without coherence. Of itself, the mind is coherence; spontaneously it constructs correlations and attributes significance. But it must have materials to construct and correlate; and if its work is not to be fanciful, its materials must be the data. Thus thought and experience are two complementary functions: thought constructs what experience reveals; and science is an exact equilibrium of the two.[12]

Working towards such an equilibrium means that "the science stands successively on a series of levels each of greater generality than the preceding." Lonergan refers to the interplay of subatomic particles, atoms and molecules sweeping the whole into unity by the theory of motion or energy. This means that in moving "from a less to a more general level of thought normally involves "a vast enlargement of the theoretical structure"[13] Since a more profound viewpoint has emerged, "a readjustment of the less general correlations" is called for. Lonergan adds that this was historically done when, for example, the Ptolemaic, geocentric theory of astronomy was eventually replaced by the scientific approaches of Copernicus, Kepler and Newton.

As to the need for a more profound viewpoint in economics, Michael Shute has noted that in calling for a new political economy,

> Lonergan joined the early theorists like Adam Smith and David Ricardo, who argue for a democratic control of economic structures. However, Lonergan's intent is clearly scientific. He starts with the data, asks all relevant questions, and answers them by verification. The difference between a strictly physical science and economics is

---

12. Lonergan, *CWL 21*, 5.
13. Lonergan, *CWL 21*, 6.

that the former grows out of sense data, while the latter also adds human meanings.[14]

In our brief allusion to the second and third functional specialties above, we stressed that Lonergan wanted to make a new beginning in economics, one that centers on "enormous facts overlooked by political economy and by specialized economics."[15] His attempt involves a new generalization, "a new study of facts, more fully grasped because more broadly seen." He adds that it is because of this, "that our general conclusions can be made a source of practical applications."[16]

We rely on the subject-object process emphases inherent in Lonergan's overall work. Briefly said, Lonergan's creative approach to an ethical economics means that he re-interprets current views of economics. In this effort, his long apprenticeship of how "the scientific or philosophic process towards discovery" works which began with his study of Plato, as revised through the influence of Joseph Maréchal in the 1930s,[17] stood him in good stead.

Transition to Second Functional Specialty by Way of an Example

As we noted, researchers gather data. In 2019, researchers in Kinshasa, the capital of the Congo, investigated what people were willing to pay for bread. Economists are called to interpret the meaning people attach to such data. In other words, why are the Congolese willing to pay a given price for their bread and why are bakers willing to make and sell their bread at that price? One must ask when was bread first baked in Kinshasa and at

---

14. Michael Shute "Preparing to Read Economic History Functionally," 1988. *Journal of Macrodynamic Analysis*, Volume 10, 88.

15. Lonergan, *CWL 21*, 10. Our study focuses on the "pure process" of the economy (the title of Chapter 2 of *CWL 21*). We relate this pure process to the processes of the human mind as addressed by Lonergan in *Insight*. In the present instance, we treat some "facts" of economics as the data of our first FS to be ethically evaluated in FS 5–7.

16. *CWL 21,* 10. Our Fig. 1 and 2 with explanations focus on a broad application of Lonergan's ethical economics.

17. See Lonergan, "Insight Revisited," *Second Collection*, 264–65.

what price did it initially sell? This involves further questions as to why Kinshasans started eating bread rather than their traditional *fou-fou* made from manioc (dumplings eaten with meat dishes)? Why do Kinshasans consume bread which they know is a staple introduced in the Congo by the despised Belgian colonizers?[18]There may also be other human factors as well, as is the case in France where the price of bread is a highly politicized issue due to that nation's history.[19] In FS 2, with Lonergan, we seek to go beyond current notions of interpreting the data of the production and exchange processes by, for example, comparing how bankers in New York differ in their expectations from those of the Congolese.

SECOND FUNCTIONAL SPECIALTY: BEYOND CURRENT NOTIONS OF INTERPRETING PRODUCTION AND EXCHANGE. CONTEXTUALIZING THE ISSUE OF JUSTICE IN THE WORKPLACE AND IN COMMUNITIES IN GENERAL[20]

In 2021, in the wake of the U.S. State of Georgia's attempt to limit voting access in ways that would disproportionately affect Black Americans, the billionaire Jamie Dimon, chairman of JPMorgan Chase, the richest bank in the US, spoke out against the attempt.[21] Dimon knows we have to interpret the signs of the times and take appropriate action. In this

---

18. Adam Hochschild, *King Leopold's Ghost* (New York: Houghton, 1998) recounts Belgium's monstrous economic injustice perpetrated upon the Congolese.

19. Abdu Gnaba, *Anthropologie des mangeurs de pain* (Paris: Harmattan), 2011.

20. The essays in *Economics as a Process in the New Institutional Economics* (Cambridge Univ. 1989, edited by Richard Langlois) are all concerned with exploring alternative theoretical approaches to the 'neoclassical' paradigm. Among the schools of thought represented are transaction-cost economics, evolutionary theories, modern law and economics, and a game-theory approach to the economics of social institutions. The essays focus on economic processes and states of equilibrium, a sensitivity to the limits of human rationality, and on the various sorts of available social institutions.

21. See Katherine Bell, *Quartz Daily Brief*, 10 April 2021. Bell adds that "Microsoft president Brad Smith's approach was more in the Jamie Dimon mold. In a blog post, Smith took on each of the law's major provisions and urged "the business community to be principled, substantive, and concrete in explaining its concerns."

instance, at least, he granted that there may be more important issues in running a business than mere profit-making. But unlike Dimon, we insist that to answer such issues, we *first have to be "mindful"* of deeper realities—as Buddhists keep reminding us.[22] In simple English, this means that we have to be ethical.

Our aim is to try bridge conflicting priorities of self-interest in economics relying on ethical principles based on justice. Lonergan reminds us that human life is a communal enterprise. "No man is an island." We depend on others to survive. This includes our dependence on such economic processes as producing goods and services. People must meet everyday life's needs while contributing to the common good. In this day and age, Westerners are so used to the underlying economic activities that produce meals, clothes, and shelter, that they rarely advert to underlying issues. They tend to take it all for granted. It is indeed hard to contemplate the reality that one's world would come crashing down if one had to live as people do in many developing nations such as in the Congo. There, the majority of the country's citizens wake up with one thing in mind: how to find the equivalent of $2.00 that will enable them to eat that day? For those with a job, this is possible, but there are still the underlying economic conditions that make life hard. In a land of vast potential resources such as the Congo where the majority of people are as poor as were slaves in ancient Rome, this calls for the political will and ability to heal the economic situation by creating the appropriate means to do so.

However, it is to the advantage of international corporations, as well as of many governments of the world, to keep life in lands such as the Congo uncertain, if not chaotic. Local Rwandan and Congolese militias rampage and often prevail. All too many politicians seek to enrich themselves while the vast resources of the land are drained away to meet the needs of far-off industries. A case in point is the building of the parliament building in Kinshasa, the Congo's capital, in 2007. Not a cent went into the local economy. Instead, all the design, the raw materials

---

22. We attempt to make Lonergan's GEM-FS approach available to the public focusing on essentials. Lonergan, *Insight*, 585–86 notes that this is difficult due to settling the differences between audiences while incorporating them in an interpretation.

and the labor came from far-off China. China offered to build the Parliament as a "gift," but it was hardly a gift. Rather it was a clever gesture to keep Congolese politicians happy while Chinese firms could join international corporations in mining the vast quantities of rare earths needed for cell phones, as well as more ordinary minerals.[23]

How best interpret such exploitation? In some ways the Congo example points to facts which everyone should know, but which actually are mired in the conflicting approaches to economic history. To survive, all human communities must build a well-functioning economy. Some facts must be noted: first, all economies are subject to local conditions; second, these are now bound up with global realities; third, understanding economics begins with rather prosaic facts; fourth, professional economists are needed to analyze complex realities such as the exploitation of the Congolese people. With Lonergan, we are in search of "terms and relations" that will spell out how a national economy can be guided democratically. Both risks and benefits cannot but accrue.[24] People across the world are not meant to merely "survive"; leaders are called upon to help them thrive. We have set out to show how Lonergan's work can help people do so by basing their lives on true values. With Lonergan, we are in search of what can make a *just economy* possible—one that gives all its members the freedom to act.

Moving beyond Mere Sentiments and Fictitious Fetters

Some pertinent questions are whether the present "science of economics" helps people act freely; how can moral reasoning be effectively applied to the rough-and-tumble facets of an economy without types of state coercion

---

23. See Andreas Exenberger and Simon Hartmann, "The dark side of globalization. The vicious cycle of exploitation from world market integration: Lesson from the Congo," Leibniz-Information Centre for Economics. Although Adrian Pabst and John Millbank, "The Meta-Crisis of Secular Capitalism," *International Review of Economics*, 62 (3) 197–212. ISSN 1865–1704, do not mention Lonergan, their argument parallels ours as to the perils of financialization and globalization today.

24. The risks include an exclusive appeal to a secular ethics that is based solely on logic or empathy and is not related to faith or religious beliefs.

exemplified in the state capitalism of the Chinese Communist Party? We seek to find adequate means to counter the greed of finance-dominated capitalism. Lonergan argued that countervailing means can, should be found. "The vast forces of benevolence," he wrote, "can no longer be left to tumble down the Niagara of fine sentiments and noble dreams. They have to be assigned a function and harnessed within the exchange system, for in no other way can that system shake off its fictitious fetters to move consistently towards its maximum."[25] The said function requires learning "the discipline of logic and of scientific reflection." This can lead to "a generalization of the exchange economy. To determine the nature of such a generalization is the aim of this inquiry."[26] It requires

> a transformation . . . of the reformers and their reforms, a move to a higher synthesis that eliminates . . . both the problem of wages and the complementary problems of trade unions; it will attack at once both the neglect of economic education and the blare of advertisements leading the economically uneducated by the nose; it will give new hope and vigor to local life, and it will undermine the opportunity for speculation corrupting central governments and party politics.[27]

Lonergan focused on how an economy can bridge by way of money (or "dummy") "the intervals, short or long, between contributing to the process and sharing in its products."[28] Having stated his aim in Chapter 3 of

---

25. *CWL*, 21, 36. Lonergan shows that a scientific economy, controlled democratically, can give "the less fortunate more than they can supply." This will require dismantling the routinely accepted "artificial nemesis" of economic realities, transforming the old guard's abuses as well as the reforms of the reformers into a higher perspective.

26. Lonergan, *CWL* 21, 36.

27. Lonergan, *CWL* 21, 36–37. Historical decisions as to where unions were to place their money have been based on various criteria. In the 1950's the International Union of Electric Workers invested their capital in developing affordable housing projects.

28. Lonergan, *CWL* 21, 37. Money is a dummy invented by humans to enable divided exchange—inasmuch as it is a promise of trust between people. Simple as money's functional purposes may seem, the determinations of how much money to create through the credit function is not well understood. There are natural limits to the supply of money; this means that the menace of the so-called Modern Monetary Theory's unconstrained printing of money is a problem challenging economists, such as when inflation could be rising when an economy is experiencing a recessionary gap.

CWL 21, in Chapter 4, he indicates that, economics "correlates the rhythms of production and the corresponding rhythms of income and expenditure. The set of such correlations constitutes a mechanical structure, a pattern of laws that stands to economic activity as the laws of mechanics to buildings and machines."[29] Money has to fulfill certain conditions such as divisibility, homogeneity and constancy as well as QE (quantitative easing) when central banks buy assets to release money into the economy. Other than the problematic Modern Monetary Theory (MMT)[30] governed by a central bank/central government paradigm, no fundamental change in practice (or theory) for supplying an economy with money has emerged since money's ties to metals were severed.[31] A fully exogenous (demographically determined) supply of currency would represent such a change.

Monetary integrity follows from closing the monetary loop. The existing economy becomes fully self-regulating with no unemployment, poverty, or public debt (the last being contingent on total government spending not exceeding its current *per capita* level). Currently, supplying the economy with money takes two forms: 1) money as credit, when banks create deposits as a result of issuing loans; 2) money as currency, when money is created for the central bank to purchase newly issued debt[32] of a national government. That the creation of money in the form of credit is determined by other economic variables is undisputed; a central bank directly determines only the creation of currency. "Price is the measure of the quantity of the dummy."[33]

---

29. Lonergan, *CWL* 21, 42.

30. Although not utopian, MMT suggests the possibility of progress in addressing poverty, despair and democratic deficits such as the deficit accompanying the boom-and-bust cycles of even a mixed capitalist economy, the underutilization of resources, and the highly-skewed distributions of economic power.

31. The difference between QE and MMT is that while QE means printing money to buy securities such as U. S. Treasuries, mortgage bonds or bad loans, MMT spends through a government funding projects; it enables governments not to rely on taxes or borrowing for spending, but to simply print as much money as they need.

32. In *The Philosophy of Debt*, (Routledge, 2016) Alexander Douglas argues that 1) we have a duty to sustain the institution of debt even if not all debts are beneficial, nor all forms of production desirable; 2) yet, some individuals may not be able to go into debt.

33. *CWL*, 21, 37.

Lonergan' approach differs radically from the traditional economics, in which the ultimate premises are not production and exchange but rather exchange and self-interest, or exchanges based on vaguely defined psychological situations. With Lonergan, we prescind from human psychology so as to first define the objective situation with which people have to deal. Only in the second place, do we address the psychological attitudes that have to be adopted if humans are to deal successfully with economic problems.[34]

Towards Coordinating the Inputs of Science and Ethical Perspectives by Way of Lonergan's "Radical Generalization"

We have set out to show how Lonergan's GEM-FS insights can also account for the deeper meanings involved in human activities. We noted that economics has some commonalities with such social sciences as philology and anthropology. It shares with these the same vague areas that occur between the humanities and physical science. The process of building a just economy needs the critical input of all socio-scientific and humanist disciplines. Lonergan held that amidst the many factors affecting human life, the facts of macroeconomics are well known, but we lack "a clear and precise understanding of the mechanism behind such obvious facts as expansion and contraction of the economy, employment and unemployment, inflation and deflation."[35] This lack is linked to the fact that millions of humans now live in grinding poverty. Traditional values of communities and nations must be respected and the means to do so should be provided. This flies in the face of those bent only on their own profit.[36] Lonergan's insistence that sane economic laws

---

34. *CWL* 21, 42; we develop this point in our treatment of Mankiw's "Principles."

35. Lonergan, *CWL* 15, *Circulation Analysis*, 12. Victor Beker, "The missing link in Keynesian macroeconomics, *Real-world economics Review*, 80, 2022, argues that in reality, prices do not behave symmetrically. Usually, "nominal wages and prices are sticky downward but a lot more flexible upward" as happens with inflation.

36. Our societies are caught in the tragic dilemma that the sources of human alienation addressed by existentialist thinkers are ignored by economists. Lonergan does not directly address alienation in *Insight*, but he does so in *MiT*.

require maintaining a standard of living for all actors in a given economy is the antithesis of Milton Friedman's view that the sole concern of a business is to maximize profits.[37] Lonergan's "radical generalization"[38] of economics is a model with some predictive power in both local micro- and macro-economic situations. His model attempts to include all types of economic activity since the beginning of our species—it does so by addressing the familiar in unfamiliar ways.[39] This differs from the methodology used in the science of physics. In a first instance, physicists gather and measure physical data. They then seek insight into the data, formulate questions and hypotheses. In a second instance, they devise ways to verify a hypothesis, then communicate the results as probably true or false. But economists have no such way of experimenting; they must interpret events as they happen.[40]

Lonergan's radical generalization treats macroeconomics as being concerned with such dynamic structures as the interrelations of aggregate rates of production and payment, of their equilibria and disequilibria, of expansions and contractions, of inflation and unemployment. Lonergan asks "What is the process by which productivity can be increased?"[41] This question is analogous to the questions he poses in *Insight* and in *MiT*. In *Insight*, he asks: "What are we doing when we know?" In *MiT*, the question is: "What are we doing in theology?"[42] He answers his question in economics as to how one increases productivity by developing his macroeconomic theory that explains the phenomena

---

37. "The Social Responsibility of Business is to Increase its Profits" *The New York Times Magazine* September 13, 1970, www.umich.edu/~thecore/doc/Friedman.pdf

38. Lonergan, *CWL* 21, 8–10, 36. We argue with Lonergan that to some extent people have to adapt to the laws of economics. This is a reversal of conventional wisdom among progressives, but not among the Friedmanites.

39. See Internet Encyclopedia of Philosophy, https://iep.utm.edu/lonergan

40. https://www.nobelprize.org/prizes/economic-sciences/2021/summary/

41. Lonergan, *CWL* 15, *Circulation Analysis*, 4.

42. The answer to the three questions all involve GEM-FS operators that foster conversions and integrate fresh data within new discoveries (*MIT*, 249–50. *CWL* 14, 234–35.) In broad terms, the GEM-FS task is to outline how Lonergan's invitation to assemble, complete, compare, reduce, classify, and select materials can be applied to the field of economics.

of business cycles—that is, the dynamic economic process of production, exchange, and finance or simply, "the pure cycle of productive process."[43]

It all starts with producing goods and services. In a capitalist or socialist economy, production is meant for sale. When one turns from production to exchange, Lonergan notes that "products that fail to be sold, despite the ingenuity of modern marketing, are regarded as just waste. It follows that acceleration in production demands a proportionate acceleration in selling and buying."[44] After distinguishing the production of producer goods from the production of consumer goods, Lonergan distinguishes two distinct markets. He adverts to the influence each exerts upon the other. The necessity of finance is twofold; it is characterized by ironic situations. First, finance transfers money from inoperative to dynamic positions in the system. Second, the economic process runs through a series of transformations and exploitations; the real flow of goods and services varies, and the "dummy flow" (money) has to vary concomitantly lest inflation or deflation arise. The real flow may attain volumes that greatly exceed previous peaks, which can be scaled[45] only if the dummy is flexible. Lonergan adds that financing is part of the effort

---

43. Michael Shute, *Lonergan's Discovery of the Science of Economics*, 18, writes that Lonergan "is able to derive a pure cycle of economic growth that would avoid the ups and downs of the trade cycle. The "pure cycle is the equivalent in economics of the ideal line of progress in the analytic conception of history. It is a projection of what would happen if all economic players observed the normative precepts which would follow from a proper understanding of the economic rhythms." To do this, Lonergan had first worked out a basic division of history based on the approximations of progress.

44. *CWL* 15, *Macroeconomic Dynamics*, 15. Paul Oslington, "Unemployment and trade liberalization," *World Economy*, 28, 8, 2005, 1139—55, observes that many economists insist that unemployment and trade issues should be considered separately. This *view cannot be justified for it ignores "the growing number of general equilibrium trade* models with unemployment. In a simple model with an exogenous wage floor, trade liberalization can lead to either gains or losses depending on the production technology, severity of the factor market distortion . . . and conditions in trading partners. Definite results can be derived about gains from liberalizing trade with lower wage floors, about relative abundance of the unemployed factor dampening losses when trade is liberalized, and about gains when the good which uses the unemployed factor is exported. The theoretical models are then linked to the policy modelling literature."

45. William Matthews, https://blogs.shu.edu/ethicsandeconomics forum/files/ 2014/ 09/5.-Mathews-TLR-V.pdf

made to solve these problems. In clarifying "the position" of his essay on economics, he appeals to some of the issues he had treated in *Insight*:

> In a universe such as ours, with its vast numbers and its enormous time intervals, one is led to think of schemes of recurrence, whose several carriers severally flow their own classical laws, whose assembly follows the probability of their emergence, and whose continued functioning follows the probability of their survival. Such in a nutshell is the evolutionary view that in *Insight* I sketched out under the name of emergent probability and, earlier in this essay, I have applied to economics.[46]

The Link between Pure Cycles and Growth

Eileen de Neeve writes that economists have recognized the link between pure cycles and growth in economics as well as the lag in the production of capital goods. For example, Finn Kydland and Edward Prescott, the 2004 Nobel laureates in economics, integrated production lags into their linear growth models. The general equilibrium linear growth model "adapts well to mathematical modelling."[47]

Economists apply this framework to the study of growth in two ways: (i) by distinguishing in the time series data between the average or trend growth rate and deviations from it (detrending), or (ii) by using growth rates of the economic variables calculated from the data. Lonergan uses growth rates, but he does not use statistical data in his

---

46. *CWL* 15, 91–93. "The Position of this Essay" begins with Lonergan's agreement with Schumpeter "that Walras' system implicitly includes the aggregates commonly considered in microanalysis, but it can hardly be credited with distinctions between basic and surplus expenditure, receipts, outlay, income, and much less with an account of their various dynamic relations. Until such distinctions are drawn and their dynamic significance understood, the aggregates and relations cannot be contained implicitly in any system." The editors, 92, note 111, emphasize the intricate connection in said *lacuna* with "Kant's idea of an analytic a priori judgments." See *Insight*, 46, 70, 491, 515.

47. De Neeve, quoting Finn and Prescott: "Time to Build and Aggregate Fluctuation," *Econometrica*, vol. 50, 6, 1345–70 in her "Interpreting Bernard Lonergan's General Theory of Economic Dynamics: Does It Complete Hayek, Keynes and Schumpeter?" *Journal of Macrodynamic Analysis* 5 (2010), 110.

general theory as it is not an empirical analysis. He does use algebra, however, to explain the relationships among the variables in the cycles of innovative growth.[48]

De Neeve adds that for Hayek and Schumpeter, the generally observed facts of growth and development theory are the following: (i) new money or credit is needed by producers to begin an expansion; (ii) labor and materials are used to build new means of production, create new organizations or markets, or provide new production services; (iii) the production lag is followed by a rising output of consumer goods or services: (iv) the production lag implies variations in consumption and investment; (v) the profit component of the price of consumer goods increases in an expansion and decreases as production is added and scarcity is overcome—a process which changes the distribution of income over the period. De Neeve stresses that these five points are all present in Lonergan's dynamic theory.[49]

THIRD FUNCTIONAL SPECIALTY: REVISITING OUR HISTORY OF ECONOMICS FROM ADAM SMITH TO MARXISM[50]

A Question of "Historical Sense"

For Lonergan, a historical sense meant apprehending a mind at work in an age very different from one's own. Reproaching classicism's inability to understand either history or the concrete, in his doctoral dissertation,

---

48. De Neeve, "Economic Dynamics: Does It Complete Hayek?, 111.

49. De Neeve, "Economics Dynamics," 111. She argues, 105, that for Lonergan, economics is "both a human and an empirical science. Within the production constraints of the economic system, outcomes depend on what or whom we choose as producers and consumers and how we understand economic dynamics. Lonergan insists that human sciences such as economics need to understand human behavior not through narrow assumptions about rationality but by assuming that people choose economic actions within a cultural framework of values that are chosen cooperatively in institutions by those involved, and with the sanctions needed to deter rule breakers."

50. Ever since capitalism separated itself from ethics the result has been dire—it has played the role of an implicit materialism. Marxism has been no better since it too is a materialist ideology. Michael Shute noted the methodological and foundational concerns that may impact on a project such as ours, but we believe that our probing "sandwich approach" is a helpful, (hopefully feasible), ethical way to meet his concerns.

Grace and Freedom in Aquinas, he sought to "re-originate the Catholic theological tradition by recovering its intellectualist origins in Aquinas."[51] The work countered the prevailing conceptualist interpretations of Aquinas; it paralleled Joseph Maréchal's faulting Kant for not having been critical enough in his critique of reason.

Marx's historical sense partly anticipated our own effort to situate natural rights from a historical perspective. According to Geoff Piling,

> Marx was among . . . the keenest students of that trend in economic thinking for which he invented the term 'classical political economy' . . . (He) used this term in a way radically different from that of many later writers, in particular Keynes. By classical political economy Marx meant to designate that strand in economic theory originating in France with Boisguilebert (1646–1714) . . . and reaching its high point with the work of Smith and Ricardo (1772–1823) who "gave to classical political economy its final shape." . . . The ideological attack upon Ricardianism after 1830 increased due to "a trend within the emerging working-class movement "which tried to deploy Ricardian theory as a weapon against the capitalist order. Ricardo's opponents seized upon . . . contradictions in the Ricardian system. In considering the deficiencies of Ricardo's work which had opened it up to these attacks, attacks which Ricardo's followers were unable to combat, Marx centered his 'entire critique of political economy on what he considered its decisive weakness, a tendency to view society *a-historically*, that is, its "inclination to treat capitalist economy as one working directly in accordance with the laws of nature.[52]

Piling concludes that Marx did not mean to imply that "the modern working class 'killed' political economy. Rather he thought that the methodological limitations of classical political economy increasingly paralyzed it in the face of this new phenomenon." That political economy

---

51. Tracy, *Achievement*, 22. GEM transposes Thomistic habitual grace; it focuses on to subjects' dynamic conversions. Lonergan, *Grace and Freedom in Aquinas* (1971).

52. Geoff Piling, *Marx's Capital – Philosophy and Political Economy,* (Routledge, 1980). https://www.marxists.org/archive/pilling/works/capital/geoff1.htm chapter 2.

"was unable to grasp the significance of the emergence of the working class and . . . its struggle against capital. For Marx, this underscored the philosophical weakness which he detected in Ricardo's work."[53]

Lonergan's New Beginning in Economics

Lonergan wanted to make a new beginning in economics. He focused on "facts overlooked . . . by specialized economics."[54] We shall outline his new start in the light of the vast changes now affecting all facets of modern life. Lonergan stresses the important roles philologists such as August Boeckh (1785–1867) played in enlarging the scope of human culture and understanding, which opened the door to the development of the science of anthropology, a science that has many similarities to economics.[55]

To understand the full, complex sweep of cultures across human history, anthropologists build upon knowledge both from the social and biological sciences and the humanities and physical sciences. Historically, anthropologists in the United States have been trained in one of four areas: sociocultural anthropology, biological/ physical anthropology, archaeology, and linguistic anthropology. Today, a central concern of anthropologists is the application of knowledge to the solution of human problems.[56]

---

53. Piling, chapter 2, referring to how *Marx* in *Capital evaluated Ricardo's achievement*.

54. Lonergan, *CWL 21*, 110. Lonergan's theories of history and economics were a significant part of his theoretical foundations—as we note in our GEM-FS sandwich approach. Both theories were attempts to "assign a function" for human benevolence within the systems of modern living. In each case it was necessary to counter prevailing theories and develop alternatives open to the possibility that human benevolence might be normative for human relationships. For Lonergan, *the self* is to be appropriated within an intricate nexus of social systems and personal relationships. If one wishes to understand that "*self*," one must face this fact with an appreciative scientific seriousness.

55. Lonergan, *CWL 15*, 10. "What Boeckh did for philology, Droysen would do for history. He moved the notion of understanding from a context of aesthetics and psychology to the broader context of history by (1) assigning expression as the object of understanding and (2) noting that not only individuals but also such groups as families, peoples, states, religions express themselves." *MiT*, 210. *CWL 14*, 197.

56. https://stars.troy.edu/gsac_anthropology.html Our text draws out some implications of applying GEM-FS insights to economics—reinforcing its ability to help humans individually and collectively integrate the mystical, ethical, and social aspects of life and to respect the planet. Lonergan argues that the canon of relevance "observes that questions

In various ways, everything is historically conditioned. On this theme, Lonergan quotes Schumpeter:

> Any treatise that attempts to render 'the present state of science' really renders methods, problems and results that are historically conditioned and are meaningful only with reference to the historical background from which they spring. To put the same thing somewhat differently, the state of any science at any given time implies its past history and cannot be satisfactorily conveyed without making this implicit history explicit.[57]

Lonergan's economics process model can have predictive power in macroeconomic situations and is relevant to local situations. Such is the purpose of his "radical generalization" of economics.[58] He discounts historical analyses that claim to offer precise predictions. Such analyses have failed to provide "a clear and precise understanding of the mechanism behind such obvious facts as expansion and contraction of the economy, employment and unemployment, inflation and deflation, and many other well-known occurrences."[59] For Lonergan, the material fabric of culture's living home is economic. Underlying the superstructure of cultural activity, "there stands as foundation the purely economic field concerned with nourishment, shelter, clothing, utilities, services and amusement."[60] Lonergan calls this purely economic field a basic

---

about final, material, instrumental and efficient causality automatically head from the data in hand" to such questions as "the psychology of the motivation of craftsmen," etc. *Insight*, 100. We also allude to some of the political implications.

57. Lonergan, *CWL* 15, 11, quoting Schumpeter's *History* (Oxford, 1954), 4.

58. See *CWL 21*, 8–10, 36. Einstein's radical generalization of physics explained certain phenomena anew. He did not start with empirical data; rather, he explored suggestive hints in several fields. His relativity model works because its predictions continue to be verified. As he started out, his model was not empirically weak, but he did attempt a leap which turned out to be highly fruitful. String theory has attempted an analogous feat but its results have yet to be borne out. We argue that Lonergan's radical generalization of economics needs to be explored and applied. Our proposed GEM-FS integration of Lonergan's economics within GEM-FS process is, we think, a step in that direction.

59. Lonergan, *CWL* 15, 12.

60. Lonergan, *CWL* 21, 12. The "purely economic field" (*CWL 21*, Chapter 2) reinforces the sandwiching aspects of a dynamic GEM-FS process and our argument for the.

"pulsating flow, the rhythmic series of the economic activities of man." He links it to "the world process, the physical, chemical, vegetal, animal, and human potentialities of universal nature which, are ever stimulated, guided, aided by human effort to the goal of human survival and enjoyment, of human achievement, waste and destruction."[61]

So as to grasp the concept of rhythmic flow, let us imagine a fountain in the gardens of Versailles, designed to spurt up water from different spigots according to a rate planned by the designer: so much water every so often, directed in specified directions to a certain height. The rhythmic flow of a given economy, whether that of a hunter-gatherer community 10,000 years ago or New York City in 2022, is so much emergence, utility, disappearance of goods and services in a given period of time, "a compound rhythm composed of many minor rhythms of varying magnitude and frequency."[62]

Bees, Smartphones and Predatory Malware

In principle, Lonergan's radical generalization of economics applies to all human communities, past and present. His generalization also has

---

need of turnarounds in economics-and-environmental policies to complement psychic, intellectual, moral, and religious conversions to foster a better social order.

61. Lonergan, *CWL 21*, 11; see *Insight*, 148, ff. This insight of Lonergan anticipates what Pope Francis writes in *Laudatio Si*, 23—connecting economic activities to the state of the environment: "A number of scientific studies indicate that most global warming in recent decades is due to the great concentration of greenhouse gases (carbon dioxide, methane, nitrogen oxides and others) released mainly as a result of human activity." To counter the free market myth, what is needed is not destroying markets but changing the institution that creates and regulates markets, namely, governments. That requires not only a new macroeconomic theory but also adept experts who would be motivated by the conversions Lonergan kept stressing. Else the situation will be exactly what The Who sang some 50 years ago: "Meet the new boss; Same as the old boss." As a counter-example, let us cite The Renewable Energy and International Law (REIL), a non-profit group seeking to implement environmental change—especially by promoting *Laudato Si*. REIL brings people together to discuss an issue and act on it. It was instrumental in launching the Interfaith Rainforest Initiative which brings the commitment, influence and moral authority of religions to efforts to protect the world's forests and the indigenous peoples that serve as their guardians.

62. *CWL 21*, 12; on compound and minor rhythms, Michael Shute, *Divyadaan*, 21/2 (2010) 183–91.

ecological implications since, in effect, all animals have a rudimentary economy. Think of bees that gather pollen from flowers to produce honey. Their pollination enables fertilization and the production of seeds. Without bees we would only be able to cultivate grains. Fruits and most vegetables would not grow. Life without honey would be much less pleasant, moreover.[63] Beekeepers build and maintain hives, giving colonies of bees strong, well-defended places to fertilize a queen, hatch eggs, feed them with honey, send out workers to gather pollen, and repeat their lifecycle. Much of the honey is retrieved by the beekeeper who takes it to market. Beekeepers also sell their bees' services as pollinators to farmers for their orchards and groves.

Recall that the development of the smartphone depended upon the invention of cellular telephones and ever-smaller, more powerful computers, as well as the Internet—themselves transformative of both the economy and cultural forms. Combining wireless phones, computers small enough to fit inside a telephone, and the Internet as well as cellular service to connect them led to Steve Jobs' popularization of the "smart" phone. At this time of writing, there are about 4 billion of these devices in the world, with several manufacturers competing for the global market. These drive the improvements of cellular speed (5G), multi-core microprocessors, and the Internet (think of streaming services). There can be no denying the acceleration of the world's economic rhythms since 2007.

Smartphones do help improve the lives of people in the developed nations but especially in the Third World. People can track crops, order goods, do their banking, borrow capital, communicate next door or across the globe, and much more—all with their phones. For instance, a woman living in Accra, Ghana, develops a thriving business in blue

---

63. Recall that Mandeville's *Fable of the Bees* (1714) was deemed to be scandalous when published. It did affect the writing of economists of the succeeding generation such as Adam Smith. Mandeville (1670–1733) criticized republicanism's emphasis on a frugal society focused on civic virtue. Only Samuel Johnson praised the *Fable* which scathingly attacked mercantilism. Mandeville wrote about a vicious hive which was the envy of all other hives due to its strong economy and large population. When honesty and traditional virtue is introduced in the hive, it undermines its power. Many bees lose their jobs. There is less economic activity due to the frugal nature of Christian virtue." See https:iep.utm/ mandevil. Christian virtue includes seeking the common good of all.

jeans, which she orders from a Chinese manufacturer on her phone, pays for them with the phone, and collects from her customers with the same telephone. In wealthy nations the same trends are accelerating the economy even more. Whatever one may think of the effects ill or good of "apps"—software for smartphones like Facebook, Instagram, etc. or malicious software—the fact is that these have created their own sub-economy, and dangers. They have indelibly affected culture and national security on a worldwide scale. Cinema, television, photography, music, predatory malware etc. have all dramatically changed, and continue to do so.

Money in History and Today

We can relate the above comments with the role of money in general. While all humans "know" what money is, the theory of money is not well understood. Attempts to create a digital currency such as the Bitcoin remind us of money's changing roles today.[64] Adam Smith wrote about the pioneering role of barter which supposedly allowed people to trade so many bushels of corn for so many eggs. David Graeber rejects Smith's view. Smith saw trading as the lifeblood of any economy: barter was essentially a matter of exchanging. It is difficult to quantify the value of what is being exchanged in such a case—beyond a single local trade. Smith maintained that barter even happened among strangers or enemies, but anthropologists have never found any economies based only on barter. Credit, what we can call today "virtual money," came well before coinage.[65]

---

64. Some economists have warned that we should not aggressively replace unjust financial systems with wildly risky alternative currencies such as bitcoin. They ask, for example, what social problem is blockchain trying to solve? One must not be naive when engaging in would-be-stop-gaps measures that some are promoting.

65. David Graeber, *Debt: The First Five Thousand Years*, 29–40. In rejecting the widespread belief that ancient economies were founded on barter, Graeber argues that it seeks to validate the notion of the "primitive savage." In fact, our ancestors were a lot more sophisticated than we give them credit for. In her *Anthro-Vision: How Anthropology can Explain Business and Life* (Random House, 2021), 160, Gillian Tett writes: "Economists often assume that societies only used barter in the past because they did not have money

Still, the case may be made that Smith and Graeber both proposed an economics narrative originating in innate human needs and impulses:

> By arguing that money derived from innate competitive (or) . . . desires, Smith sought to separate money from the state. Graeber seeks instead to prove that money arose from the innate moral and social qualities of our debt to each other, as understood and articulated since the beginning of human existence.[66]

For Lonergan, as we saw, various people decide upon what he calls a "dummy," (money). The dummy bridges "the intervals, short or long, between contributing to the process and sharing in its products. . . . If this dummy is to work satisfactorily, if it is to bridge the intervals fairly and adequately,"[67] then it must fulfill the following four processes which we illustrate by way of examples. First, it is divisible, so that x bushels and

---

or credit—which implies that once modern finance was invented, barter disappeared." However, "our standard account of monetary history is precisely backward," argues Graeber. Instead of humans using barter first, then "evolving" to adopt money and credit, "it happened . . . the other way round." This might seem hard to believe. But there is no evidence that ancient societies operated as Smith imagined. "No example of a barter economy, pure and simple, has ever been described, let alone the emergence from it of money; all available ethnography suggests that there had never been one." Instead, communities without money have had extensive, complex "credit" systems since households create social and economic debts." Tett adds: "The crucial difference is that "Graeber amassed a mountain of evidence, Smith had none."

66. Margaret Hefferman, "David Graeber's Debt Shows Us How to Think about Post-Pandemic, Climate Crisis Economy," *Financial Times*, July 2021. Hefferman adds: "Graeber dug deep, taking it upon himself to do what economists mostly avoid: trace what money has meant to societies from prehistory to the present day and from the Nambikwara of Brazil to the IMF. He kicks off with a convincing demolition job on economists' origin myth that money grew out of the barter. But barter is so obviously unworkable—what would you do when you needed milk but your neighbor with the cow had no need of your roses?—that, to this day, nobody has found anywhere it actually existed. No example of a barter economy, pure and simple, has ever been described, let alone the emergence from it of money; all available ethnography suggests that there has never been such a thing." Yet the myth is continuously perpetuated in economics textbooks, from Adam Smith to Joseph Stiglitz. Why? Because it positions economics as a discipline whose foremost concern is competitive advantage. . . . All deeper human motivation—passion, adventure, curiosity, sex or death—is neatly erased. Money, Graeber concludes, has 'no essence'; it is 'something that can be turned into anything.'"

67. *CWL* 15, 37.

y eggs are the trading equivalent of z dummies—that is, the *price*. Second, it is homogeneous, in that the dummy is the same here and there. Third, it has to have a reasonably steady trading value, neither more nor fewer bushels and eggs per unit of dummy. Fourth, it must be acceptable tender for everyone in a given region. This is a trust issue. If the dummy is not a precious substance like gold, or paper money backed by precious metal, then it must be backed by something else: today's U.S. dollar is backed by the "full faith and credit of the United States."

Money is and has always been a social construct, an expression of mutual trust.[68] For many years in the USA, the expression "sound as a dollar" was popular. Many dollar bills were labeled "silver certificate"; this meant that the paper could be exchanged for a certain quantity of silver. In other words, "trust but verify." Today, there is no physical means of checking a dollar's value against a standard commodity: one can only "trust the government" when buying and selling. Money is now a "fiat currency," because its value is what the government issuing that currency claims it is. The existential question is how much money do I need to buy eggs in the face of increasing inflation?[69]

The move away from cash to electronic banking has added more wrinkles to the "trust but verify" adage essential to the dummy's usefulness. A stack of bills is anonymous. A credit or debit card is not—you need to provide some proof that it is your card that is being used, e. g., by furnishing the code numbers associated with it. An online transaction will require more identification, not only with the card numbers but also your name and address. A separate measure of identification is more and more required, a text message asking you to authenticate that it is in fact you using your card, for instance. We also have to trust that when we authorize a draw on our account, the bank will debit the correct amount and accurately credit it to the merchant.

Behind this ability are the governmental bodies that write the rules for such transactions—in effect, setting up the terms and conditions that

---

68. See Lonergan's discussion of the "dummy," *CWL* 21, 37–41.

69. The US dollar has lost 93% of its value since 1913. See https://fred.stlouisfed.org/series/CWUR0000SA0R

allow a market to function. They want to protect the bank, merchants and customers from online fraud. They want to know what is happening in one's accounts for tax purposes. They try to counter money laundering. Communist China monitors your politics.[70]

The social media revolution that the smartphone has greatly facilitated is another source of distrust. By using a free service to exchange information with "friends," we give away details of our personalities that are then "harvested," analyzed and then sold to advertisers, who can then pitch the product directly to you knowing that you will pay with a digital transaction, which increases their possession of data on you.[71] This practice, known as "surveillance capitalism," chips away at the fundamental trust that is the *sine qua non* of any exchange economy.[72] There arises a further question of trust in the issuers of currency.

Bitcoin is the first truly digital currency (there are now thousands). Digital currencies attempt to create a currency that is controlled neither by a government nor a bank. Transactions are anonymous; no third party needs to authenticate them or censor them. There is a limit set to the number of Bitcoin tokens that can be "mined" (21 million), so it is not fiat.[73] Bitcoin uses a public ledger (the "blockchain") hosted by hundreds of computers linked via the Internet, which is simultaneously updated with every transaction. The ledger records the coin holders' accounts using cryptography. A Bitcoin is in fact a unique digital file. It is spent by

---

70. China is where it's at now due to Deng Xiaoping, who after Mao's death and the machinations of the group of four, gradually rose to supreme power. Deng led China through a series of far-reaching market-economy reforms, resulting in his being called the "Architect of Modern China." Today, XI Jinping allows just enough freedom that does not threaten his controlling most aspects of life, including the development of blockchain and cryptocurrencies.

71. Josh Hawley, *The Tyranny of Big Tech* (Regnery, 2021) details (114–21) how Facebook, Google etc. have taken over from the corporate robber barons of a century ago. They use our personal data and information to make fortunes while stifling competition; they protect themselves by currying favor with governments. More controversial is Hawley's attack on Woodrow Wilson as being the architect of American corporatism, 39ff.

72. Cory Doctorow, *How to Destroy Surveillance Capitalism*, at https://onezero. medium.com/how-to-destroy-surveillance-capitalism-8135e6744d59

73. The terms and relations for the Bitcoin are set and maintained on its blockchain by its "decentralized autonomous organization" or DAO. On DAOs, see below.

the account holder who uses a unique private code[74] to unlock the "wallet" where the coins are "held" so as to pay it to the receiver's wallet.[75] A "decentralized autonomous organization" oversees the overall functioning (see Appendix G).

We comment on Lonergan's radical generalization of economics so as to phrase it in contemporary terms. It is important to note that what Lonergan calls the rhythmic flows of an economy still rhythmically cycle together in the same basic ways they did in ages past. Whether one were to buy an amphora of fine wine in 164 A.D. in Rome or to buy wine from a dematerialized market in 2021 that accepts Bitcoins, the structure of that "pattern of laws that stand to economic activity as the laws of mechanics to buildings and machines"[76] is still operating. What is missing are, for example, the different meanings relating to drinking wine and the pertinent judgments of value. Such judgments are some of the hidden drivers of the economic rhythms that our ethical GEM-FS process approach seeks to promote by way of the *six transformational turnarounds*—still-to-be-fleshed out—from Lonergan's integral lifework.

Towards Group (Socio-Communal) Economics Turnarounds

Lonergan's inquiry into economics differs radically from traditional economics, in which the ultimate premises are not production and exchange but rather exchange and self-interest based on vaguely defined situations. He first defines the objective situations with which humans have to deal, then the needed "psychological attitude that has to be adopted if man is to deal successfully with economic problems."[77] His is a type of a Copernican revolution that involves some of the philosophical premises we laid out in Part I. Lonergan differentiates between the economy as a means of survival,

---

74. If the unique private key or password to "open the wallet" is lost, the tokens are irretrievable.

75. A useful introduction is Anthony Lewis' *The Basics of Bitcoins and Blockchains: An Introduction to Cryptocurrencies and the Technology That Powers Them* (Coral Gables, FL: Mango, 2018). It also gives a helpful account of the history of money.

76. Lonergan, *CWL 21*, 42.

77. *CWL 21*, 42.

and the "psychic factors of meanings and values integral to human life."[78] Optimizing[79] these are integral factors of Lonergan's approach. He writes:

> Instead of taking man as he is or as he may be thought to be and from that 'deducing' what economic phenomena are going to be, we take the exchange process in its greatest generality and then attempt to deduce the human adaptations necessary for survival.[80]

CWL 15 and 21 sketch economic processes in several versions of Lonergan's rates of flow diagram,[81] some of which we show in FS 4 and in

---

78. See https://functionalmacroeconomics.com/2020/05/31/elements-of-analysis/

79. Optimizing was not the aim of the reparations imposed on Germany at the Versailles Treaty after WWI; it led J. M. Keynes to resign from the Versailles negotiations. The techniques of optimizing efficiency such as supply chain management known as a RACI Matrix (which stands for Responsible, Accountable, Consult and Inform) would be an acceptable form of optimizing economic processes. GEM-FS would maximize not profit but the good.

80. *CWL 21*, 42–43. At first, the "greatest generality" alludes to communist command economies as well as socialist and capitalist economies; Lonergan soon stops considering the former due to his perception that bureaucrats cannot anticipate changes in demand and supply, leading to the necessity of maintaining an increasingly unsound (and unrealistic) exchange system until a crash occurs. See pp. 36–37. Lonergan's equation of the two economies shows the underlying analysis that appeals neither to a capitalist nor a socialist ideology, but to concrete realities of the circulation of money in a productive process. He points out that command economies cannot have an intelligent grasp of the reality on the ground, since even the best communist economist would always be reacting to situations in the past instead of the present. Nor does it help anyone to equate economics to physics, since it is primarily a human science. Mathematical models are important to further understanding, but we know of no math that accounts for human decision-making *per se*. When Lonergan decries ignorance rather than greed as the cause of crashes, it isn't because he discounts greed but because he knows how humans act when panicked. On the other hand, we cannot ignore the sense of unreality pervading today's mood in Western markets when, for example, in mid-summer 2021, "the cryptocurrency market (just the cryptocurrencies themselves, not related businesses) hit a level that was worth more than the market value of Walmart, Home Depot, Disney, Exxon Mobil, Netflix, Nike, McDonald's, and Goldman Sachs combined!" See https://orders.stansberryresearch.com/?cid= MKT554814 ?cid=MKT554814 &eid=MKT558437&assetId=AST189957&page=2. Since then, the market capitalization of cryptocurrencies has declined by two-thirds from its peak.

81. There is no date as to when Lonergan first integrated production, exchange and financial flows in the two-circuit rates of flow diagram. That he had the notion of two circuits by 1941 is clear from his article "Savings Certificates and Catholic Action'" which appeared in the *Montreal Beacon*, 7 February 1941.

Appendix D; we argue that there is a "process mode" at the heart of Lonergan's GEM-FS method, including his economics. We stress that in basing his work on economics upon the rhythmic cycling of the two economies there are two circuits, not just one.[82] Lonergan is by no means reviving the equilibrium theories of the 19th-century political economists such as those of Walras, Ricardo, or John Stuart Mill. Much to the contrary. Lonergan opens the way to the possibility and need of what we name *group economics conversions*. Lonergan's two circuits are, in effect, two interconnected economies, a "basic" or consumer circuit, and a "surplus" or production circuit, incarnated in the four monetary functions.[83] These are likely to be partially out of phase with one another. Understanding why and how to handle accelerations and decelerations of these is at the heart of Lonergan's original circulation analysis. GEM-FS processes can lead to ethical insights to adjudicate the claims of macroeconomic[84] theories–a type of redistribution process which, we argue, can be a basis for our proposed "group economics turnarounds." The example we gave of the Mondragon corporation in Spain's Basque region exemplifies such a type of authentically-motivated group turnarounds in economics.

Let us quote Lonergan to the effect that measurement becomes less important as one advances to the higher levels of intelligibility:

> In physics and chemistry, measuring is a basic technique that takes inquiry from the relations of things to our senses to their relations to one another. But when one mounts to the higher integrations of the organism, the psyche, and intelligence, one finds that measuring

---

82. The distinction between circuits is functional; it categorizes a good or service into the basic or surplus circuit—depending on how a product *is used*. When a car is sold, we ask who is going to use it? If it is going to be used privately, then it is a basic-circuit transaction. If it is going to be used as a taxi, then it belongs in the surplus circuit since it will accelerate other activities. That is, Lonergan replaced the single circuit of economic textbooks with the credit-centered, double circuit of functional macroeconomic dynamics. See Paul St. Amour "Introduction to Lonergan's Macroeconomic Theory."

83. Lonergan identifies the *four monetary functions* in his description of "Rates of Payment and Transfers," *CWL*15, 45–51. The four functions "form two circuits connected by a crossover and the role of the redistribution function." See fig. 4–5.

84. See Stephen Morris and Hyun Song Shin, "Rethinking Multiple Equilibria in Macroeconomic Modeling," Macroeconomics Annual, Vol. 15 (2000), 139–61.

loses both in significance and in efficacy. It loses in significance, for the higher integration is, within limits, independent of the exact quantities of the lower manifold it systematizes. . . . There is also a loss in efficacy. Classical method can select the functions that solve differential equations by appealing to measurements and empirically established curves. What the differential equation is to classical method, the general notion of development is to genetic method. But while the differential equation is mathematical, the general notion of development is not. It follows that, while measurement is an efficacious technique for finding boundary conditions that restrict differential equations, it possesses no assignable efficacy when it comes to particularizing the general notion of development.[85]

Aware of Lonergan's caution as to the nature of development, we turn to examine his GEM-FS integrative approach to economics. We shall give several examples, some encompassing and some more restricted, on how to counter claims that capitalism should focus only on making profits. A GEM-FS economics focuses on the good of all.

FOURTH FUNCTIONAL SPECIALTY: SOME DIFFERENCES IN APPROACHES TO DIALECTIC AND THE NEED FOR CHANGES IN ECONOMIC THEORIES

An underlying reality that makes it difficult to apply GEM-FS to economics is that religious people today are confronted with the demands and requirements of *two diverse systems*, namely those of those of secular economics in a changing era, on the one hand, and those of their faith. This means that to be authentic, religious people must try to reconcile[86] within

---

85. *Insight*, 488. Lonergan adds: "What the differential equation is to classical method, the general notion of development is to method." While measurement is efficacious for finding boundary conditions that restrict differential equations, "it possesses no assignable efficacy when it comes to particularizing the general notion of development."

86. "It is the inner dynamism of inquiry that provides the reconciliation, both general and completely concrete, of the interdependence of other fields and of the universal relevance of theology. In principle, other fields alone are competent to answer their proper

their everyday life "the alphabets" of both secular and religious systems. This is a core problem begging for a solution. In Parts I and II, we laid a ground to address this dilemma. In Parts III and IV, we seek credible solutions. That is, we shall delve into how people of good faith, including secularists, both individually and communally, might counter the presuppositions of a Marx or a Freud—as well as the profit-maximizing mentalities of capitalists—by means of a GEM-FS process approach to economics. In FS 4, we continue to summarize the arguments Lonergan makes in *CWL* 15 and 21 in order to "sandwich" them within the inner achievements of his better-known writings.

In *CWL 21*, Lonergan begins his study of the pure process of the economy using his notion of the basic and compound rhythmic flows of economic activity, and how these flows affect the laws of increasing and decreasing returns.[87] His understanding of these laws, however, is not typical due to the very original and unique manner by which he relates the acceleration or deceleration of economic rhythms to more encompassing sociological processes and ethical issues.[88] Michael Gibbons points out that Lonergan, by using the technique of implicit definition, shifts the emphasis "from trying to define the relevant variables to searching heuristically for the maximum extent of interconnections and interdependence." The variables discovered in this way "might not resemble very much the objects"[89] or the aggregates which, in the first instance, one was thinking about.

The collective historical West, which has influenced all and everyone for 500 years, must face the fact that this era is irrevocably passing,

---

questions. In fact, men in other fields do not triumph over all the various types of bias to which polymorphic human consciousness is subject unless they . . . answer successfully the further questions that belong to ever further fields." *Insight*, 766.

87. Lonergan, *CWL*, 21, 12. In *CWL* 15, 125, he notes: "While any concrete realization of the capitalist idea is subject first to increasing and then to decreasing returns, the series of new capitalist ideas cannot be said to be subject to either."

88. Lonergan, *Grace and Freedom*, *CWL* 1, Univ. of Toronto, 15, writes: "Everyone is familiar with the common notion of going faster. Few understand what you mean when you explain that an acceleration is the second derivative of a continuous function of distance and time." See also Michael Shute "Functional Collaboration as the Implementation of Lonergan's Method," Part 2, January, 2015.

89. https://functionalmacroeconomics.com/table-of-contents/five-images/sublation

even as some people try to hold onto what's slipping away by artificially slowing down, as it were, the objective process of forming a multipolar world. In the face of this, we seek a transformative-process approach to world problems rather than one only intent on maximizing profits. As to this, let us point to a passage on the productive process by Lonergan in *CWL* 15 that can be easily misunderstood:

> The productive process of the exchange economy is a process of production for sale. Already it was remarked that the productive process included sales management as well as production management. The remark has now to be completed. The productive process includes not only sales management but the sales themselves. What is produced and not sold either does not appertain to the exchange economy at all or else it is an unfinished product. Inversely, in any section or stage of the productive process, goods and services are completed only if they are sold. . . . For in the exchange economy production is not a matter of art, of doing or making things for the excellence of the doing of or the making; it is a matter of economics, of doing and making things that other people want and want badly enough to pay for.[90]

In a related passage, the editors of *CWL* 15 caution that

> It would be unfair to ascribe to Lonergan, on the basis of these sentences, a modern, secularist utilitarianism of the type whose foundations were laid by Hobbes, Locke and Smith. Lonergan's whole life work makes clear that he does not identify the general idea of value, which has a transcendental range (*MiT* 34–36, 101–03), with economic value . . . Lonergan is making a distinction based on not eliminating or reducing non-economic values. This distinction has to do with the fact that, given property rights as the means of correlating particular persons with particular objects and given money as the medium of exchange, the modern industrial dynamic configuration of surplus and basic production will function on the basis of decisions to exchange in such a way as to concentrate upon production

---

90. *CWL* 21, 247.

as for sale, thus turning economic value into exchange value. . . . Lonergan's concern for the dynamic mechanism of macro-equilibria is for the sake of intelligently *subordinating* economic to other social, cultural, personal, and religious values.[91]

Two steps are needed to subordinate economic values to other values. The first is to oppose those who try to manipulate the system in favor of the rich embodied in the claim of a "third economy," a patently false claim.[92] We would expose its falsity by recalling that money is and has always been a social construct, an expression of mutual trust. Markets and exchanges depend on such trust. This is why systems of checks and balances were developed. Modern economies need covenants—based on mutual trust—in order to function at all. Lonergan insisted that these should be considered part of the moral aspects of capitalism. Recent economic crises have eroded trust in the markets that should be serving the needs of the surplus and basic economies. Lonergan's schematic account of the rhythms of capital (illustrated in fig. 4–5) can be used to indicate the ethical dilemmas of the huge inequalities in our world, in which just 28 people own as much wealth as do over three billion other persons.[93]

A second step toward subordinating economic values to other values focuses on two ways to counter inequalities by 1) reinvesting the social dividend to ensure that future goods and services will be produced; 2) implementing the framework of a pure cycle, with its differences between the two phases—expansion in the means of production followed by expansion of consumable goods and services. *These two points are key to understanding Lonergan's economics.* Eileen de Neeve stresses that Lonergan's innovative growth process approach includes no negative acceleration of the productive process:

---

91. *CWL* 15, 40, note 46.

92. Capitalism has told us that the American dream means becoming a mega-millionaire or more. Instead the American dream should be to collectively build a society where nobody starves or goes homeless. Our book seeks to promote the latter version. Countering tax evasion is one indispensable means to make the dream come true.

93. With the intent of helping resolve such dilemmas, we refer the reader to our discussion of the ethical implications of the redistribution function and Lonergan's notion of a social dividend (income over and above the standard of living).

It is entirely a forward movement which . . . involves a cycle inasmuch as in successive periods of time the surplus stage of the process is accelerating more rapidly, and, again later, less rapidly than the basic stage.[94]

Lonergan's view of the acceleration of the productive process, which introduces new and better producer goods, emphasizes the growth in equilibrium output that innovations, for example, make possible. The larger equilibrium output ensures that resources and labor, diverted from firms that are made redundant by the rise in productivity, will be put to use in a growing economy.

Developing the Implications of a "Generous Hand"

Lonergan insisted that an economy should provide for all "with a generous hand." What does that mean? In the following pages, we shall cite two encompassing examples and several down-to-earth examples (e. g. on beekeeping), to illustrate how GEM-FS strategies can ethically help provide for the needs of all. Unfortunately, our first "would-be" encompassing example was coopted when, in 2021, COP26 failed to advocate the need to combat climate change. Instead of an ethical strategy, COP26, an industry-led and UN-convened alliance of private banking and financial institutions, announced plans to overhaul the role of the world's global and regional financial institutions—including the World Bank and IMF—as part of a broader plan to "transform" the global financial system. The officially stated purpose of the proposed overhaul is to promote the transition to a "net zero" economy. Sadly, COP26's proposed reimagining of international financial institutions would seek to merge these institutions with the private-banking interests that

---

94. Eileen de Neeve, "Interpreting Bernard Lonergan's General Theory of Economic Dynamics. Does it Complete Hayek?" (2010), 109 (referring to *CWL* 15, 35). In the words of Paul St. Amour, "Introduction to Lonergan Macroeconomic Theory," "Lonergan has two main criteria for balanced growth in the normative case: 1) that new money and credit flow to producers; 2) that entrepreneurs "reinvest the extraordinary profits of an expansion—profits beyond normal returns to labor, management, material, and lenders.""

compose the alliance,[95] thus creating a new system of "global financial governance," while eroding national sovereignty among developing countries by forcing them to establish business environments deemed "friendly" to the interests of alliance members. In other words, the powerful banking interests that compose this group want to recreate the entire global financial system for their own benefit under the guise of promoting sustainability.[96] We may link this emphasis on subordinating economic values to private interests to what we wrote in FS 3, and to our comments on smartphones.

Our second encompassing—this one positive—example for providing for the needs of all touches on Lonergan's use of a pure cycle and a trade cycle; it reinforces our GEM-FS integrative sandwich approach. We noted some aspects of the dynamic economic process:

§ The dummy (money) "must be constant in exchange value."

§ Prices alone do not explain the economic process. Prices must be interpreted in the light of the significant variables able to actually explain the economic process.

§ The economic process of production and exchange is the current, purely dynamic process. It is an organic whole with an exigence for a normative pure cycle of expansion.

§ Equilibrium requires balancing the interdependent flows of products and money.

§ A too high supply of money is the normal cause of inflation.

§ Maladjustment of incomes is a maladaptive cause of inflation.

§ "Just as the surplus phase of the expansion is anti-egalitarian in tendency, postulating an increasing rate of saving, and attaining this . . .

---

95. Treasury Secretary Janet Yellen called for a "wholesale transformation" of carbon intensive economies at COP26. She urged that the private sector capitalize on an opportunity to help developing nations transition to a carbon free economy. "Rising to this challenge will require the wholesale transformation of our carbon-intensive economies," Yellen stated. "It's a global transition for which we have an estimated price tag" between $100 and $150 trillion over the next three decades." Undoing climate change is the greatest economic opportunity of our time, which we stress needs six turnarounds.

96. Interpreting comments made in *Investigative Reports*, Nov. 5, 2021.

so the basic expansion is egalitarian in tendency; it postulates a continuously decreasing rate of saving."[97]

§ The central adjustment to the respective phases of the process may be formulated as adjustment of I"/(I' + I"), the ratio of surplus income to total income.

§ Interpreters of price changes must distinguish between real and relative price increases monetary and absolute changes in prices.

Lonergan warns of the "psychological effects" of the arbitrary procedure of making the exchange system "an exclusive club for businessmen . . . It produces the split personality of the business man in his office and the respected citizen in his home. It turns out the pure types of the uplift worker who cannot get down to business, and of the common cynic who takes a business view of larger issues. But these psychological aberrations are but symptoms of a deeper malady."[98] Needless to say, this malady calls for socio-communal policy turnarounds.

Exploring Some Implications of Economic Theories Calling for Turnarounds

Sir David Attenborough and Alexandre Antonelli have stressed the need for economics and environmental turnarounds, arguing that biodiversity can provide the compass that we urgently need. They show that by brining economics and ecology together, we can help save the natural world and ourselves. We quote:

> We are facing a global crisis. We are totally dependent upon the natural world. It supplies us with every oxygen-laden breath we take and every mouthful of food we eat. But we are currently damaging it so profoundly that many of its natural systems are now on the verge of breakdown. Every other animal living on this planet, of course, is similarly dependent. But in one crucial way, we are different. We can change not just the numbers, but the very anatomy of the animals

---

97. *CWL* 15, 139.
98. *CWL* 21, 35–36.

and plants that live around us. We acquired that ability, doubtless almost unconsciously, some ten thousand years ago, when we had ceased wandering and built settlements for ourselves. It was then that we started to modify other animals and plants (Attenborough).

It's time to say farewell to one of the biggest and longest running myths in the economy, the myth that social development must come at the cost of nature. That this dichotomy is false has long been articulated and promoted by the conservation movement, but to little avail. Around the world, countries and businesses have continued to empty natural resources for short-term economic profit. Now, more than ever, someone is needed to tell them this cannot continue—but who would they listen to? (Antonelli).[99]

On the Scissors Metaphors and Some Implications

Alfred Marshall rejected cost-of-production theories of value. In doing so, he introduced a "scissors metaphor" to convey the fact that both supply and demand simultaneously determine value. He wrote:

We might reasonably dispute whether it is the upper or the under blade of a pair of scissors that cuts a piece of paper, as whether value is governed by utility or cost of production. It is true that when one blade is held still and the cutting is effected by moving the other, we may say with careless brevity that the cutting is done by the second; but the statement is not strictly accurate, and is to be excused only so long as it (recognizes that) . . . it is not a strictly scientific account of what happens.[100]

---

99. *Dasgupta Review*, Feb. 2021.

100. https://conversableeconomist.blogspot.com/2020/08/supply-and-demand-scissors-banana-and.html quoting Alfred Marshall's *Principles of Economics*, 1890—the dominant economic textbook in England in the early 20th century. It brings the ideas of supply and demand, marginal utility, and costs of production into a coherent whole. The Marshallian scissors seeks to concretize the scissors metaphor, reversing the abstract and the real. Lonergan, *Insight*, 337, relies on his notion of the heuristic structures of empirical method that "operate in a scissors-like fashion" and from which we draw some ethical implications by way of our reliance on our "theory-praxis-FS-sandwich approach" developed in Parts III and IV.

Lonergan developed a precise notion of a scissors movement as an analytical tool that differs from Marshall's view of it. He relied on his notion of the heuristic structures of empirical method that "operate in a scissors-like fashion"; the lower blade "rises from data through measurements and curve fitting to formulae, but also there is an upper blade that moves downward from differential and operator equations and from postulates of invariance and equivalence." This quote comes within the context of Lonergan's examination of mathematical judgments and the enriching role of insights which

> Go beyond images and data by adding intelligible unities and correlations . . . which, indeed, contain a reference to images or data but nonetheless add a component to knowledge that does not exist actually on the level of sense or imagination.[101]

A GEM-FS economics can reinforce notions of culture and a social ethics, both of which Lonergan links to the basic aspects of the human condition—rooted in his key notions of operator[102] and of cosmopolis.

---

101. *Insight*, 336–37.

102. Operators are one of the key, integrative factors in the entire GEM-FS effort. Yet, they are seldom addressed systematically by Lonergan's students. In Lonergan's *opus*, the notion of operator first appears in *Insight*, Ch. 15, 465. He writes that in the general case, the operator "is the upwardly directed dynamism of proportionate being that we have named finality." Among other functions, "operators form a flexible series along which the organism advances from the generic functioning of the initial cell to the flexible circle of ranges of schemes of the mature type." The difficulty in studying the operators lies in the complexity of its data. In contrast to this very general notion of operator, Lonergan develops a notion of operator which can help us change the future. In dialectic, operators develop positions and reverse counterpositions. Phil McShane, *Bernard Lonergan, His Life and Leading Ideas* (Vancouver: Axial Press, 2010, 76), stresses that this operator is one of "discovering operatively." It is a "serious forward speaking . . . a direct speaking. Otherwise one becomes a sort of a two-way signpost." The book details how Lonergan was able to integrate the implications of his writings on economics with his concerns for truth in philosophy and ethics. Lonergan's work relates "to the deep issue" of the procedures and content of science. Our path in this book is similar: bridging seemingly unrelated issues so as to arrive at a comprehensive synthesis. Today such a path includes tracing the insidious path of "dark money." For example, a right-wing dark money group controlled by Leonard Leo—a legal activist who has played an outsized role in packing the U.S. Supreme Court with conservative ideologues—was the beneficiary of a massive, possibly unprecedented donation of $1.6 billion from a shadowy electronics mogul with ties to the Koch

Integrating Lonergan's Notions of Cosmopolis and Economics[103]

For Lonergan our knowing-doing operations imply an operator—a self-transcendent subject.[104] Unfortunately, it is not the case that most people are self-transcendent: most of us have neither the time nor the ability to consistently act in self-transcending ways. Still, there is a need for human solidarity. Lonergan's notion of cosmopolis—as a higher

---

network. The enormous infusion of cash, first reported on August 22, 2022 by *The New York Times*, could bolster and embolden right-wing efforts to drag the U.S. judicial and political systems even further to the right for decades to come, imperiling the climate and human liberty that have come under growing threat from the GOP and conservative judges. "With this fortune, Leo can grow his singular influence in near perpetuity." According to the *Times*, the donation to the Marble Freedom Trust from former Tripp Lite CEO and longtime Republican benefactor Barre Seid is "among the largest . . . single contributions ever made to a politically focused non-profit. "The Times reports how the gift, based entirely on funds generated by the sale of Tripp Lite, "was arranged through an unusual series of transactions that appear to have avoided tax liabilities" for both Seid and Leo's non-profit. Citing an unnamed source with knowledge of the matter, the *Times* explained that "rather than merely giving cash, Mr. Seid donated 100% of the shares of Tripp Lite to Mr. Leo's non-profit group before the company was sold for $1.65 billion." A sad example of "non-profit profiteering" abuses.

103. In FS 4, we seek to show that *MiT*'s dialectic can help us develop Lonergan's notion of justice which provides helpful contexts for reinforcing the ethical aspects of Lonergan's economics. The structure of dialectic occurs on an upper level and a lower one. On the upper level, there are the two operators or precepts whereby one develops positions and reverses counterpositions. "Positions are statements compatible with intellectual, moral and religious conversion; they are developed by being integrated with fresh data and further discovery. Counterpositions are statements incompatible with [such] conversions; they are reversed when the incompatible elements are removed." One must assemble, complete, compare, reduce, classify and select the relevant material; this entails the different horizons within which various investigators operate. If investigators' horizons differ, further objectifications of horizons are needed. GEM-FS operators foster the conversions and integrate fresh data within new discoveries (*MIT*, 249.50. *CWL* 14, 234–35). See Philip Hold and Andrew Barden, "Justice and Ethics" in *Journal of Security Education*, 2, 2007, 81–106. We study the evolution of economic theories to ascertain how they may shed light on implementing cosmopolis. Francisco Sierra-Gutierrez, (www.bu.edu/wcp/ Educ/Educ Sier.htm) stresses Lonergan's approach to the higher viewpoint of culture: "The integrating form of education is involved in the general tension between limitation and transcendence." The global challenge is to be met in terms of cosmopolis and the conversions." See *Insight*, 263–67.

104. In Appendix A, we link Lonergan's crucial notion of self-transcending operators with economics. For Teilhard de Chardin, self-transcendence is "se replier sur soi"—to fold back on oneself. GEM-FS economics may be an instance of such inasmuch as it can help solve the global structural climate and economic crises confronting humanity.

viewpoint of culture—can serve as a half-way house to foster human solidarity. Cosmopolis is not a new kind of organization, structure, or hierarchy. Rather,

> It is a withdrawal from practicality to save practicality . . . It is
> not *simpliste*. It does not leap from a fact of development to a belief
> in automatic progress nor from a fact of abuse to an expectation of
> an apocalyptic utopia reached through accelerated decline. It is the
> higher synthesis of the liberal thesis and the Marxist antithesis.[105]

Cosmopolis promotes people's ability to develop needed horizontal transformations. Lonergan noted how unresolved tensions afflict both individual persons and the communities they live in. Our GEM-FS aim is to suggest how caring communities throughout the world can help resolve such tensions ethically. Cosmopolis can reinforce the attitude of people of good will—intent on overcoming injustices. It can help reinforce the ethical principles of the world's major religions. As GEM-FS generalizes the notion of data to include the data of consciousness, so too it generalizes the notion of method. It wants to go behind the diversity that separates the experimental method from the quite diverse procedures of hermeneutics and of history. It would discover their common core.[106] As a needed dialectical-foundational breakthrough, cosmopolis is a notion Lonergan developed to promote the good of order.[107] It can help us overcome the *social surd*[108] by reaching beyond politics. It would help undo illusions that mark perfidious

---

105. *Insight*, 266. See Dennis Gunn "Teaching for Cosmopolis: Bernard Lonergan's Hopeful Vision for Education in a Globalized World," *Religious Education*, 113, 2018, 26.

106. Lonergan, *A Third Collection*, "Religious Knowledge," 141. Inasmuch as Lonergan did discover their common core, the GEM-FS world can credibly claim that Lonergan has retrieved one missing link that has afflicted Western thought since Descartes. The "GEM-FS world" should show a united front in spelling out the implications of the GEM-FS link. As of now, a "GEM-FS global team" tends to be voices crying in the desert.

107. The good of order includes cooperative efforts among suppliers of particular goods.

108. "The general bias of common sense generates an increasingly significant residue that (1) is immanent in the social facts (2) is not intelligible, yet (3) cannot be abstracted from if one is to consider the facts as in fact they are." *Insight*, 255.

cycles of decline.[109] As an integral GEM-FS component, cosmopolis can help us cope with the general bias generated by mere commonsense. Biases stem from an incomplete development of intelligence. A problem is that good ideas often fail to be implemented because people are all too likely to exalt "the practical . . . the cult of the class." He adds

> What is necessary is a cosmopolis that is neither class nor state, that stands above all their claims, that cuts them down to size that is founded on . . . the disinterestedness of every intelligence . . . that is too universal to be bribed, too impalpable to be forced . . . too effective to be ignored.[110]

Protest is a form of pressure, which could be effective in mitigating the worst effects of group bias but it is ineffective against the general bias of common sense.[111] In view of this, cosmopolis can help artists, religious persons, philosophers, and journalists free themselves from having to justify their efforts to practically-minded persons. This is so because the practical mind is subject to the biases of common sense[112] and social

---

109. "To ignore the fact of decline was the error of the old liberal views of automatic progress. The far more confusing error of Marx was to lump together both progress and the two principles of decline under the impressive name of dialectical materialism, to grasp that the minor principle of decline would correct itself more rapidly through class war, and then to leap gaily to the sweeping conclusion that class war would accelerate progress. What in fact was accelerated was major decline, which in Russia and Germany leaped to fairly thorough brands of totalitarianism." *Insight*, 260.

110. *Insight*, 263. We argue that cosmopolis requires that as many as six turnarounds are required to fully implement Lonergan's vision. Our dynamism of consciousness cannot overcome all the diverging series of biases to which it is subject without a cosmopolis.

111. Richard H. Thaler and Cass R. Sunstein, *Nudge* (Penguin, 2009) show that no choice is ever presented to us in a neutral way. We are all susceptible to biases that can lead us to make bad decisions. But by knowing how people think, we can use sensible "choice architecture" to nudge people toward the best decisions for ourselves, our families, and our society, without restricting our freedom of choice.

112. The reason we need mathematics is the same reason Lonergan felt bound to begin *Insight* with illustrations of mathematical understanding. He writes: "If one's apprehensions of those activities [that define the successive levels of consciousness] is to be clear and distinct, then one must prefer the fields of intellectual endeavor in which the greatest care is devoted to exactitude and in fact the greatest exactitude is attained. For this reason, then, I have felt obliged to begin my account of insight and its expansion with mathematical and scientific illustrations, and while I would grant that essentially the same activities

engineering—making it captive to them as it were. Keeping in mind that the first phase of the FS lays a path for implementing the second phase of functional collaboration, we argue that the structure of dialectic[113] in FS 4 can help people of good will develop cosmopolis so as to give a sound ethical basis for Lonergan's economic variables outlined in *CWL* 15 and 21. Economists would do well to emulate physicists' successful method by relying on the basic principles Lonergan used in revising notions of economic processes. Cosmopolis, based on a higher viewpoint, suggests a way to do so. In his succinct expression of his economics principle found in his "Healing and Creating in History,"[114] he lays out an ethical basis for his economics. Since his approach to economics differs in *CWL* 15 and 21, we turn to sort out, reconcile some of the differences to highlight Lonergan's integral development of an ethical GEM-FS economics.

Above, we touched on how Lonergan's notions of emergent probability and schemes of recurrence are relevant to understanding evolution

---

can be illustrated from the ordinary use of intelligence that is named common sense, I also must submit that it would be impossible for common sense to grasp and say what precisely common sense happens to illustrate." *Insight*, 14–15. One problem is that mathematicians do not properly understand the relevance of insight to their own subject. They may have an intuitive notion of insight and understanding, but they fail to grasp its relevance until they have applied it to a mathematical problem.

113. Dialectic rests on the concrete unity of opposed principles. Great physicists achieved their breakthroughs using experimental methods. Lonergan suggested how economists could emulate physicists' successful methods—though economics has its own methodology and principles as we shall show in our delineation of *CWL* 15, *Macroeconomic Dynamics*, 21. For one thing, economists have no way to verify hypotheses experimentally, but must react to developments of the economy itself.

114. Lonergan, "Healing and Creating in History, *Third Collection*, 100–110. The article should be studied within the context of Lonergan's deeper notion of religious conversion. In *MiT*, 245, *CWL* 14, 228, Lonergan writes: "Religious conversion goes beyond moral. Questions for intelligence, for reflection, for deliberation reveal the eros of the human spirit, its capacity and its desire for self-transcendence. But that capacity meets fulfilment, that desire turns to joy, when religious conversion transforms the existential subject into a subject in love, a subject held, grasped . . . owned through a total and so an other-worldly love. Then there is a new basis for all valuing and all doing good. In no way are the fruits of intellectual or moral conversion negated or diminished. On the contrary, all human pursuit of the true and the good is included within and furthered by a cosmic context and purpose and, as well, there now accrues to man the power of love to enable him to accept the suffering involved in undoing the effects of decline."

and how humans strive to develop their knowledge of how economies grow. Economic patterns over the millennia have changed drastically affected by both slow forms of evolution and abrupt revolutions. Neanderthals were organized to find food, shelter, and clothing before the appearance of *homo sapiens*. Our species replaced them for reasons still being debated; most likely *homo sapiens* was better at organizing. Our species went from hunting, fishing, and fruit-picking[115] to agriculture. It developed the concepts of property, went from simple exchange to developing complex trade relationships involving long-distance travel, from animal husbandry to today's global industrialized agriculture. Concomitantly, humans have gone from informal credit and money to establishing banking, lines of credit to finance projects, and the capital markets. Economists, in evaluating all these changes, have had to change their views, as we noted in Part II.

Briefly stated, Lonergan's move in economics was to replace the single circuit by a credit-centered double circuit. For him,

> The world process with all the potentialities of universal nature, (is) ever stimulated, guided, aided by human effort . . . All such human activity occurs rhythmically in a series of impulses . . . But though the whole is rhythmic, not all is economic . . . All of this is a rhythmic transformation of natural potentialities by human effort. None of this is strictly human activity. Yet, conditioning all culture and inextricably connected with it, there is the economic factor.[116]

It is at this point that Lonergan first introduces and develops in *CWL* 15 his notions of a credit-centered double circuit and of rhythms and flows in the economy which we shall develop below.

We have been arguing that Lonergan's dynamic version of economics proposes an alternative based on phase-based-economic processes—a method that reinforces what we call Lonergan's overall GEM-FS process approach. We now proceed to reassess Lonergan's approach to

---

115. Lonergan, *CWL 21*, 19. He distinguishes the common sense of a primitive culture from that of an urban civilization; this, of course, affects his treatment of the transformations that need to be integrated.

116. *CWL* 15, 11–12.

an economy's phases from a socio-ethical viewpoint. This will involve reflecting on the phases of an economy based on a GEM-FS dynamic economic process. This reassessment and reflection are core elements of how our notion of an economic sandwich seeks to foster a democratic, ethical socio-communal economics "abetted" by needed turnarounds in environmental policies.

How Lonergan Understood the Phases of an Economy

For Lonergan, money facilitates "the production of goods and services. In a well-run economy, the circulation of money adjusts to the rhythms of production, that is, money circulation is concomitant with the steps of the production process."[117] Lonergan refers to the basic rhythm, measured in exchange units over some interval, as DA, where A stands 'for economic Activity' and D recalls that the activity is a series of events, a flow of impulses, a compound rhythm composed of many minor rhythms of varying magnitude and frequency.[118] Lonergan notes that since DA is but the first of a dozen or so similar terms he will use, he spells out that DA refers *not* to an average but to "an aggregate rate of rhythm or volume of flow," a quantitative rate. It means "so much so often." It also refers to the longer or shorter period of utility, and the disappearance . . . or waste of an aggregate of meals, clothes . . . ships and hospitals"[119] and other functions of daily life. DA refers to an objective quantity, but it is not a mathematical symbol. Lonergan is content "with distinguishing quantities *qualitatively*," in the way "we distinguish the quantitative differences of the several wavelengths of light by the qualitative differences of the spectrum.[120] DA is the total rhythmic flow, the total aggregate of all rhythms at any instant t.[121] It is composed of DA' and DA". DA' is the aggregate of *primary rhythms*, of the routines that

---

117. Michael Shute, "Real Economic Variables," *Divyadaan*, 21, No. 2, 2010, 188.

118. *CWL* 21, 12.

119. *CWL* 21, 13.

120. *CWL* 21, 13.

121. Based on *CWL* 21, 16.

are productive factors on the lowest level. By definition, any increment in the primary rhythms tends to yield a proportionate increment in the field of ultimate products. If a family of Inuit, for example, catches one more fish per week, they will tend to eat one more per week. DA" is the aggregate of *secondary* rhythms or flows. We can write these relationships with the expression

$$DA = DA' + DA''\,^{122}$$

which helps us understand the four phases of an economy. When DA', the basic or consumer stage, and DA", the surplus or productive stage, are both in unchanging rhythms (at the "effective zero" when there is no change in the rate "of every so often" in the secondary rhythms, that is, when "they do not produce anything"), the overall economy is in the static phase. The capitalist phase begins when DA" accelerates but DA' does not.[123] When DA" is constant but above the effective zero, the surplus can increase DA'; this is the materialist phase. Finally, the surplus of DA" can increase "overhead" DA', resulting in a "cultural" phase.[124] The economic history of the United States from 1800 on gives plenty of examples of such changes of phases, although statistics on gross national or domestic product do not identify them except as being "up" and "down" movements.

How The Four Phases Affect Notions of GDP

GDP is the value of a nation's finished domestic goods and services during a specific time period. It does not measure the different flows of basic

---

122. *CWL* 21, 16. Still, as some have noted, a primitive economy can do without money. See also *CWL* 21 Index under "G: distributive multipliers" and its various entries.

123. "Capital is capital because its utility lies not in itself but in the acceleration it imparts to the stream of useful things." *Lonergan Reader,* 124. The context is that for Lonergan, there is a need to seek beyond higher viewpoints, that is to search "for a religious integration and transformation of concrete human living." The dynamic structure of our conscious, intentional operations is what enables us to transform our lives.

124. DA, concomitance and rhythmic flows are analogous notions and play a central role in *CWL 21*; that is why we make a special effort to link the three notions.

and surplus circuits, nor does it indicate monetary flows. Lonergan, on the other hand, does measure monetary flows (see fig. 4–5), which are, strictly speaking either part of the productive process itself ("operative payments") or else are in the domain of the redistributive function, which moves money in and out of the productive process (in or out of savings, for instance). We seek to supply a value-based link for how one uses money so that an ethically-based redistributive function may operate effectively.[125] Lonergan's approach to such an ethical framework differs somewhat in *CWL* 15 and 21. His use of diagrams, symbols and abbreviations also differs in the two volumes—making our task a somewhat difficult enterprise. For example, he has several, slightly different versions of the rates of flow diagram in which he sketches the underlying contributions that make up the aggregate flows of goods and services and money.

His earlier tome, *CWL* 21, written in the 1940's, focuses on economic activity as a series of events where DA stands to economic activity with D recalling "that the activity is a series of events, a flow of impulses, a compound rhythm composed of many minor rhythms of varying magnitudes and frequency."[126] At the beginning of *CWL* 21's treatment of the productive process, Lonergan declares that he is not yet concerned with specific amounts; he is simply identifying a *flow of activity* that can be loosely divided into two parts. As simple as this formula is (and at the risk of over-simplifying), it is nonetheless at the heart of Lonergan's understanding of what an economy is. While there will be much more to say about how the two circuits interrelate[127] and about the ratio of DA′ to DA″, we stress that it is the functional differentiation of the two distinct circuits of work that places Lonergan's theory on a unique footing.

---

125. Eileen de Neeve, "Interpreting," 107. For Lonergan, "A cycle starts when innovating producers obtain the credit and initiate production. The normal entry of new money into the circuits is through transfers from the redistributive function to the supply functions."

126. Lonergan, *CWL* 21, 12.

127. Relevant here, especially in terms of Lonergan's own intellectual biography, is Christopher Dawson's account of human prehistory in *The Age of the Gods* (New York: Sheed and Ward, 1928). Lonergan read *The Age of the Gods* in the early 1930s. Dawson was an influential source in his discovery of the two circuits. See Michael Shute, *Lonergan's Discovery of the Science of Economics*, 149–50.

Many economists make a nominal distinction between consumer goods and production goods, but that distinction is not crucial to their theoretical underpinnings. With Lonergan, we distinguish between basic and surplus circuits and their rhythmic dynamism. In both *CWL* 15 and 21, there is a real, functional distinction between the basic and surplus circuits. Without this distinction, there is no economic science.

In the earlier *CWL* 21, DA stands for the total aggregate of all rhythms at a given time. There is the material structure and a dynamic structure, a primary rhythm and a secondary rhythm, which are distinct but interdependent. DA' stands for the aggregate of primary rhythms, and DA", the aggregate of secondary rhythms. One might think that DA equals DA' plus DA", but these are not to be taken in a strictly mathematical sense. Lonergan uses the example of a piston of a steam engine, in which the total quantity of steam is equal to the steam on either side of the piston. DA' also stands for final products of an economy, which are goods and services not made for the economic process itself but leave it: honey for eating, automobiles for transport, smartphones for all sorts of information-sharing (including phone calls), and so on. By definition, "DA" "attends to the acceleration of DA."[128] It does so through three secondary rhythms or flows:

First, by a *"widening"* which requires adding workers to e. g. make more hives or farm implements.

Second, by a *"deepening"* requiring less labor, because existing firms need fewer workers; but newer and larger firms grow and employ them. Here, innovation has a crucial role. Deepening can happen without widening: transitional deepening occurs to make further widening possible, while final deepening gives people more leisure.[129]

Third, the work of maintenance, repair and replacement at all levels. Here, Lonergan posits a new term, "the effective zero of DA" which obtains *when there is no change* in the rate "of every so often" of DA'

---

128. *CWL* 21, 17.

129. Lonergan, *CWL* 21, 19. He distinguishes the common sense of a primitive culture from that of urban civilization; this, of course, affects his treatment of leisure and of the transformations that need to be integrated.

and DA". With more widening, there is needed more maintenance, repair and replacement—leading to a rise in the effective zero.

Our approach to Lonergan's radical generalization of economics began with a non-human economic structure—the transactional symbiosis between honeybees and flowering plants, which is in fact a rudimentary "exchange economy." Beekeeping focuses on harnessing this "economy" to adapt it to human use. Most people love honey and buy or trade for it. Whence all the arcana of the profession: hives, combs, smokers, frames, extractors, and so on. The production of honey and its trade which can be designated as (DA') is an example of what Lonergan calls the "basic" economy, the production cycle entailing the concomitant process of the "surplus" economy (DA"). Of course, beekeeping is but a tiny part of the overall functioning of an economy, its DA. Note that economies do not necessarily depend on money—for millennia people traded on credit. Things become more complicated when we do add money.

Understanding how households and the furnishing of goods and services—microeconomics *à la* N. Gregory Mankiw—is one thing. Exploring the macroeconomic implications of universal economic rhythms, and the dynamics of these rhythms, as Lonergan does, is quite another.[130] We do not refer to the "bee economy" as a microeconomics phenomenon, but as a pointer to help explain Lonergan's pure cycle. In contradistinction to the practice of some economists, Lonergan is primarily interested in how humanity can survive and thrive—not in how people or firms can maximize profits. [131]

---

130. Mankiw's first four principles address efficient causes (the subjective psychology of persons making decisions in microeconomic matters). Lonergan focuses on objective macroeconomic situations to which we must adapt without neglecting an economy of scale. Paul Hoyt-O'Connor, "Economic Development and the Common Good: Lonergan and Cobb on the Need for a New Paradigm," *Worldviews*, 11. 2 (2007), 203–25.

131. We agree with David Oyler's argument in his homepage that a market economy is not a market. A prevalent view of the economy combines modeling it on market dynamics (which are a subset of, but distinct from, economic dynamics). We argue that a capitalist market economy can survive if it is understood that the capitalist phase (in Lonergan's sense) is only one phase which is both limited and transitory, though productively recurrent. It is a strawman to link a capitalist economy to the short term pursuit of wealth—any economic system can be led astray. In fact, the economy exists within the context of, and embodies values, collective or not, explicit or not. It is not to be confined

The later *CWL* 15, *Circulation Analysis*, features two versions of the diagram of rates of flow. Lonergan points out the fact that *CWL* 21 referred to "a universal economic rhythm, DA, a rate or volume of unmeasured, pulsating flow."[132] Then there arises the question as to why he abandoned his earlier use of DA.[133] The answer may help us grasp Lonergan's meaning of cycle and phase. In both *CWL* 15 and 21, Lonergan speaks of the cycles and phases of the economy:

> By a cycle is meant a more or less necessary succession of phases. By a phase is meant a series of intervals in which certain defined characteristics are verified. By a cycle of the productive process is meant a concatenation of phases defined by relations between quantity indices and their increments.[134]

Reconsidering GDP[135] and the Basic Rhythmic Flow

Gross Domestic Product (GDP) is generally considered by economists to be the total market value of the goods and services produced by a country's economy during a specific period of time. It includes all final goods and services—that is, those produced and ready for use. GDP is calculated using the value of goods and services made only during a particular period,

---

by market dynamics but should respond to human aspirations, to group economics conversions. Economic growth depends on population growth; this fact can have negative implications. Economic growth is more sustainable (environmentally and economically) if based on innovation.

132. *CWL* 21, 26.

133. In *CWL* 21, Lonergan explores the possibility of different types of phases, the main criterion of which is derived from the relation between basic and surplus acceleration. Note the confusion that stems from the fact that the *earlier 1944* book is numbered *CWL* 21 while the *later 1983* book is numbered 15 in the *CWL* series.

134. *CWL* 15, 113.

135. GDP and GNP differ. GDP is the value of a nation's finished domestic goods and services during a specific time period. GNP is a related but different metric. GNP is the value of all finished goods and services owned by a country's residents over a period of time. The expenditure approach defines GDP as the sum of goods and services purchased. A mutually exclusive and exhaustive approach is to decompose GDP as (private) consumption, investment, government spending, and net exports (exports minus imports). Both GDP and GNP represent the total market value of all goods and services produced over a definite period.

typically on an annual basis. It is used throughout the world as the main measure of output and economic activity. "The investment element of GDP is where the animal spirits of the economy bark and where a recession first bites."[136] For Lonergan, due to his notion of two flows[137] (consumer and capital investment) in the economy, GDP is not the most effective measure of economic success—nor does it take in the ethical aspects of a just economy. The two-flows notion enabled him to approach GNP and the possible implications for avoiding a basic Marxist objection to capitalism. In 1979, in his course on macroeconomics, Lonergan partially disagreed with Robert Gordon's three equations in his *Macroeconomics*:[138]

$$GNP = PQ = Y; Q = Y/P$$

where P is the price level, and Q the real income.

But in the two-stage productive process, P' and Q', P" and Q" are distinguished; Y' and Y" are the basic and surplus gross products.

$$Y' = P'Q'; Y'/P' = Q'$$
$$Y" = P"Q"; Y"/P" = Q"$$

With the circuits distinguished, the crossover[139] makes it manifest that it supplements the wages paid in the basic circuit, so that profits are

---

136. Jonathan Haskel and Stian Westlake, *Capitalism Without Capital: The Rise of the Intangible Economy*. See *Book Reviews*, 2018, 13, 1 (Princeton Univ., 2018). Economics today is a fixed culture of one-flow analysis, emphasizing GDP. See also Paul Hoyt-O'Connor, "Economic Development and the Common Good, *Worldviews*, Vol. 11. 2 (2007), 203–25.

137. Phil McShane's *Profit: the Stupid View of President Donald Trump* (Axial Publishing, 2016) examines how Lonergan's radical pedagogy seeks to correct misguided views on profit. Such economists as Schumpeter, Michal Kalecki, and Joan Robinson had admitted that there is a deep flaw in modern efforts at economic analysis. Schumpeter's dynamic analysis failed to develop refined scientific distinctions in the productive process. Kalecki and Robinson came nearer to such a refinement, but the question remains "What is the flaw?" McShane answers by drawing a parallel between Newton's transformation of astronomy through his theory of gravitation and Lonergan's approach to the two flows that inevitably occur in the productive cycle.

138. Gordon, *Macroeconomics* (Boston: Little, Brown,1978). Lonergan used Gordon's book in his class as an example of some clear thinking in the field.

139.Generally speaking, economists speak of a crossover a) as a point on a trading chart in which a security's price and a technical indicator line intersect, or b) when two

not robbing workers of part of the labor value of their contribution. If so, there is no need for government subsidies to supplement workers' basic wages.[140] This underlines Lonergan's contention that "Of itself, the productive process can give the fortunate more than they desire; moreover, it would like to treat all with a generous hand, for only by such generosity can it attain its maximum."[141]

Lonergan's and Rianne Eisler's Approaches to the Economy

The historian and economist Rianne Eisler[142] (1931–) has proposed an alternative view of how "partnership economics" could work. She sets aside the GDP as a fake indicator of a nation's "success," and uses instead measures of caring, relationship values and happiness to indicate a nation's success, that of a "Social Wealth Index." She makes a strong case for her alternative system. She offers an entirely different way of thinking about economics as a real-world system that affects the lives of ordinary people and families. Like Lonergan, she re-focuses economics to make it work for us, not against us by inviting global participation in rethinking an economy that works in the interest of all the people it pretends to serve. She points to the real problems of our economic system and offers actual solutions that can benefit real people.

The Bees, Again

Going back to our example of keeping bees (FS 3), with Lonergan we measure economic success in terms of $DA = DA' + DA''$. A stands for "economic activity" and D recalls that the activity is a series of events,

---

economic indicators cross. Lonergan has his own meaning of crossover. Economists also speak c) of crossover adjustment methods in the context of economic evaluation, Lonergan assigns to crossover an important function that mediates between his two basic circuits or basic flows in the economic process.

140. *CWL* 15, 71–72, note 87.

141. *CWL* 21, 36.

142. Eisler is the only woman among 20 major thinkers including Hegel, Adam Smith, Marx, and Toynbee listed in *Macrohistory and Macrohistorians* (1997) in recognition of the lasting importance of her work as a cultural historian and evolutionary theorist.

a flow of impulses, a compound rhythm composed of many minor rhythms of varying magnitude and frequency. "The basic rhythmic flow" is DA (a measure of the aggregate of redistributional activity measured in exchange units over some interval), while DA' measures the aggregate of sales at the primary final market in a similar interval; DA" measures "the aggregate of sales at the secondary final market over the same period of time."[143] In our example of honey-production, DA signifies the aggregate rate or rhythm or volume of flows; while it is a quantity, quantitative differences are distinguished not by measurement but qualitatively as are colors in the spectrum. When money enters into the picture, it brings easily-tracked units of measurement. What DA refers to must be clearly understood, for it is the most basic concept and it is dynamic. This is one aspect of DA—DA'. But there are also the companies that furnish hives to beekeepers, combs for the bees' incubators, bottles for the honey—DA". And there are the few companies that build the hive-making and bottle-making factories. The bees and their domesticators form a material structure which has a basic rhythm of so many bottles of honey every so often. But they depend on the dynamic structure of the hive- and bottle-makers, who depend in turn on the builders of their factories and the furnishing of the machines, and furnishers of the raw materials for both activities that supply other producers of goods.

Successive levels in production *accelerate* a previous level:

> A ton of iron may be employed at any of three levels. Employed at the lowest level, one ton of iron yields one ton of automobile parts or farm implements. Employed on the second level, one ton of iron yields one ton of machinery for making one ton of automobile parts or farm implements or what you please. Employed on the third level, one ton of iron yields one ton of machinery for making the machinery with which machines for making automobiles or other implements are made. Here, plainly, each level accelerates the preceding.[144]

---

143. Lonergan, *CWL* 21, 45. It is at this point that Lonergan introduces the symbol DA* to refer to the redistributional activity but in *CWL* 15, he no longer uses DA*.

144. Lonergan, *CWL* 21, 14.

There occur the secondary flows of widening, deepening and the work of maintenance, as well as repair and replacement at all levels that we noted above. These can lead to an economic transformation.

> The new leisure created by the combination of agriculture, the mechanical arts, and commerce at once stimulates and makes possible the study of science; but science brings applied science, finance and mass production to transform agriculture, trade and the crafts and to unite men in an economic interdependence that stands at the opposite pole of the self-sufficiency of the primitive.[145]

The human ability to innovate drives economic emergent probability. Yet, "for society to progress," it cannot be stupid, like a titanothere "with a three-ton body and a ten-ounce brain."[146] Economies must glory not in the widening that adds more food and goods but in the "pure deepening that adds to aggregate leisure." Being liberated from our ancestors' hard labors allows us to devote more time and energy to the cultural overhead. "All the functions of the primary and secondary rhythms are integral to the universal progress."[147] Culture is all too often overlooked in economics although it is essential to the rhythms of economic transformations. Nor will it "suffice to have some highest common factor of culture . . . to have the physical sciences but not bother with their higher integration on the plea that this is too difficult, too obscure, too unsettled, too remote."[148]

Lonergan's Use of Mathematics in his Writings on Economics

Consider again, the suggestive description DA $\to$ DA'+DA'' of *CWL* 21. It expresses Lonergan's theory as a mathematical differentiation.

---

145. *CWL*. 21, 19–20.

146. *CWL*, 21, 20. The titanothere *Megacerops* was the largest of the Brontotheres, (large ungulates, or animals with hooves living in North America 50 million years ago).

147. *CWL* 21, 21.

148. *CWL* 21, 21.

Acceleration can be described either as "going faster" or (in Leibniz notation) as a second-order derivative:

$$a=\frac{\delta^2 x}{\delta t^2}$$

The equation means that acceleration or the change in speed is equal to the change in distance divided by the length of time squared. In high school, students learn that an object falling in the air goes faster and faster at the rate of roughly 9.8 meters (32 feet) multiplied by the length of time multiplied by itself (minus the drag or friction of the air). The above equation works equally well for "going slower." In a way, Lonergan's economic theory describes economic terms as "going faster or slower" using the formula $a=\frac{\delta^2 x}{\delta t^2}$. To explain his reasoning requires some exposure to further equations, which we attempt to keep at a minimum in the main body of our text.

What is it that "goes faster or slower"? Lonergan often referred to flows or rates of "so much every so often," that is, flows of money within the exchange economy, as well as to goods and services that are created, sold, delivered, but move out of the economy.[149] Humans have immediate needs: food and drink, shelter, adequate clothing, education, health-maintenance, and amusements. The economy provides these; it supports the procreation and nurture of children and ensures their survival. The goods and services of the productive process affects the standard of living; they are direct "improvements upon nature, increasing its power and efficacy. Through this increased power and efficacy, "they affect the standard of living by . . . increasing the supply of consumer goods and services."[150] The surplus economy has the same overall aggregate of rates as the basic—with allowances made for production errors and lags. But, because its products do not enter into the basic stage, it is only indirectly related to the standard of living, being composed of successive stages of production. The example we gave of a ton of ore illustrates that the standard of living is consumer to the basic stage, which

---

149. However, a used car can be resold; it thus reenters the economy. See *CWL* 15, 45.

150. *CWL* 15, 22. "Since the form of the relation between them is a double summation, the emergent standard of living and the basic state of the process are not identical aggregates of rates." See *CWL* 15, 42.

is consumer to the lowest surplus stage, which is consumer to the next stage, and so on. "Producer goods and services are . . . consumed by producers. Not passengers but railway companies consume rolling stock and rails. Passengers consume transportation."[151]

Differentiating the Pure Cycle from the Trade Cycle

We discussed earlier the "widening" and "deepening" in productive processes. These correspond to "short-term" and "long-term" accelerations of the whole process. A short-term acceleration may happen when existing capital equipment is utilized more effectively, when labor and management duly cooperate, or when existing stocks decrease. It is when deepening begins to happen primarily through innovation that a long-term acceleration becomes possible. When the basic stage acquires more and better equipment from the lowest surplus stage, and its demand is strong enough, all the successive stages begin to produce more and in improved ways: there ensues a type of *transformational wave* of the capital equipment in the whole economy, basic and surplus. The wave is not only cyclical: in its wake everything adjusts itself. Labor is transformed, people move about, retrain for new jobs; they can change professions. This leads to an increase in the standard of living. The wave then settles down. This movement throughout the whole economy Lonergan calls "the pure cycle"—not to be confused with the trade cycle which is, "the successions of booms and of slumps, of positive and then negative accelerations of the process."[152] *The heart of the matter is* Lonergan's contention that there is a pure cycle "at the root of the trade cycle."[153] The trade cycle is a general movement of expansion marked by lags in

---

151. *CWL* 15, *Macroeconomic Dynamics*, 32.

152. *CWL* 15, *Macroeconomic Dynamics*, 35.

153. For mainstream neoclassical economists, the trade cycle was the norm. Depressions were 'explained' as a consequence of a prior boom. Even Schumpeter, an exceedingly talented and creative economist, accepted the inevitability of the cycle. On the other hand, Marxist economists regarded periodic recessions and depressions as the inevitable series of crises that lead to the eventual breakdown of the capitalist machine. See Michael Shute, *Lonergan's Discovery of the Science of Economics*, 1.

accelerations: surplus expansion, then basic expansion, and then a proportionate expansion of both.[154]

Lonergan summed up his meaning of a trade cycle in a 1979 paper:

The trade cycle:

Exaggerates the surplus expansion phase into booms, thus reducing the basic expansion to a slump leaving a notable proportion of the population in the state of unemployment. The exaggeration into booms follows from the "one precept" of classical economics: "thrift and enterprise" implying that most firms can make a profit for a while; everyone does their best to get into the act.

The transformation of the surplus expansion into a slump is due to the fact that the thrift precept works less and less well, as the above-normal profit, the "social dividend," as Schumpeter called it, has to shift from anti-egalitarian tendency of the surplus phase to the egalitarian tendency of the basic phase.[155]

Lest the pure cycle degenerate into yet another trade cycle of boom and slump, humans have to make some adaptive decisions. At the time when the Soviet Union was still extant, Lonergan wrote that the "free economies of the present day are over-adapted to the surplus expansion, which they exaggerate into booms, and under-adapted to the basic expansion, which they then convert into slumps."[156]

For Lonergan the meaning of such terms as supply, demand, profit and redistribution are set within a theoretical construct of a "pure cycle"

---

154. See Arthur F. Burns and Wesley C. Mitchell, "Measuring Business Cycles," National Bureau of Economic Research, 1946, 3.

155. *CWL* 15, *Macroeconomic Dynamics*, 115, note 148.

156. *CWL* 15, 115. While discussing the occurrence of the "final crash," and lack of a recovery, Lonergan writes that the triple crisis per cycle may "correspond" to how Schumpeter combines the three small Kitchin cycles in a larger cycle named a Juglar with a ten-year period. The pattern of six Juglars in one sixty-year Kondratieff would seem to result from the quasi-logical connection between successive long-term accelerations," eventually leading to a "fundamental transformation of the capital equipment of an economy," *CWL* 15, 162. Kondratieff's "long waves" mean that economic cycles come in regular waves ("K-waves"). See www.researchgate. net/publication/294086817_Kondratieff_Waves_Juglar_-_Kuznets_-_Kondratieff

of economic activity. His theoretical construct includes a basic consumer cycle of economic activity in addition to a surplus productive cycle inaugurated by new ideas that spark entrepreneurial activity and the creation of pure surplus income.[157] Pure surplus income, often erroneously identified as "profit," *can only play a socially beneficial role if it is oriented towards the final goal* of expanding the basic consumer cycle—thus *raising the standard of living*. It will be helpful to illustrate our meaning in figures 1 to 6.[158]

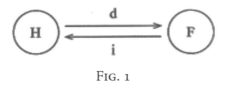

FIG. 1

Fig. 1 represents a type of diagram that is a basic fixture of economic texts. But it hides a problem. You can see the essential relationship between households H and firms F. The firms provide an income i which engenders a demand d. This is the basic economy of goods and services that we all depend upon, and it sets the *standard of living*. For example, households find honey desirable for all sorts of reasons, and beekeepers launch firms to fulfill that desire. But honey-producing firms F also require goods and services to make them viable. They build and maintain hives, retrieve honey, clean and bottle it, and take it to market. Besides the firms that furnish hives to beekeepers, there are firms that supply combs for the bees' incubators, bottles for the honey. And there are the few firms that build the hive-making and bottle-making factories. The bees, their domesticators, and their customers form part of a productive process which has a basic rhythm of so many bottles of honey sold every so often at a certain price. The process also depends on the dynamic structure of the hive-and-bottle-makers also selling every

157. Lonergan's notion of surplus income differs from Marx's use of surplus value as an exploitative mechanism. It is what Schumpeter called "the social dividend." Our "twin theory-ethical-praxis sandwich" addresses this issue.

158. See Pierre Whalon, "Desperately seeking a macroeconomic theory that works," Dec.6, 2017, https://www.huffpost.com/entry/ lonergan-economic-theory_b_1185449

so often at a certain price. They are *part of the secondary economy* that depends in turn on the firms building their factories and furnishing the machines, selling every so often at a certain price and finally firms that furnish the raw materials for both activities that supply multiple producers of other goods. This secondary economy is the "surplus economy" diagrammed in fig. 2:

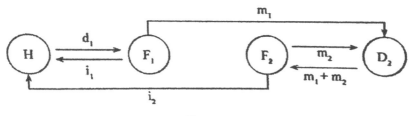

FIG. 2

In Figure 2, m_1 stands for the need for e.g., replacements, which creates demand D_2 for the firms F_2 providing the necessary goods and services for the producers of the basic economy's goods and services, e.g., honey. Let m_2 fill the same need for F_2, and $m_1 + m_2$ be the sum of what F_2 firms need to provide. In fig. 2, i_2 is the income that F_2 firms provide for households H.

Fig. 2 may be more meaningful if we re-shuffle it to arrive at figure 3 on "How Money Changes Hands":

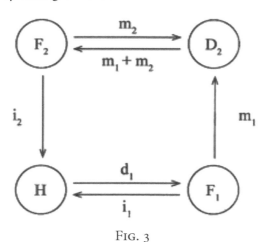

FIG. 3

Money changes hands, so much every so often, in different markets at different rates depending on the segment of the productive process—basic or surplus.[159] There are qualities and quantities of goods and services produced and sold at different rates along the process. A good is changed from its natural state through manufacturing thus turning raw materials into a finished product such as a bottle of honey. When the bottle is purchased, it leaves the process.

Exchanges in an Economy and Classes of Payments

We turn to discuss classes of payments, their cost, and the ratio of money to quantity of goods or services. Money circulates as payments are made. Consumers (H) buy (d_1) from shopkeepers (F_1); shopkeepers buy (d_1) from wholesalers: wholesalers buy (d_1) from beekeepers (F_1); beekeepers buy (D_2) from bottle-hive-and-technical equipment manufacturers (F_2); manufacturers buy (D_2) from various furnishers of raw materials. In fig. 3, firms 1 and 2 pay income to H; i_1 designates the income of H from F_1, what firms in the basic stage pay their employees. i_2 is the income paid by F_2 firms to their employees in the surplus stages which then enters into the standard of living.

All these payments are essential to the production of honey: they are called "*operative*" payments. They occur repeatedly at regular intervals as long as the process is maintained. The volume of honey trade determines whether the payments increase, decrease or stay the same. "They are the index of its prosperity as also of its misery. They provide the one common measure of all its elements, a measure that is intrinsic to the [honey trade] as completed."[160] One unusual feature of our example is that the "exchange economy" of the blossoms and the bees provide

---

159. Appendix D outlines the redistributive function (RF) as adapted to our encompassing GEM-FS approach. It suggests how the RF is key to economic justice and how it fits in to the productive process. The RF insists with Pigou on the need for fair redistribution of goods within and among nations. RF is key to the circulation of money in an ethical economics.

160. *CWL* 15, 41.

the essential raw material for free.[161] It is people who set up the entire process from there. The only reason it exists is that people like to eat honey, cook with it, sweeten foods, distill it into mead, etc. However, the demand for it will always be secondary to the demand for foodstuffs that actually maintain life.

This illustrates the complexity of our needs, real and felt. *Real* needs are the basis for every economy in human history. *Felt* needs exist at the invisible border between an economy and its superseding culture; advertisers make a living exploiting and creating them. Our illustration is meant not so much to detail the particularities of the honey trade as to suggest an economy's essential structure. The standard of living is the direct result of the basic stage, and the indirect result of the surplus stages. The standard of living is also the measure of economic justice as we have defined it, that is, an economy that enables all the members of society to be actors in it, not only to survive but to thrive. This does not mean that this will end the divides between rich and poor, but that the levels of inequality will not be as outrageously high as they are now. As we shall see, investment is at the heart of economic justice.

Payments within the productive process are not just *operative* in either the basic or the surplus stages. They can also be *redistributive*. These are for durable goods that are resold, either in a one-off exchange or in an organized secondhand trade. In such cases, traders provide the goods they have collected in various ways. They receive a redistributive payment for the cost of the goods, since those have left the productive process. They make their living from the mark-up; this means that part of the payment is operative.

The most important types of exchanges are financial ones, when sums of money are paid for or received. If they are equal, the payment is redistributive: it is not part of the productive process. If they are not equal, as in a bank loan, then the payment of principal is redistributive

---

161. As noted, beekeepers also receive income from renting hives to farmers; this would enter into a more complex scenario than we are addressing at present.

and the payment of interest is operative—for the banking service rendered. This applies also to the sale of real estate, which is redistributive except for the agent's payment. Beyond the initial investment (a topic we examine below), sales of stocks, bonds and other financial instruments are redistributive. We now need to add to our initial diagram the stepwise movements of payments, not only among the four functions by adding the *redistributive function* RF, and the maintenance costs M. Let "D_1" replace "H" since consumer demand is wider than just that of households. Let 'f'' and 'f''' indicate incomes (replacing "i_1" and "i_2"). Further, notice that incomes f' and f" are reduced by maintenance costs M_1 and M_2.

Figure 4 is a more complex graphic representing exchanges in an economy. It is *a "snapshot" at time* t:

From lower left, counterclockwise:

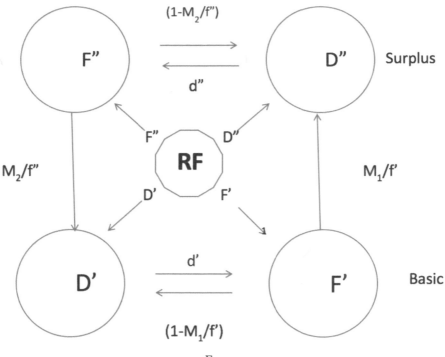

FIG. 4

D' = consumer demand

F' = basic firms

d' = consumer demand

f' = salaries

M_1 = maintenance expenditures of basic firms

D" = basic firms' demand

d" = surplus demand

M_2 = maintenance expenditures of surplus firms

f" = salaries within surplus firms

F" = surplus firms

M_2/f"= income to consumer (e.g., wages from surplus firms into base economy)

RF = redistributive function activities

Fig. 4 shows schematically the two crossover flows of monies in a productive process at time t, in a closed economy (i.e., no foreign trade, deficit government injection of monies, or taxes).[162] The RF refers especially but not exclusively to finance's role; a productive "so much every so often"[163] takes place in a wider context. Savings, loans and lines of credit, dividends, rents, interest, royalties, resale or secondhand markets, stocks, bonds, in short, all exchanges that take place outside the productive process fall in the redistributive process. It should now be clear that the basic and surplus stages are connected by two crossover flows of goods and services and money, "so much every so often." Lonergan's model distinguishes two circuits in the production cycle: a basic circuit which directly supplies goods and services for the standard of living and

---

162. The schema is virtually the same used in Terry Quinn and John Benton, *Economics Actually: Today and Tomorrow. Sustainable and Inclusive*, 17. Phil McShane helped us (and Quinn and Benton) create our schemas. See McShane's *Economics for Everyone: Das Jus Kapital* (Vancouver: Axial Publishing, 2017), 56–67. Lonergan's own diagram appears in *CWL* 21, 258. See also "A history of the diagram," *CWL* 15, 177–202.

163. A quantity in a given time, a flow interrelated to rates *within a cycle*.

a surplus circuit which sets up and maintains the means of production. It differentiates the production from the redistributive function in the economy. It establishes a new notion of dynamic equilibrium located in the ratio of crossover flows between the two circuits. [164]

A. C. Pigou's Pleas for some Redistribution of Wealth

In his *Economics of Welfare*[165] and other writings, Pigou, vigorously urged economists to address the problems of poverty. He insisted that the complicated analyses economists make of the dire poverty afflicting many are "instruments for the bettering of human life." The misery

---

164. https://functionalmacroeconomics.com/explanatory-macroeconomics-relevant-in-any-instance lays out crucial notions of Lonergan's economics. In the always-current, purely dynamic, objective economic process, there are two sets of general, purely-relative, and always-relevant primary relativities. The first set regards a) the double summation of quanta of production in outlays, b) the pattern of lagged acceleration (lag between the net investment decision and the acceleration of output) in the productive process to which the corresponding monetary flows are joined, and c) the explanatory interdependencies among monetary flows represented by the channels and nodes in the diagram of rates of flow." The terms and relations of the primary monetary relativities "are symbolized in algebraic equations, the upper-case symbols represent rates . . . i.e., velocities of so much or so many every so often, d/dt and $\Delta/\Delta t$." *The Diagram is a* double-circuited, credit-centered one. The immanent intelligibility of the process is the interrelations among rates of interdependent functional flows. "Functional" is a technical term pertaining to the realm of explanation, theory; it does not mean "who does what" in some commonsense realm of activity." Rather, it identifies the contemporary notion of a "function" as a basic kind of implicit definition—one that specifies "things in their relations to one another." The basic terms are rates of productive activities and rates of payments. The objective of the analysis is to discover the underlying intelligible and dynamic (accelerative) network of functional, mutually conditioning, and interdependent relationships of the rates to one another. A second set of primary relativities specifies intelligibilities immanent in an expansion, that is, the differentials explaining how the pure cycle of expansion works out over time. It treats the cycles of basic income, pure surplus income and the aggregate basic price spread. *CWL*, 15, 26–27; 76–81.

165. Pigou, London: MacMillan, 1920; for a facsimile: http://pombo.free.fr/pigou1920. pdf. By "welfare" Pigou meant what we would call now "well-being." Pigou's influence continues to this day. See e.g., Ian Kumekawa, *The First Serious Optimist: A.C. Pigou and the Birth of Welfare Economics*, (Princeton Univ., 2017). Gregory Mankiw invites people to join the Pigou Club: "Smart Taxes: An Open Invitation to Join the Pigou Club," *Eastern Economic Journal* (2009) 35, 14–23. https://scholar.harvard.edu/files/mankiw/files/smart_taxes.pdf

surrounding us . . . the luxury of wealthy families . . . are evils too plain to be ignored. . . . It is possible that they be restrained."[166]

John Kenneth Galbraith's theory of the "dependence effect" in his *The Affluent Society* provides a way to rescue Pigou's argument for wealth redistribution from a powerful objection.[167] For Alexander Douglas, this means that "The objection is based on the unprovability of statements making interpersonal comparisons of utility. Galbraith's dependence effect theory allows him to present a version of the Pigouvian argument that requires no such statements to be made." Douglas argues that "Galbraith's main piece of advocacy in *The Affluent Society* was for income redistribution, despite the fact that he claimed to be in favor of greater spending in the public sector rather than redistribution as such."[168] Douglas then shows how his reading of the dependence effect theory helps defend it against objections from Hayek and Rothbard. He ends by discussing what improvements in economics a proper test of the theory would require and showing how his reading of it helps reveal the ongoing importance of *The Affluent Society* to the understanding of political economy. Mark Thoma, for his part, has noted that "There has been a lot of support for the ideas that Pigou (successor of Alfred Marshall at Cambridge University) set forth in his book *The Economics of Welfare*. Thoma asks whether Pigou fans—enthused about Pigouvian taxes—[169] will also endorse his argument for redistributing income from the rich to the poor:

It is evident that any transference of income from a relatively rich man to a relatively poor man of similar temperament, since it enables more intense wants to be satisfied at the expense of less intense

---

166. Pigou, *Economics*, vii.

167. Pigou's welfare book sought to explore the effects of economic activity upon the total welfare of society and its various segments.

168. Alexander Douglas, *European Journal of the History of Economics*, "Contrived desires, affluence and welfare, J. K. Galbraith's Pigouvian redistribution argument reconsidered." Vol. 23, 2016, Issue 4.

169. A Pigouvian tax is a tax on any market activity that generates negative externalities. It is meant to correct inefficient market outcomes by being set equal to the external marginal cost of the negative externalities—including private cost and external cost.

wants, must increase the aggregate sum of satisfaction. The old 'law of diminishing utility' thus leads securely to the proposition: Any cause which increases the absolute share of real income in the hands of the poor, provided that it does not lead to a contraction in the size of the national dividend from any point of view, will, in general, increase economic welfare.[170]

Lonergan's Notion of Redistribution of Income Differs from David Harvey's and Chris Hedges' More Radical Redistribution Notions

In the Marxist view, a redistribution of income or wealth cannot resolve the fundamental issues of capitalism—only a transition to a socialist economy[171] can do so. We have touched on the radical notion of Chris Hedges' criticism of neoliberalism. Hedges was influenced by David Harvey who has written on "accumulation by dispossession (ABD)" which refers to the "continuation and proliferation of accretion practices" that Marx had designated as "primitive accumulation." Harvey sought to update this Marxian theory by considering the ways in which dispossession occurs in capitalist practice. But Harvey's view of ABD has been rejected as being mistaken and chaotic.[172] Lonergan's notion is altogether different—more in tune with Pigou's notion. It is a logical component of what we name "his own GEM-FS approach" to the two circuits in the production cycle as in indicated, e. g., in our fig. 4 and 5.

170. Mark Thoma "Pigouvian Redistribution," Nov. 2006, https://economistsview.typepad.com

171. Lonergan's economics is not about capitalism or socialism, but about the laws binding any economy; the surplus phase was anti-egalitarian, as much in Communist Russia as it still is in today's socialist countries.

172. See https://roape.net/2018/03/19/imperialist-realities-vs-the-myths-of-david-harvey/

Lonergan's Focus on the Productive Process

Economics today focuses on capital's marginal efficiency. This allows both market theorists and Marxists to push aggressive agendas that neglect self-transcendence. Lonergan offers a way to avoid people's marginalization. He remaps ideologies that short-circuit ethical approaches to economics. Our own hope is that economists and ethicists cooperate in addressing the need to go beyond marginal efficiency. Socialists would rein in market ideology with collective projects in which many participate as something constructed by their own energies and belonging to them. Socialist planning, which sets social priorities, "would have to be a part"[173] of such collective projects. As the economy cannot really be a project, since economies are compounds of elements of progress, decline and recovery.[174] Lonergan analyzes these elements and develops grounded norms to order the elements; still, it is easier to generalize about "universal order"[175] than to carry it out! Lonergan helps us see how skewed econometrics' use of statistical and mathematical analyses can be. He argues that in setting economic policy such analyses only play a subsidiary role. For instance, Wassily Leontief's input-output model has only limited usefulness in dynamic periods when final products are shifting rapidly. Lonergan partly offsets this limitation by going beyond the price mechanism. Focusing on a long-term acceleration in

---

173. Frederic Jameson in "Postmodernism and the Market" in Zizek, ed., *Mapping Ideology*, 295. David Bentley Hart in *Commonweal*, July 16, 2021, reflects on Peter Sloterdijk's view that Christians should live in a world "after God"—one in which modern culture has lost the encompassing horizon of ultimate meaning that formerly shaped and sustained human existence. Without shared meaning in understanding the world, we have lost what Sloterdijk calls "co-immunity" against the historical pathogens that threaten us. But Sloterdijk may be giving too much determinative power to the forces of history. Hart writes, "Christian thought can always return to the apocalyptic *novum* of the event of the Gospel in its first beginning and, drawing renewed vigor from that inexhaustible source, imagine new expressions" of love in its apostolic endeavors.

174. Standard analysis generalizes the correspondence principle Samuelson imported from physics into economics. Lonergan favors Schumpeter's ideas of innovation over Samuelson's notion of optimization. Still, one cannot avoid the need to reconcile Lonergan's treatment of business cycles with the longer cycle of decline, *Insight*, 250.

175. Lonergan, *Insight*, 629.

the production process, he uses "matrices of interdependence" to suggest why we should expect a long-term acceleration to be a massive affair. Such matrices involve the concrete conditions necessary for their implementation.

> Any objective change gives rise to series of new possibilities, and the realization of any of those possibilities has similar consequences; but not all changes are equally pregnant, so that economic history is a succession of time periods in which alternatively the conditions for great changes are being slowly accumulated and, later, the great changes themselves are being brought to birth.[176]

Lonergan combines a set of approximations to the real situation.[177] His economics' normative implications involve an interrelated set of schemes of recurrence. Its terms "form a closed circle in which terms are fixed by their relations, relations fix the terms, and the whole is justified by the degree in which it and its implications are verified."[178] Democratic

---

176. Lonergan, *CWL* 15, 36. Our example of the development of the smartphone and the subsequent growth that continues to follow is consonant with this.

177. *Lonergan's CWL* 15 studies production and money circulation in terms of his notion of schemes of recurrence. Michael Shute uses the scale of value to situate the *Analysis* within the FS. Unlike Nietzsche's eternal recurrence or economists' equilibrium analyses, schemes of recurrence explain what is going forward in actual or potential economic cycles. Part of income *could be* adjusted to the laws of economic structure by way of the RF. This adjustment would be an adaptation of the Church's social justice message and of liberation theologians' agenda. The need is to counter inequalities income while also protecting the environment. Lonergan's economics incorporates a moral perspective that can mediate the conflicting economic theories of Marxists, on the one hand, and of market theorists such as Schumpeter on business cycles, on the other.

178. Lonergan, *Circulation Analysis*, 9. For Peter Burley, "Lonergan, Economics, and Moral Theology," *Method, Journal* 15, Spring 1997, 51–55, Schumpeter's theory of the role of money in a technologically developing economy can be formalized in terms of an evolutive model. Incorporating credit money into that model permits additions to the input-output matrices in a Schumpeter-Lonergan model. "An arbitrary number of fixed capital goods can be accommodated in processes corresponding to a hierarchy of machines making machines. A cluster of innovations can be represented by a set of new processes which become available at a given time. Eileen de Neeve, *Decoding the Economy* (Thomas More Institute Papers, 2008), uses notions of unimaginable particles to mediate and apply the data of consciousness to ethics and economics.

rules can only prevail if economics succeeds in uttering not counsels to rulers, but laws which *We the People* can implement through rationally chosen rules and policies. This goes beyond the price mechanism; money is only an indispensable *means* in adjusting production to monetary flows. GEM-FS's eight-step process method allows us to evaluate an economy's functional circuits so that we may cooperatively remove barriers detrimental to the common good. Like the family, the economy is a dynamic base for human cooperation—one that changes slowly since new common forms of consent take time. The same economic setup can lead to prosperity or to recession. Lest Malthusian population growth wipe out productive gains, a GEM-FS stance on capital flows supports systems of production where investments fluctuate more than consumption goods.

Studying the possibility of a differential acceleration of the various stages of the productive process, Lonergan correlates the dynamics of said stages with the role of money in an exchange economy. Key to this correlation are monetary payments and their classification. Using the basic unit "so much every so often" (a quantity in a given time, a flow interrelated to rates *within a cycle),* Lonergan correlates the complex process of the exchange of various goods and services in terms of flows of payments through a production process' different stages. The productive process and monetary circuits intersect in dynamic ways. Lonergan explains how a uniform expansion in an advanced economy can avoid booms and slumps by correlating *relations* connecting flows of goods to circulations of payments made and received. Classes of payments become rates of payments. The payments stand in the mutual conditioning of an *internal* circulation. From this internal conditioning, there arises an *external* conditioning due to transfers of money from one circulation to another. Lonergan correlates this twofold conditioning with the rhythms of production.

From the foregoing dynamic configuration of conditions during a limited interval of time, he deduces possible types of change in the configuration over a series of intervals. Lonergan envisages any total movement of an economy as a function of variations in rates of payment. The variations define the conditions of desirable movements and deduce the causes of breakdowns.[179] Lonergan classifies goods and services according to *where they stand in production's dynamic chain*—not according to common-sense microeconomic properties.

From Studying Pure Process to the Functioning of an Exchange Economy

Having given an account of the pure economic processes with their two cyclic phases in Chapter Two of *CWL* 21, in Chapter Three Lonergan begins to study an exchange economy. His is a dynamic conception that focuses on the nexus of differentials applicable to any concretely functional economy:

> In this inquiry we are concerned never with what happens to be or to have been, always with abstract generalities, with functional significance, with the pure laws and correlations that are the inevitable structure of an exchange process. The finance of London in 1830 or of New York in 1930 does not concern us, but only the pure purpose or function to be found in both those cases and, as well, in the activity of totalitarian technicians financing a five-year plan. Similarly we are concerned not with the concrete details but with the abstract explanatory residue of significance that underlies property, exchange, value, markets, and money. The result of the inquiry will be knowledge of the pure type of exchange economy.[180]

---

179. GEM-FS can help humanity solve some of its problems in various areas of life—if carried out in full *diphase* GEM-FS fashion. This means that Lonergan's transcendental method should be implemented as a generalized two-phase feedback *process* at the heart of our human knowing-doing operations. This generalized "self-correcting" GEM-FS feedback process is at the core of Lonergan's overall achievement as outlined in our Part III and IV, featuring *MiT*'s two interactive mediating-mediated phases. Both US Fed Chairman Jerome Powel and his counterpart in Europe, Christine LaGarde, have given urgent warnings as to the need of raising interest rates to avoid a recession. Further, the COVID pandemic has affected the planet, making it clear that the world needs global cooperation of the type developed in *MiT*'s diphase procedure. This would require going beyond the profit motive, e. g. by waiving vaccine patents during the emergency.

180. Lonergan, *CWL* 21, 29.

Lonergan's intent is to provide a normative analysis of economic process—normative in the sense of providing a model of a properly functioning economy. His model, having investigated what happens in the recurrent schemes of material production, recognizes that the proper end of these schemes is an emergent standard of living. It distinguishes the rhythms of production from those of finance. It identifies, as crucially important for a well-functioning economy, the need to adapt financial rhythms to underlying production rhythms.

Understanding the Price Mechanism: Correlating DA as Pure Process with the Freedom of Exchange

The flow of goods and services involves two stages whose ratio of DA' to DA" is the functional differentiation of the two circuits of work; this places Lonergan's theory on a unique footing. The present state of mainstream economics pivots on a *fixed notion of one-flow* analysis, symbolized by talk of GNP and GDP. Lonergan's key insight was to identify, after a more than a decade of historical and theoretical work, the historical reality and scientific *fact of two flows*.[181] If economies fail to adjust the rates of activity, the two stages of boom-slump cycles will recur. Systematic profits usually increase in the earlier stages of long-term accelerations of the productive process but fall back to zero in later stages. Slowdowns in long-term acceleration or in profits cause variations in capital's marginal efficiency. Increases or decreases of systematic profits call for corresponding changes in subordinate rates of spending or

---

181. Various thinkers have realized that neither pure forms of capitalism nor of socialism/communism are acceptable, insisting that we must find the right compromise between them—as if all possible options are somewhere on a one-dimensional continuum from capitalism to socialism/communism. So as to move forward, we need to recover what we've lost: the understanding that ethics, politics and economics should not be separated, and that the purpose of business/economic activity is to enable us to achieve goods more important than material wealth. In a way, Lonergan attempted to recover the wisdom of the perennial philosophy that was discarded during the Enlightenment. But some argue that he merely fine-tuned, neo-classical (i.e. capitalist) economics. Even though his point about two flows instead of one may be correct, such naysayers argue that his economics is too much concerned with financial wealth and material goods.

saving. Prices are *not* to be the ultimate norms of economics; "they are merely a mechanism to overcome the divergence of indifferent preferences." Since not all decisions "possess this indifference," the exchange economy must either eliminate itself by suppressing the freedom of exchange or it must augment "the enlightened self-interest that guides exchanges."[182]

A GEM-FS economics helps us understand the price mechanism, and how a pure cycle enables a uniform expansion of an exchange economy. It would avoid boom-bust cycles by not misjudging the various types of systematic profits and by making corresponding changes in subordinate rates of spending needed to adjust the rates of accelerations in production. Traditional theory looks to rates of saving and to shifting interest rates to adjust the productive process; for GEM-FS economics, what a surplus expansion calls for is not simply more saving but a *continuously* increasing rate of saving. The rate of saving must not only be bigger for a surplus expansion; it must consistently increase. Because rates of savings do not equal rates of investment, the relevance to increments in interest rates is not in their intermittence but rather in the increase in interest rates themselves.

Lonergan's economics uses crossover channels to link and interrelate the dynamics of both the productive process and of money circulation. Classes of payments are correlated to rates of payments constructed from the classes. Both of these are linked to the productive process' stages, to analyses of monetary circulation by way of channels. The channels show the conditions under which partial equilibrium can be valid. As distinct but *not* separable from the price mechanism, the channels determine the circulation within which the price mechanism works. They account for such phenomena as booms and slumps, inflation or the distortions of deficit government spending.[183] The channels coordinate a vast, ever-shifting manifold of otherwise independent

---

182. Lonergan, *CWL* 15, 6.

183. Today, too many Americans struggle daily to stay afloat on a sea of red ink, threatened by wave after wave of debt. The phenomenon was aggravated in 1978, when the US economy was sailing into dire straits—due among other causes to the Arab oil embargo, the Vietnam war and stagflation.

choices from supply and demand decisions. Humans are not to be passive cogs within a pricing system but should be autonomous agents, external to it.   .

How Multinational Corporations (MNCs) Impede Social Justice[184]

Identifying the patterns of evolution of the American labor movement, John Commons noted that rules are needed to stem group actions.[185] GEM-FS economics extends Commons' insights to today's global markets. It respects the "Invisible Handwriting" in our hearts as being more basic than Smith's invisible hand. If impervious to that writing, people look not at but through victims, making them "invisible."[186] Economic policy must be conducted in solidarity with the poor, because the presence of poor people means that the economy is not functioning at its greatest efficiency.[187] MNC resources are an unequal match for developing nations or for small farmers. In *The Visible Hand*,[188] Alfred Chandler traced the development of vertically-integrated U.S enterprises that coordinated the flow of goods on global and national scales in the

---

184. Robert Reich, *Saving Capitalism For the Many not the Few*, (Knopf, 2015) argues that to change capitalism we must change the ways the government sets market conditions. This means finding ways to limit multinationals' influence over government. Reich adds that since the 1990's, firms seek to increase profits by keeping wages down. We view Lonergan's economics as being a model. Like relativity: it makes predictions, but those predictions must be verified. Reich's book fits into Foundations. In keeping with our view of FS 4, Reich's macroeconomic theories have an implicit impact on foundations. For us, the overall Lonerganian corpus provides adequate foundations. But implementing FS 5 to economics will depend on actual-and-hoped for possible-and applied ethical GEM-FS imperatives.

185. John R. Commons, *History of Labor in the United States* (NY: Macmillan, 1918).

186. Our biases make us prey to Ralph Ellison's "I-am-an-invisible-man" syndrome.

187. For Matthew Lamb, *Solidarity with Victims: Toward a Theology of Social Transformation* (Crossroad, 1982), Marx's concern for social praxis prefigues Lonergan's efforts to deal with massive economic oppression.

188. Chandler, *The Visible Hand, The Managerial Revolution in American Business* (Harvard, 1977), argues that Smith's "invisible hand" requires his *Theory of Moral Sentiments* to justify it.

historical drift toward mammoth MNCs. As Social Darwinists[189] turned *laissez faire* into antisocial greed, so MNCs have people subordinate their ethical principles in pursuing unlimited growth.[190] By overlooking the complementarity between the subjective and objective criteria of decision-making, they negate our ability to see beyond a drive for profit, "delivering value" to shareholders. They preempt poorer nations' development and make it difficult for their economies to take off.[191] Lobbyists push projects that prop up bloated sectors. Investors focus on quick returns rather than on production for long-term growth. This leads to stagflation, rising national debts[192] and cyclical poverty in poorer nations instead of a pure economic cycle. GEM-FS economics would ward off stagflation by insisting on policies that gauge world supply and demand in equilibrium markets. Its equilibrated production and consumption circuits channel profits equitably[193] while tempering greed.

Leaders of the world religions have encouraged a spirit of living simply. Moral ideals will remain ineffectual if not translated into feasible

---

189. In *The Origin of Species*, *Great Books of the Western World*, 49, p. 7, Darwin writes that having studied "Variation under Domestication," he will "pass on to the variability of species in a state of nature. . . . Unfortunately, I shall be compelled to treat this subject far too briefly." To Darwin's "far too briefly" one can contrast Lonergan's "Species as Explanatory," *Insight, CWL* 3. Chapters 2, 8, and 15 delve into coincidental aggregates, schemes, conjugates, the psychology of animals, man as explanatory genus and species as transition from the intelligible to the intelligent, etc. These are all parts of a larger emergent probability.

190. For John Kenneth Galbraith, *The New Industrial State* (Boston: Houghton Mifflin, 1967) such subordination, common in our "mature corporations," undermines communities' authentic values. Unlike machines, humans evaluate their positions in relation to others, accepting others' goals as their own; see James March & Herbert Simon, *Organizations* (New York: Wiley, 1958), 65.

191. Stephen Haggard, *Pathways from the Periphery* (Ithaca: Cornell Univ., 1990) 21, notes that both the dependency and liberal perspectives ignore how domestic political forces constrain economic policy; they use a normative benchmark to assess government-induced distortions, but overlook what results from underdevelopment itself. The dependency view harbors a determinist strand that downplays the importance of countervailing state strategies.

192. https://www.project-syndicate.org/commentary/kenneth-rogoff-is-convinced-that-economic-recovery-will-require-some-form-of-debt-restructuring-or-rescheduling

193. On seeking to equitably distribute goods today see Diane Saintsbury, *Welfare States and Immigrant Rights: The Politics of Inclusion and Exclusion* (Oxford, 2013).

precepts.[194] If politico-economic interests disregard ideals, GEM-FS economics can help free societies delegitimize unjust "legitimations." But that *presupposes implementing* the second mediated-healing phase of Lonergan's process method. In Part IV, we proceed with GEM-FS' mediated-healing phase based, in part, on Lonergan's dynamic-equilibrium approach to economics at the core of which stand the productive and exchange processes and the redistribution function (RF). We contrast GEM-FS's key insistence on the need of a personal self-appropriation of one's own rational self-consciousness with views defending the "legitimacy" of *Homo Economicus* as motivated only by self-seeking. We can hardly be economically just unless we develop the needed transformational horizons—a very difficult task! [195]

One key for solving such complex problems is the notion of the redistribution function (RF) between the basic and surplus circuits outlined in the "snapshot," and developed further in Appendices D and E. Also to be reckoned with is the distinction between the two cycles affecting group bias and common sense. The shorter cycle is due to group bias. The longer cycle[196] originates in the general bias of common sense. "The

---

194. Lonergan, *CWL 15, Circulation Analysis*, 106. In "Healing and Creating History," 108, he explicitly calls for linking moral and economics precepts by experts in these fields.

195. Does credibility come with authenticity? Being "authentic" is at the core of religion, ethics and GEM-FS. How can a society—even small groups—be "authentic"? Small Christian Communities (SCCs) across the world have been engaged in trying to authentically live the Good News of Jesus within complicated capitalist and even communist lands. Communist regimes make it even more difficult for SCCs to be authentic since they prioritize ideology.

196. Michael Shute in his *Discovery*, 12, notes that "the longer cycle of decline distorts normative economic process." This distortion has harmed the environment, social institutions, and cultural life. "Lonergan provides an adequate foundation for a proper science of economics (which) . . . would dramatically aid efforts to achieve a just economy." His decision to study economics was a strategic choice within the context of his understanding of the Church's 'social mission,' the compelling problem of the day. He foresaw that the general outline of a solution was possible, using the partial insights gathered in the history of economic theory. "The result is the beginning of a science to replace" theories that tended "to make human life unlivable." "The totalitarian has uncovered a secret of power. To defeat him is not to eliminate a permanent temptation to try once more his methods. Those not subjected to the temptation by their ambitions or their needs will be subjected to it by their fears of danger and by their insistence on self-protection. So in an uneasy peace . . . one totalitarianism calls forth another." (*Insight*, 257).

shorter cycle turns upon ideas that are neglected by dominant groups only to be championed later by depressed groups. The longer cycle leads to the neglect of ideas to which all groups are rendered indifferent by the general bias of common sense."[197]

An equally important point to be made as we transit from the mediating phase of a GEM-FS process approach to the mediated phase is that our approach to the second phase is intimately related to our attempt to develop the deeper meaning of a GEM-FS economic which has not been sufficiently pointed out by Lonergan interpreters. We emphasize that GEM-FS process has a reduplicative aspect to it that can enable one to connect or interlink the sciences and humanities with economics and religion. This is due to the fact that Lonergan's process method includes the "hoped-for" aspects of life, not just the reasonable expectations of daily life, but the longer-term outlook that religion has offered mankind throughout the ages. Fig. 5's RF (illustrated in Appendix D) suggests one such possible aspect of a GEM-FS process approach that fosters self-transcending lives and is reinforced by a redistributive function. It is not easy to understand how authenticity can be incorporated within an organized collaboration of individuals—considering the reality that people are subject to various pressures and influences from outside. Lonergan contrasts what he calls the minor authenticity of individual persons with the major authenticity or unauthenticity of the tradition that sustains them.[198] Given an empirical notion of culture, the question becomes, how can a community become authentic in the face of a general cycle of decline? The answer for Lonergan, a man of faith, lies within his heuristic solution to the problem of evil:

> The new and higher collaboration will be, not simply a collaboration of men with one another, but basically man's cooperation with

---

197. *Insight*, 252. We draw the conclusion that to achieve transformative change, it is necessary to initiate GEM-FS-inspired reforms. Being unphilosophical does not mean being unconverted. But conversion is a journey to be made; we are all on different stages in that journey. Human authenticity is never some pure and serene and secure possession. It is ever a withdrawal from inauthenticity, and every successful withdrawal only brings to light the need for still further withdrawals. *MiT*, 106. *CWL* 14, 102.

198. *MiT*, 77. *CWL* 14, 80.

God in solving man's problem of evil. For if men could collaborate successfully in the pursuit of truth that regards human living, there would be no problem, and so there would be no need of a solution. But the problem exists, and the existence of a solution is affirmed because of divine wisdom, divine goodness, and divine omnipotence. It follows that the new and higher collaboration is, not the work of man alone, but principally the work of God.[199]

We cannot achieve a "collective authenticity" simply by human efforts. Whether one is religious or not, one's attitude to this should be one of humility. Such an attitude is part of the presuppositions underlying Part IV (beginning with FS 5), which we shall now develop in terms of the GEM-FS second mediated-healing phase.

---

199. *Insight*, 780.

PART IV

———◦◦▸◦◦———

The Second Mediated-Healing Phase of Lonergan's Process Method.
The Relevance of the Last Four FS to Economics:
Addressing the Harm Done to the Planet[1]

---

1. Part IV is meant to invigorate Lonergan's economics as a partner in renewing society on the basis of a just distribution of goods.

W̲e have alluded to differing macroeconomic theories. In the second phase, beginning with FS 5, we suggest how economists might adopt a GEM-FS approach to their specialty—even though such an approach is more a heuristic than a full-blown theory. This will involve an adequate discernment of GEM-FS's radically-healing potential in the second healing phase. As noted, pure surplus income is what requires the "anti-egalitarian" investment in the surplus economy in order to innovate; once it is exhausted, the basic expansion takes off and the standard of living is raised. Economic justice requires that movements of capital beyond ordinary profit (the accountant's idea of it) be directed toward innovative projects that can help raise the standard of living so as to give everyone an opening to a better life. In Part IV, we deploy the last four FS focusing on non-coercive, foundational democratic measures that could lead to viable economic policies systematically and adequately communicated.

FIFTH FUNCTIONAL SPECIALTY: REINSTATING THE FOUNDATIONS OF ECONOMIC JUSTICE BY BROADENING GEM-FS' TRANSFORMATIVE HORIZONS[2]

Lonergan's macroeconomic field theory provides a solid relational basis for macroeconomics.[3] In FS 5, we seek to justify this claim. We

---

2. Pre-intentional levels of healing emerged long before humans arrived on the scene—a point that we must not forget when addressing economic processes. Technologists tend to ignore this aspect. Lonergan would have us understand the interrelatedness of and the dynamic movements among the FS. Theology is ordered by "a fully conscious decision in foundations about one's horizon . . . , one's worldview. It deliberately selects the framework, in which doctrines have their meaning, in which systematics reconciles, in which communications are effective." *MiT*, 268; *CWL* 14, 251–52. With Lonergan, we invoke the levels of *personal and communal* commitments needed as the foundational reality for transcending previous horizons, even in economics. We shall spell this out on the lines of *MiT*'s second mediated-healing phase which implies a need for apophatic insights.

3. Macroeconomic field theory is a set of invariant relations explaining the formal cause of the double-circuited macroeconomic process, just as electromagnetics is a set of invariant relations explaining the formal cause of the combination of electro-magnetic phenomena. Tad Dunne, https://functionalmacroeconomics.com/page/2/. Each case of stagflation boils down to, or can be explained as, an imbalance of the crossovers between

argue that Lonergan's "GEM-FS economics" provides a new standard model[4] for economics—one that stresses the need for economic justice for all. This might require measures such as adopting a basic income for all, income equality by gender and race, etc. That would be part of the role of the Redistribution Function (RF) we explore in fig. 4 and Appendix D. With Lonergan, we seek a nonviolent approach to social justice, one requiring horizonal transformations.[5] We seek to discern the natural rhythms of economic processes that are part of the larger rhythms of history.

A Need for Economic Reforms in Tandem with Self-Appropriation

Lonergan's contribution to a standard model in economics invites us to work for economic reforms reinforced by intellectual conversion. However, his view of credit-centered double economic circuits has been ignored by economists. It is not yet a factor that could ensure the needed transition to a genuine scientific approach to economics. As a result, at present there is no operative standard model for economics.

---

the basic and the surplus circuits. Whether due to a) dis-equilibrated taxation and spending, b) a rise in oil prices and reduced investments, or c) stimulus flows escaping intended channels, stagflation is a disequilibrium within a set of flows which should be interdependently coordinated. In *CWL* 15, 175, after sketching a particular possible configuration of stagflation, Lonergan adds: "what cannot. . . . be sustained, is for one circuit to be drained by the other. That is the essence of disequilibrium."

4. Michael Shute, "Preparing to Read Economic History Functionally," *Journal of Macrodynamic Analysis*, Volume 10, expresses an approach similar to ours.

5. As did Heinrich Pesch in his *Teaching Guide to Economics*. 5 vols., (Lewiston, NY: Mellen, 2002). Pesch was an ethicist and economist of the Solidarist school. His work is the source of Pius IX's *Quadragesimo Anno* on social justice issues. Influenced by Pesch, in the early forties, Lonergan wrote that he was convinced that to deny the possibility of a new science of economics and new precepts is to deny the possibility of the survival of democracy. Echoing *Quadragesimo*, Lonergan wrote: "What is at stake with economics is the renovation of society." The reconstruction of the social order envisaged in *Quadragesimo* was premised on a properly functioning economy. Lonergan noted that there were "technical matters" in economics independent of the Church's moral authority. Despite the theoretical orientation of his 1944 *CWL* 21, Lonergan's economics emerged out of practical concerns. It was a withdrawal from practicality for the sake of practicality.

A potential turnaround can only happen through a shift in economics affecting local, national and global transactions. Such a shift to a scientific economics would need to adopt a "GEM-FS" generalized empirical method, functionally specialized. As of now, people are still in a sort of fantasyland.[6] "The question is how to move beyond the tyranny of evaluating corporate quarterly reports to a more realistic type of evaluation of sustainable long-term thriving for all, one that reaches out to developing nations?"[7] Lonergan wrote that it was not impossible "that further developments in science should make small units self-sufficient on an ultramodern standard of living to eliminate commerce and industry, to transform agriculture into a super-chemistry, to clear away finance and even money, to make power over nature the only difference between high civilization and primitive gardening."[8] Lonergan thus advocated ways whereby a sound economics could help ensure a viable future for mankind.

Terry Quinn depicts Lonergan's circular-flow economics as the interactions between goods, services and expenditures, on the one hand, and income and labor on the other."[9] Quinn adds:

> One doesn't need to be an economist to know that there is something terribly wrong with mainstream economics. In recent years, world stock markets have been thriving. Yet . . . major chain stores have filed for bankruptcy; nations struggle with international debt; the global arms trade is booming . . . ; there are apparently interminable wars and humanitarian crises; and technologies are being

---

6. Our book seeks to counter fantasylands: it is premised on insights that to some may appear to be a fantasyland. In fact, with Lonergan we seek to promote the good of all.

7. Quoted from Lonergan Archive, File 697, p. 14.

8. *CWL*. 21, 20. Due to the contemporary shift in sensitivities toward the environment, the phrasing "power over nature" should be changed to reflect the new sensitivities.

9. This differs from the current view that the circular flow of income is a model of the economy in which the major exchanges are represented as flows of money, goods and services between economic agents. The flows of money and goods exchanged in a closed circuit correspond in value, but run in the opposite direction. The difference is that the is a latter is a mere instrumental view of the exchange process. Lonergan offers a foundational approach that transcends such instrumentalism to reform economics.

implemented that are destroying the environments on which we depend for our survival.[10]

For Quinn, CEOs prioritize increasing the wealth of shareholders over workers' wages; the reigning circular-flow model of economics is *not explanatory*. The existential questions are "How should wealth be distributed? Do we not need *a plurality* of models? What can we do to help ensure individual and collective happiness? What is a reasonable number of work hours per week? No doubt, greed has been institutionalized in western corporations. A chief executive officer is not asked to think of the well-being of the world's economies nor to help grow jobs and wages. The aim, instead, is to increase the wealth of shareholders.[11]

Interfaces between Governments and What They Should Regulate

While Communist regimes tend to protect their cadres,[12] in a capitalist system, the rich stand to benefit most since they dominate the legal process. Let us cite five examples that illustrate or touch on some of the official policies of Western capitalist countries.

First, recall fictional heroic figures such as Robin Hood and Zorro esteemed for having opposed aristocrats' oppressive laws.

Second, we decry what are known as SLAPP suits (Strategic Lawsuits Against Public Participation). The suits are brought against

---

10. Terry Quinn, "Anatomy of Economic Activity," *American Review of Political Economy* 13(1), 2019. Compare the relentless technological drive with how Walmart and the Walton family are investing billions into new technologies that could radically transform not only Walmart, but everything about the way we live. Walmart is operating a pilot program called "Alphabot" in New Hampshire—a series of autonomous carts inside a warehouse that radically overhauls the world of online grocery shopping.

11. Quinn, "Anatomy of Economic Activity," 3. Quinn's view that "orthodox economics has been causing great damage to world cultures and ecosystems," https:// arpejournal.com/ article/id/157/, lays a basis for the turnarounds in environmental policies we advocate.

12. See Brigitte Stude and Berthold Unfried, "At the Beginning of a History: Visions of the Comintern after the Opening of the Archives," in *International Review of Social History*, Vol. 42, 3, Dec. 1997, 419–46.

individuals who publicly expose industrial wrongs as did Ralph Nader against General Motors in the 1960's. The use of SLAPP by European firms is meant to silence or intimidate their critics who are often of significantly lesser financial means. In one instance, an activist woman in Kosovo was slapped with a fine of 100,000 euros for so-called defamation of a hydropower plant owner.[13] European courts have overwhelmingly backed firms in the nefarious use of SLAPP suits to silence and intimidate those who would expose their malpractices.

Third, finance-dominated capitalism seeks to avoid low interest rates for the wealthy; high interest rates benefiting rentiers[14] should be eliminated.

Fourth, the history of rich countries plundering developing nations is described in a paper that quantifies the drain from the global South to the North through unequal exchange since 1960. The authors, relying on exchange-rate differentials, found that recently the advanced economies of the global North appropriated from the South commodities worth $2.2 trillion. Over a longer period, the drain from the South totaled $62 trillion dollars ($152 trillion in terms of lost growth). Such a drain

> is made possible because rich countries have a monopoly on decision-making in the World Bank and IMF; they hold most of the bargaining power in the World Trade Organization; they use their power as creditors to dictate economic policy in debtor nations . . . Northern states and corporations leverage this power to cheapen the prices of labor and resources in the Global South.[15]

In effect, this allows them to appropriate goods through trade. The authors contend that during the 1980s and 1990s, IMF structural

---

13. A notorious example is that of Daphne Caruana Galizia murdered in Malta in October, 2017 for reporting on the doings of a power plant on that island. Her son said 47 SLAPP suits had been lodged against her.

14. Eckhard Hein and Achim Truger, "Finance-dominated Capitalism in Crisis" in *New Economics as Mainstream Economics*, 190–230. Rentier capitalism is a term used to describe access to properties so as to gain a significant amount of profit.

15. Jason Hickel, Dylan Sullivan, Huzaifa Zoomkawala, "Plunder in the Post-Colonial Era: Quantifying Drain from the Global South through Unequal Exchange, 1960–2001," *New Political Economy*, 30 March, 2021, abstract.

adjustment programs cut public-sector wages, while rolling back labor rights and other protective regulations, all of which cheapened labor and resources. Today, poor countries are structurally dependent on foreign investment and have no choice but to compete with one another to offer cheap labor and resources in order to please the barons of international finance. This ensures a steady flow of disposable gadgets and fast fashion to affluent Northern consumers, but at extraordinary cost to human lives and ecosystems in the South. The authors do suggest some potential solutions. One way to fix this problem would be to "democratize the institutions of global economic governance, so that poor countries have a fairer say in setting the terms of trade and finance." Another, "would be to ensure that poor countries have the right to use tariffs, subsidies, and other industrial policies to build sovereign economic capacity."[16]

Fifth, neoliberalism is distinct from liberalism insofar as it does not advocate *laissez-faire* economic policy. In fact, it is highly constructivist; it advocates a strong state to bring about market-like reforms in every aspect of society. In the words of Michel Foucault which parallel the views of *CWL* 15, 20, "Neoliberals had to subject classical liberalism to a number of transformations" such as dissociating the market economy from the political principle of *laissez-faire*. Foucault adds that the neoliberal theory of pure competition, "in which competition was not presented as . . . naturally given, as the very source and foundation of society (had) to be allowed to rise to the surface and be rediscovered." For neoliberalism, competition was a structure with formal properties. "It was these formal properties of the competitive structure that assured, and could assure economic regulation through the price mechanism . . . Neoliberalism should

---

16. *Al Jazeera*, 6 May, 2021, commented that "achieving these goals will not be easy: it will require an organized front among social movements toward a fairer world, against those who profit so prodigiously from the status quo." Here we note that we place this report on plunder and exploitation in FS 5 rather than in FS 6 on policy because of the further problem that the elite of developing nations profit from this reality. The issue becomes a foundational one requiring a change in ethical behavior by those who profit from a system of politically and economically built-in preferential systems.

not therefore be identified with *laissez-faire*, but rather with permanent vigilance."[17]

With Lonergan, we are concerned with those excluded from having a say about their destiny within the global economy. GEM-FS stresses ethics and faith-inspired spiritualities rather than divisive beliefs[18] or ideologies that dominate the thinking and acting of many governments across the globe. Faith and love are gifts we have to acknowledge so as to keep us humble.

Examples of Lonergan's Scientific Two-Circuit Approach to Economics

In *CWL* 21, Lonergan outlines his scientific approach to economics. He pays attention to the fundamental aspects of any human economy, insisting that there are always two economies, not just one, in play. The one we all participate in is the basic economy of selling and buying goods and services. The second distinct surplus economy is that of producing the means for those goods and services. Since mainstream economists rarely pay attention to this fact, they usually cannot account for the total reality of any economy. One exception is Schumpeter,[19] who did not develop his insight.

> In reality, there are always two economies, two types of firms, two interrelated processes that move at differing rates or velocities. Indeed, accelerations and decelerations are indicative of booms or busts. Each economy functions on the basis of equal exchanges:

---

17. Michel Foucault, "The Birth of Biopolitics: Lectures at the College de France, 1978–1979." (New York: Palgrave Macmillan, 2010).

18. Lonergan, *MiT*, 119, *CWL* 14, 119, implicitly relies on Wilfred Cantwell Smith's distinction between beliefs and faith. Faith is oriented to the mystery of love; it can unite believers in different creeds—transcending divisive beliefs.

19. Joseph Schumpeter, *The Theory of Economic Development*, (New Brunswick, NJ: Transaction, 2012), 16: "It is usual to classify goods in 'orders,' according to their distance from the final act of consumption. Consumption goods are of the first order, goods from combinations of which consumption goods originate are of the second order, and so on, in continually higher or more remote groups."

selling and buying, or income and expenditure. Expenditures also occur at each stage in the parallel productive processes, but income only comes at the final stage when the finished product or service is purchased. Expenditures include not only raw materials and implements but also utilities, maintenance, wages, and taxes. Producers' expenditures are spread over time at each stage, and there is always a series of lags with revenue. Yet, the process outlined in the DA = DA′ + DA″ formula leaves us with two difficulties: the lack of an effective science of economics, and an out-of-control finance sector.[20]

Lonergan's Insistence on the Concrete

Lonergan insisted that one must always attend to the concrete since that is where we live our lives. We alluded to the honey business. Phil McShane asked people to imagine a "Spud Island" which depends on growing potatoes.[21] Its small economy also involves a schematic cross-over flows of monies in a productive process—although it is a theoretical closed static system, like our "snapshot at time t." On the island, a woman wants to improve her potato-farm's production with a horse and spade. A banker hears of her plan. He believes in the planned project and the farmer herself. He lends her the needed money. As her firm works out a design for a plow, leather-and-metal-working production expands; earnings are up. But for a while increased production of potatoes and other crops lags behind. The surplus economy is heating up; the basic economy hasn't surged ahead yet. It catches up some time later as the surplus growth calms down (enough plow-making equipment is now available) and the plow-production increases as farmers buy plows. Then that levels off as well. Related industries that repair and replace equipment get a boost. Plow retailers spring up. Horse-breeders profit. Farmers increase output of all their crops, allowing them some leisure for improving their

---

20. Pierre Whalon, "To Help the Poor," Academia, June 2015. https://www.academia.edu/19555839/To_help_the_poor. In effect, when the finance department controls a firm, the firm may be on its way to extinction. It must be avoided at all costs through monetary and fiscal policies that the global economy become prey to irresponsible financial dealings.

21. McShane, *Piketty's Plight*. His *Economics for Everyone* alludes to a similar example but much more diffusely.

crops' quality. Hopefully each phase has occurred in such a way that all islanders are better off. But in the short term there will be ups and downs in income, and things can go badly.

The first period's new income flowing into consumer purchases that simply raises the cost of producing potatoes (or other short-circuiting of the island economy), can happen. Here is where intelligent, democratic regulatory and financial processes are needed to achieve concomitance in both economies, surplus and basic. Two noteworthy aspects about the imaginary Spud Island are that first, innovation will create an increase in the standard of living of all the Spud Islanders, if it can proceed from surplus economy expansion to basic economy expansion to leveling off. Income inequality is not eliminated, but the poorer citizens[22] benefit significantly as well, and not just because a rising tide lifts all. Second, the role of credit here is richer than is the case with typical economic textbooks.

Credit is a promise (from the Latin *credere*, to believe), just as money itself is basically a promise. It denotes the real implication of finance, a central redistributive function, in creating economic activity. This example should make it clear that the success of the plow-woman and her collaborators means coming up "with credit needs that are related to the best aggregated turnover in reference to the island's requirements."[23] This means learning how to fine-tune production *turnover* with the minimum necessary credit. The fact of turnover—"so much every so often"— is rarely addressed in economic textbooks. But the matter is intensely practical: how many plows to manufacture, and how often?

Spud Island helps exemplify one aspect of Lonergan's scientific economics. The bank's credit implies a willingness to share the risk; the banker *trusts* the plow-woman enough to take a chance on her ability to repay based on the potential value of her invention. The funds it

---

22. We argue that the "nuts and bolts" of Lonergan's economics lead to questions of justice; some people will have to accept the growth of pure surplus income in that stage. We want to convince them that the purpose is not to "rip off" the poor, but to prepare for a much larger expansion in the standard of living, which is the "generous hand" Lonergan addresses. See *Going Beyond Essentialism*, ed. Cloe Taddei Fratelli. Istituto Italiano per Gli Filosofia, Naples, 2012.

23. McShane, *Plight*, 50.

extends seem to come from the savings of the Spud Islanders, but this is only apparently so. In fact, modern banking has not depended on loaning actual cash reserves for centuries. In our example, the actual risk the bank takes is crediting the woman's account by simply increasing the number of units of currency in her account. The bank adds a corresponding debit on its balance sheet. The risk is that it may be forced to call the loan prematurely. If the bank were a modern private commercial bank, the loan would be funded by creating the money. While central banks issue banknotes and coins (tangible instruments of trust), commercial banks are licensed to create money when they extend credit. This does not depend on cash reserves which are hardly ever loaned out or spent down.

Exemplifying Lonergan's Two-Circuit Economy and "Turnover"

The issue of turnover is rarely treated in economics textbooks.[24] In his *Economics for Everyone*, Phil McShane gives an example of a lawn-mower factory owned and operated by a woman named Hannah.[25] When Jane goes to Rhoda's lawn and garden shop, she pays $1600 for one of Hannah's machines. This is the exit of that particular mower from the productive process.[26] But that $1600 final payment includes a whole lot of payments, initial and transitional, enabling Rhoda to buy her stock from William's Wholesale Supplies, who buys machines from Hannah.

We imagine Hannah's factory to be completely (but quite improbably) vertically integrated: she makes every component of her mowers: rubber wheels; steel bodies, ball bearings, and blades, aluminum engine blocks, and so on. She has capital outlays first for her factory building and assembly line, and then machine tools, which all require maintenance, repair and replacement. For every mower made she has to buy semi-finished steel, aluminum, plastic, etc., from suppliers. Those firms

---

24. See McShane, *Plight*, 51ff.

25. McShane, *Economics for Everyone* (Vancouver: Axial, 2017), 139–51.

26. It exits the process, but the mower could return to the redistributive function if it is resold secondhand.

had to buy ore, bauxite, petroleum, etc., from extraction companies. Her initial capital came from her savings and a bank loan. Every month she has to make payroll for herself and her employees, and pay for electricity, water, natural gas, various insurances on her factory and employees, including herself. And she has to make monthly payments on her loan, both principal and interest, and maintain the bank line of credit that makes up for the inevitable lags between payments and income that are the most basic credit needs of any enterprise. Finally, she has to make up for errors in production, late arrival of materials, etc. Let us simplify further, specifying that Hannah estimates she needs to make 10 lawnmowers a week on average—this is her *frequency of turnover*. If it takes four weeks to make one machine, then at the end of one week, she has ten finished, ten three-quarters finished, ten half-done, and ten just begun. Her *magnitude* of turnover is therefore forty. She estimates that four weeks per mower is the shortest turnover frequency she can afford: if each took eight weeks to construct, she would need twice as much circulating capital, i.e., pay more to the bank at the end of the turnover.[27] For every mower made she has to buy semi-finished steel, aluminum, plastic, etc., from suppliers. Those had to buy ore, bauxite, petroleum, etc., from extraction companies.

When she began her business, Hannah had first envisioned selling her mowers at a factory outlet. But that would have required a storefront and a place to store the production in the off-months of fall and winter when no one buys mowers. Making a deal with William's Wholesale reduced but did not eliminate those costs, since Hannah has to compensate William for his purchase and storage of items he can't sell during part of the year. So she gets payments from William for every mower she sells him, minus his compensation. William gets payments from Rhoda and other retailer clients. Rhoda is paid by customers; when a machine rolls out her door, the productive process that began with Hannah ends *for*

---

27. McShane, *Plight*, 51. This directly impinges on the quantity theory of money, which is at the heart of the rivalry between monetarists like Milton Friedman and John Maynard Keynes and his followers. Lonergan's analysis takes a different route from both schools, focusing on where the money goes and how fast, rather than to begin with how much. "Follow the money" is not just good criminology.

that mower. So many mowers "every so often," requires a complex series of operative payments: initial payments, transitional payments and final payments.[28] In our example, all three enterprises are in the basic stage, providing both a consumer good and the service of making it available for purchase. Hannah's suppliers of machine tools also have their manufacturing needs, as do the extractor firms which belong to different levels of the surplus stage. As Lonergan points out, machine tools and raw materials can enter either into the basic consumer stage or into the surplus capital stage.[29]

Each of the above three enterprises has a different frequency and magnitude of turnover. Hannah's turnover determines part of both the surplus firms' turnover and a portion of William and Rhoda's turnovers. At each step, the said frequencies are an estimate of consumer demand at a future time. In regard to labor, management and use of capital, all three firms are risking what is in the longer term their very existence on that estimated future, including indirectly the creditors of all those firms.[30] Not merely production, but both production and sales enter into the estimate.

Before generalizing the extract from McShane's homespun example, it will be well to note that if we are to "make the practical economist as familiar a professional figure as a doctor, a lawyer, or an engineer,"[31] then studying economics should include a healthy dose of real-world cases. On this point, Thomas Piketty has argued that economists must give up their "infantile passion for mathematics and speculations that are always theoretical and very often ideological, to the detriment of historical studies and join the other social sciences." Piketty adds that unless they do so they will continue to play with "little mathematical problems of interest only to themselves, which allows them to have an appearance

---

28. See appendix F for the mathematics of circuit acceleration.

29. Utilities such as electrical and gas suppliers are part of both stages. *CWL* 21, 278.

30. In Lonergan's words: "The bookkeepers are wise after the event. But if the entrepreneurs are to be wise, they have to be wise before the event, for their payments precede their receipts, and the payments may equal the receipts but they may also be greater or less, to give the entrepreneur a windfall profit or loss." *CWL* 21, 142.

31. *CWL* 21, 37.

of being scientific while avoiding having to give answers to the more complicated issues of the world which surrounds them."[32] We, too, seek to avoid little mathematical problems of interest only to ourselves.

In order to follow Lonergan's analysis, let us resume our account of Hannah's manufacturing business. Let E_1 stand for Hannah the entrepreneur; she has outlay O_1 per turnover period n, or n *times* O_1, where n is 12 (months/year). For the total enterprises involved, E_i, total outlay will be nO_i. We restrict the problem to the three firms of Hannah, William, and Rhoda, or H, W, and R. Let us assume that total aggregate outlays DO for the three firms equal DE, the aggregate of final sales.

$$DO = DE$$

Hannah has only initial payments—vertically integrated ones:

$$\Sigma n_h O_h{}^{33}$$

William has transitional payments $\Sigma n_w T_w$ to Hannah and receives transitional payments $\Sigma n_r T_r$ from Rhoda:

Rhoda makes transitional payments to William and receives final payments DE:

$$DE = \Sigma(n_r O_r + n_r T_r)$$
$$\Sigma n_r T_r = \Sigma(n_w O_w + n_w T_w)$$
$$\Sigma n_w T_w = \Sigma n_h O_h$$

Thus, total outlay $DO = \Sigma(n_h O_h + n_w O_w + n_r O_r)$

Despite the Σs, one can readily understand that DO does equal DE. (The math is easier than it might seem). The economic reality these

---

32. Piketty, *Capital*, 63. We suspect that some business leaders are willing to detect Government and Wall St nonsense. What Piketty underlines is that economists are not paying attention. (See https:www.academia.edu/19555839/help_the_poor). Piketty's *Une brève histoire de l'égalité* documents in unvarnished detail those economic arrangements (bolstered by cultural approval) that we all deplore. The question is how best empower the poor.

33. (The symbol Σ is the Greek letter for a capital S; it stands for summing up, or summation).

equations represent is quite another matter. The equality depends on maintenance and replacement costs. The issue is whether the crossover flows in this particular production balance—are they concomitant?[34] Not to be forgotten is that there is a factor of indeterminacy in this matter since estimates are not real until they prove to be accurate. Estimates do have a decisive influence as to what drives turnover frequencies and magnitudes. Production is always for the future.

Back to the Pure Cycle: Prices and Quantities

The pure cycle occurs when there is an expansion in both basic and surplus stages, in consumption and production. This "proportionate expansion" is akin to an economy coming out of recession. It corresponds to the "widening" discussed above when more efficient use of production resources in both stages creates a short-term acceleration of the process. However, the expansion will end since there are limits to widening: there are limits to increases in efficiency. Two conditions must hold for further development or acceleration. First, innovation in production of goods and services is necessary; second, new money must enter into the circuits.

> The development of long-term acceleration in the surplus stage and its lag in the basic stage leads to a surplus expansion. The emergence and generalization of a long-term acceleration in the basic stage, together with the impossibility of maintaining the increasing rate of acceleration in the surplus stage, gives a basic expansion.[35]

Here, we are not merely discussing lawnmower businesses; we seek to draw some implications for an overall national economy. We can now state our reason why Lonergan's "radical generalization" is really not so radical. Undoubtedly, a requirement of justice is that a society be able to adapt to the laws of economics so that all its able members can find work; productive members able to work should not only survive but thrive. The reasoning is simple; making it come to pass is anything but

---

34. McShane, *Economics*, 143–44.
35. *CWL* 15, 128; *CWL* 21, 281.

simple. Societies in general do not yet have the intellectual tools that would allow humans to adapt to the underlying realities of economics; our GEM-FS stresses the needed socio-cultural conversions to remedy this lack.

On one level, Lonergan's explanation of the two stages of flows of goods and services and money, each with its demand and supply functions, two crossover circuits along with the redistributive function of banks, stocks, bonds, sinking funds, etc., is an original approach to economics stemming from his engagement with Hayek, Keynes, Kalecki and Schumpeter among others.[36] On another level, Lonergan's intent in measuring the productive process is a heuristic; it is not merely empirical since the kind of statistical analysis necessary to give empirical understandings of the rough-and-tumble dynamics within two interrelated economies is not available. His hope was 1) that his analysis itself would provide some rather convincing indicators; 2) that "as expertise develops the new tricks of a new trade would lead to the discovery of methods of sufficient accuracy for practical purposes."[37] Those practical purposes are not only economic; they have wider, cultural consequences. When a society learns that it can do better not only for the fortunate but for all citizens, the rising tide will finally lift all boats—if the pure cycle is not only respected but implemented. It is nevertheless inevitable that some will still be better off than others due to political limitations, but also, as Marx pointed out, because differences in ability are endemic to the human condition.

We conclude FS 5 by stressing Lonergan's express inclusion of economic growth in *CWL* 15, 21. The surplus and basic phases of Lonergan's

---

36. Eileen de Neeve, "Interpreting Bernard Lonergan's General Theory of Economic Dynamics: Does It Complete Hayek, Keynes and Schumpeter?" *Journal of Macrodynamic Analysis* 5 (2010): 94–113, points out that recently, economists have begun to follow the trail Lonergan laid down (110).

37. Lonergan, *CWL* 15, 72. One wonders what may happen when researchers begin to analyze economic behavior from a fundamental two-stages, two-crossovers model. For a pointer, see, Joshua D. Angrist and Jörn-Steffen Pischke, "The Credibility Revolution in Empirical Economics: How Better Research Design is Taking the Con out of Econometrics" *Journal of Economic Perspectives*, 24, 2 (2010), 3–30. The econometrics "con" is still alive and well; see Imad A. Moosa, *Econometrics as a Con Art: Exposing the Limitations and Abuses of Econometrics* (Northampton, MA: Elgar Publishers, 2017).

pure cycle parallel the view of Schumpeter on booms and a depression. For both men, a surplus phase or expansion is marked by a surplus profit beyond the normal returns to management and other factors of production. The surplus phase requires reinvestment of profits to ensure that the social dividend of extraordinary profit benefits all of society. Lonergan uses the term social dividend in Schumpeter's sense that profits in an expansion are "certificates for future services or goods yet to be produced."[38] Reinvestments of the social dividend are part of the FS 5 foundational context of a GEM-FS economic outlook. The framework of a pure cycle, with its differences between the two phases—expansion in means of production followed by expansion of consumable goods and services—is the key to understanding that redistribution is in large part the role of finance—including its role in economic growth on a basis of justice.

SIXTH FUNCTIONAL SPECIALTY: POLICIES[39] SEEKING JUSTICE FOR ALL

John Kenneth Galbraith left us a cautionary note:

> Regulation and more orthodox economic knowledge are not what protect the individual and the financial institution when euphoria returns, leading on as it does to wonder at the increase in values and wealth, to the rush to participate that drives up prices, and to the eventual crash and its sullen and painful aftermath.[40]

---

38. Schumpeter, 1931, 101. Quoted by Eileen De Neeve, "Interpreting," 102.

39. One may ask 1) how do government across the world create and regulate markets; how do they officially subsidize democratically governed public-sector enterprises? We argue that the Lonerganian corpus provides adequate foundations to do so ethically. It has the transformational potential that could make a difference. Our FS 6 seeks to address the said two policies.

40. John Kenneth Galbraith, *The Essential Galbraith*, edited by Andreas Williams (Houghton, Mifflin, Harcourt, 2001), 249. As we've noted Lonergan was also influenced by Marshall, Schumpeter, John Bates Clark and others in his views on economic policy. We argue that there are Christian, interfaith and mystical facets that inform GEM-FS itself as well as our attempt to apply these perspectives to economics. Overall, Lonergan wanted to modify economic processes for the better. Part of our strategy is to examine how the just noted economists laid paths for Lonergan. Lonergan's notes from the 1940s on Schumpeter

In his first joint address to Congress, President Joe Biden in 2021 laid out his vision for the U. S. He seemed to both echo and challenge Galbraith's cautionary tale when he questioned the forty plus years of politico-economic orthodoxy claiming that government is the problem, while the free market can solve everything. Biden then laid out his policy that contradicts the baseless claims of Ronald Reagan's "trickle-down" economic policy that has never worked. Rather, than help the middle class, Reagan's fanciful "trickling-down" led to enriching corporations and the 1% that owns them.[41] Let us note that since the appearance in 2013 of the original French version of Thomas Piketty's *Capital in the Twenty-First Century*, the theme of inequality has been widely discussed in many parts of the world. Such notable world figures as Pope Francis and Barack Obama have declared inequality to be the defining issue of our time. How to fight it is now an essential topic in electoral debates everywhere—even in many South American countries such as Brazil where the perennial income inequality has begun to decline. Moses Naim recently wrote that "peaceful coexistence with inequality will end." Demands "to fight it will become fiercer and more widespread than they have been since the end of the Cold War."[42] That is, in fact, what has been happening. In recent years, "the *1 percent versus the 99 percent*" became a global catchphrase. In 2012, there were 25 percent more academic articles written about inequality than in the previous year and 237 percent more than in 2004.[43]

---

are transcribed in Michael Shute's *Lonergan's Early Economic Research*. For Lonergan's later use of Schumpeter, see various transcriptions of his lectures in "Macroeconomics and the Dialectic of History," 1979–1982 available in the Lonergan Archives, Regis College Toronto and online at Bernard Lonergan Archives.

41. *Common Dreams*, June 23, 2021, commented on the seeming return to "normal" when Covid-19 was fading—the narrative that the corporate media is selling. "But there's a problem; 'normal' is destroying our planet, threatening our democracies, concentrating massive wealth in a tiny elite group, and leaving billions of people without access to life-saving vaccines amid a deadly pandemic . . . The super-rich have seen their median wealth increase 2824% since 1983, while in some cases paying $0 in taxes."

42. Moses Naim, *The Atlantic*: "Thomas Piketty and the End of Our Peaceful Coexistence," May 19, 2014.

43. Jake Johnson wrote in *Commonweal* August 10, 2021 on an analysis issued by the Economic Policy Institute in early August, 2021 found that CEO pay in the United States rose by a staggering 1,322% between 1978 and 2020—a sharp contrast to the pay increase

The main themes of Piketty's dense tome, *Capital in the Twenty-First Century,* are that economic inequality is the inevitable collateral effect of capitalism, and that if governments do not act decisively to contain it (mostly through higher taxes on wealth and incomes), the crises will steadily grow until they provoke a crash. According to Piketty, inequality grows when the rate of return on capital ("r") is larger than the rate of growth in the economy ("g"); or, in his well-known formulation: inequality grows when "r > g."[44] The book has been praised as an invaluable reconstruction of inequality but criticized inasmuch as it does not correctly assess the causes of inequality: uneven bargaining power, political corruption,[45] globalized labor and capital markets, and the ineluctable progress of technology. Piketty is accused of only waving his hands around the all-important question of whether economic inequality undermines democracy. He says nothing about how much inequality is too much, or which kinds of inequality are the worst—in accessing education, health care, or political power, for instance. Piketty's most well-known work illuminates a vast unexplored landscape but leaves his readers with no compass to navigate it. In his recent *Une brève histoire de l'égalité,*[46] Piketty argues that we need better statistical tools

---

of the typical worker, which was just 18% during that same period. Exorbitant CEO pay is a major contribution to rising inequality. Johnson, *Commonweal,* July 7, 2021, had argued that taxing multinationals at 15% would still leave them facing a lower rate than the average American pays in state and federal income tax.

44. Piketty, *Capital,* chapter 10. Philip McShane, *Piketty's Plight and the Global Future* (Vancouver: Axial, 2015), 50ff, writes that the quantity theory of money is at the heart of the rivalry between such monetarists as Milton Friedman and their followers, and the school of John Maynard Keynes. Lonergan differs from both schools; rather than beginning with the quantity of how much is involved, he focuses on where the money goes, on how fast the funds circulate (note his title of *CWL* 15, *Circulation Analysis*).

45. *The New York Times,* Sept. 19, 2021, recounts how accounting giants craft favorable rules from inside the government. Lawyers of top accounting firms do brief stints in the US Treasury Department, with the expectation of big raises when they return. It cites the example of a woman who worked briefly in the Treasury Department to help write rules on federal tax rates that would benefit her employer to the tune of billions of dollars. She returned to the firm and was promoted to partner. Such revolving-door complicity exploits wrinkles in the U. S. tax regulations system. A question is whether tax laws and Piketty's suggestions could serve as a means to implement the redistribution function.

46. Piketty, *A Brief History of Equality* (Paris: Éditions du Seuil, 2021).

to address environmental and economic crises: "Humans need to live in harmony with nature . . . they also need to have lodging, to eat, to clothe themselves, to have access to culture. And above all, they need justice."[47] Piketty calls for democratic control of the economy, much as did Lonergan. Similarly to Lonergan, he writes that educating people is at the heart of the matter. "Economic issues are too important to be abandoned to others. Citizen appropriation of this knowledge is an essential step in the combat for equality."[48]

Raising the standard of living was Lonergan's main aim of his economics. This presupposes a grasp of new ideas; it needs serious re-education. It is the greatest challenge to the modern economy.[49] In FS 6, we consider Lonergan-inspired policies that could help remedy the problems Piketty has documented. Urgent issues such as changes in the climate also impact upon economic inequalities. This implies that GEM-FS policies must consider parallel solutions to interrelated problems. There are inherent links between attempts to bring about policy changes in the domains of economics and the environment—links that we argue call for policy changes on the economy and the environment. Our book touches on this issue only in an embryonic way.

Lonergan's Revisions of Modern Economists' Views

GEM-FS is an *overlooked* method best suited to address today's many societal dilemmas. We have alluded to Lonergan's perceptive approaches to the dilemmas and to how some of his students have sought to apply his views on said issues. We believe that his efforts parallel those of Michal Kalecki, who according to Joan Robinson explained that "if monopolistic influences prevent prices from falling when wage costs are lowered . . . reduced purchasing power causes a

---

47. *A Brief History*, 43. Our translation.

48. *A Brief History*, 350. Our translation.

49. *CWL* 15, 119. A step in the right direction is the CORE educational project, which emphasizes presenting real-world problems to students. It is also provided gratis. However, the *sine qua non* for empirical data from the two stages and the crossovers between them is still not understood. https://www.core-econ.org

fall-off in sales of consumption goods, so that higher profit margins do not result in higher profits."[50]

Paul Oslington and colleagues have also studied *CWL* 15 and 21 within the context of his overall achievement.[51] For Lonergan, an adequate economic theory contributes to democracy by helping people understand how economies function and how business cycles actually work. Citizens must be educated to decide wisely in promoting the common good. If citizens do not understand how economies work, then promoting the human good will fail. The failure to understand economic processes leaves society prone to crises—opening the way for undemocratic forces.[52]

In both *CWL* 15, 21, Lonergan criticized the state of economics. In his 1940s economic manuscripts, his criticism was fairly restrained. He concentrated on constructing an alternative macroeconomic model. Michael Novak notes that when he returned to economics in the 1970s, he offered more strident criticisms of mainstream economics' emphasis on "choice theory" and its associated call for micro-foundations of macroeconomic models. Instead he sought to discern the natural rhythms

---

50. Joan Robinson, "Kalecki and Keynes," 337 quoted in the Editors' Introduction to *CWL* 21, p. ii. See also Hiroshi Nishi, "A two-sector Kaleckian model of growth and distribution with endogenous production dynamics," in *Economic Modelling*, 88, June 2020, 223–43. Nishi "extends a two-sector Kaleckian model of output growth and income distribution by incorporating endogenous labor productivity growth. The model is composed of investment good and consumption goods production sectors." The impact of a change in wage and profit shares on capacity utilization and output growth rates at the sectoral and aggregate levels are identified. The study reveals short-run cyclical capacity utilization rates and productivity growth dynamics. Even if the short-run steady state is stable, the capital accumulation rate in the consumption goods sector must decrease more than that in the investment sector for long-run stability. When simultaneous rises in profit shares in both the sectors affect long-run aggregate economic growth differently at a steady state, the distributional interests between the same class in different sectors may hamper the long-run economic growth. A policy message is that the effect of income distribution on industrial output growth is not always beneficial. These phenomena are specific to two-sector models and cannot be observed when using conventional aggregate growth models."

51. Neil Ormerod, Paul Oslington, Robert Koning, "The Development of Catholic Social Teaching: Bernard Lonergan and Benedict XVI," *Theological Studies* (73) 2012, 395.

52. Paul Oslington, 3 Nov. 2020, Web reprint from "The Economics of Bernard Lonergan: Context, Modelling and Assessment," in *Journal of Macrodynamic Analysis*, 3, 2008.

of the economic process, which is part of the larger rhythm of history. While most contemporary economists focus on the consistency of decisions in satisfying arbitrarily determined preferences, Lonergan studied how economic agents do or do not act rationally, whether they recognize the intrinsic intelligibility of economic processes and conform to that intelligibility. For Lonergan, the economic process has an end or telos. Unfortunately, teleological discussion has not been part of mainstream professional economics for many years.[53]

In *CWL* 15 and 21 Lonergan kept revising his equations and diagrams—a problem that the editors of these two volumes had to resolve. Our own solution has been to treat the equations and diagrams to ensure consistency. This shows Lonergan's own limitations as well as those of his interpreters. Let us note that Lonergan died before the word "glocal" came on the scene, but, in fact, his writings did anticipate the need to connect global events with their repercussions on local realities in glocal fashion. Fig. 5 in Appendix D is a simplified diagram of fundamental exchange variables for macrodynamic economics.[54]

Lonergan's account of the pure cycle includes a stationary phase, a surplus expansion and a basic expansion. In the stationary phase, there is no appreciable growth. In the surplus expansion, there is a massive investment in new production for the sake of more efficient production in the future. The basic expansion gradually exploits the benefits of the surplus expansion ideally returning to a new stationary phase with a higher standard of living. We are approaching these implications through the lenses of promoting justice. Lonergan focused on the intelligibility of the rhythms of production and monetary circulation of an advanced economy as well as of a pure business or trade cycle. Fred Lawrence has noted that capitalist economists speak of business or trade cycles while Marxists focus on crises in the economy in terms of surplus value and exploitation. For Lonergan, a pure business or trade cycle involves

---

53. Michael Novak, "Memories of Bernard Lonergan, S.J.", *Journal of Macrodynamic Analysis*, Vol. 3, 2003.

54. Our fig. 4–5's GEM-FS versions attempt to integrate Lonergan's Redistribution Function within the way he approaches self-transcendence in *Insight* and *MiT*.

the anti-egalitarian flows proper to new surplus or productive goods expansion and the egalitarian flows proper to basic or consumer goods expansion, which Marxists correctly complain are not fully carried out. Crucial to the smooth expansion are 1) the crossover payments between surplus and basic monetary circuits in harmony with the phases of economic development; 2) re-understanding of profit, not as a criterion of economic activity but as involving "a group interest that does not strictly 'belong' to capitalist entrepreneurs, and yet cannot be negotiated by socialist bureaucracy. The issue is not greed, . . . but ignorance."[55]

With Lawrence and other insightful Lonergan commentators, we seek to reverse the ignorance that has impeded Lonergan's proposals being understood, let alone implemented. A GEM-FS "healing-creating" approach emphasizes the need to understand real values and to practice justice in ways that avoid the extremes of mere profit-seeking on the one hand, and communist command-economy policies which have largely floundered, on the other. Government policies must promote justice for all; every person must be free to act in their economy. Such a focus is far from being the aim of prominent textbooks used in Western colleges and universities.[56]

Criticisms of University Textbooks on Economics

McShane argued that most textbooks on economics fail to correctly identify within enterprises divisions like management, sales departments, services, etc. They misdiagnose the problem of double counting and "middlemen." They fail to make the distinction that we, too, insist on:

---

55. Lawrence, *Revista Portuguesa Di Philosophia*, 63.4, (2007), 941.

56. David Albertson and Jason Blakely argue in *Commonweal*, May 28, 2001, that social bonds in the U. S. "have been steadily dissolved by decades of neoliberal capitalism that starved the public sphere and trained us to view neighbors as competitors or threats. The Left has policy solutions to some of these problems, but if they want to succeed, they must also address this crisis of civic belonging. . . . In the absence of ethical transformation, achieving policy goals may prove to be a Pyrrhic victory—swapping out institutions and incentives but keeping the same damaged social body underneath."

the difference between buying a consumer good like bread and buying something such as a dough mixer that makes bread, the consumer good. Lonergan went to great pains to show that this distinction is empirically workable. Part of our task has been to stress these key distinctions. Our allusions to Quesney, Cantillon, Ricardo, Marx, Kalecki, etc., are meant to clarify some of the lacunæ that crop up on the first day of Economics 101. McShane explained that this was part of his own effort to help teachers of grade 12 economics give three "good" subversive classes before they help the kids get through the prescribed course. McShane believed that this could be a strategy that might eventually emerge in teaching economics in some universities.[57]

"Would-be-Scientific" Views of Economics: The Case of N. Gregory Mankiw

Bruce Anderson and Phil McShane have argued[58] that despite claims by the enormously influential economist Gregory Mankiw that his analyses are "scientific," in fact they are not.[59] As to the two pages Mankiw devotes to the pros and cons of whether policymakers should try to stabilize the economy, Anderson and McShane write:

> Before he plunges into the pro argument Mankiw makes a single key statement: "left on their own, economies tend to fluctuate." He has already devoted an . . . unscientific chapter to this topic in which we meet with no serious attention to data, but rather a range of

---

57. www.philipmchane.org; "Grade 12 Economics: A Common Quest Manifesto."

58. Bruce Anderson and Philip McShane, *Beyond Establishment Economics: No Thank-you Mankiw* (Halifax, Nova Scotia: Axial, 2002). McShane, *Sane Economics and Fusionism* (Axial, 2010), endorses Schumpeter's critique of Keynes; he appeals, 27, to Heilbroner to the effect that "Behind all the symbols . . . there rests the central requirement of faith. Money serves its indispensable purposes as long as we believe in it."

59. They also review the pros and cons of some of Mankiw's recommendations on monetary and fiscal policies and tax laws. Monetary policy is primarily concerned with the management of interest rates and the total supply of money in circulation; it is generally carried out by central banks, such as the U.S. Federal Reserve. Fiscal policy is a collective term for the taxing and spending actions of governments.

suggested causes and effects, starting with the Pigou effect, and swing-
ing on through the twentieth century's various "theories" of interest,
prices, . . . that obviously relate to the problem on hand, the problem
of stabilization.[60]

Anderson and McShane reproach Mankiw for "immediately and
simple-mindedly" cutting off "empirical analysis," based on a model
of aggregate demand and aggregate supply.[61] They dispute Mankiw's
claim that almost everyone agrees about his "Principle 1" that a more
unequal distribution of income leads to higher economic output.[62]

Peter Bofinger has also argued to the contrary.[63] Citing Mankiw,
Principles, 429, Bofinger writes:

> As "Principle 1" . . . students are taught that a more unequal dis-
> tribution of income leads to higher output. "This is the one lesson
> concerning the distribution of income about which almost everyone
> agrees." But there is no evidence for this. OECD data on income dis-
> tribution (measured by the Gini index for net household income)
> show very high inequality in very poor countries such as South
> Africa, Chile, Mexico, Turkey or Bulgaria. In contrast, the econom-
> ically very powerful Scandinavian countries—measured by gross

---

60. Anderson, McShane, *Beyond Establishment Economics*, 205.

61. N. Gregory Mankiw, *Principles of Macroeconomics*, 1991, 408.

62. One of our book's goal is to seek to restore ethical values in economics using
a GEM-FS approach. There are many examples reaching back beyond 2000 to refute
the *myth of capitalism lifting all boats*. For us, Mankiw's textbook is just the visible tip
of the iceberg of deceptions—an opinion that agrees with Michael Hiltzik, Feb. 17,
2014, *Los Angeles Times*. Peter Cassar-Torreggiani suggests that Pedro Casaca's *On
the Value of Money: Unmasking Economics' Deception*, (Adin: 2021) and on the unpre-
dictability about changes in the value of money "leaves the intelligible field open to
innovation, . . . to a transcendent fiduciary structure that may be what is needed for
opening political and financial mindsets across digital econometrics." See also Pope
Francis, *Fratelli Tutti*.

63. Peter Bofinger, "Best of Mankiw; Errors and Tangles in the World's Best Selling
Economic Textbooks," *Institute for New Economic Thinking*, Jan. 3, 2021. In "Friday for
Keynesianism, Feb. 17, 2020, Bofinger www.socialeurope.eu/fridays-for-keynesianism
adds that "Keynes recognized the key role of the financial system in modern capitalist
economies . . . The 2008 crisis must bring the demise of neoclassical economics."

domestic product per capita—are characterized by very low inequality of household incomes.[64]

We stress that whereas Mankiw's first four principles address the notion of an efficient cause, that of the subjective psychology of persons making decisions in microeconomic matters, Lonergan first addresses the objective macroeconomic laws to which persons must adapt. This is why we have undertaken to develop for Lonergan's economics a GEM-FS approach that emphasizes the need to understand real values and to act justly as a *sine qua non* for reforming economics *according to its all-too-often misunderstood inherent laws.* The world needs a viable notion of economics that can help devise policies that avoid the extremes of both capitalism and communism—policies that can help overcome systemic shortcomings of both extremes. Fortunately, some bankers have also been writing on capitalist shortcomings—suggesting steps to help remedy the situation. The banking industry's periodical *Global Finance* has featured articles on the topic.

Angela Berg, a leader of the Diversity, Equity and Inclusion (DEI) movement, stresses the need for more-proactive corporate leadership on human equity. She writes:

> It's time to challenge the most senior leaders to participate in a new way. We've heard a lot about the importance of empathy in organizations, but I think we need to move now to humility. It's time for senior leaders, and board members to . . . admit that, even if they had good intent . . . in their organization, there's still a lot of work to be done . . . New actions are needed . . . acknowledging that to actually progress and have change around DEI in the future requires new behaviors and mindsets. If a DEI strategy hasn't achieved the desired results, then it's time for new and different actions.[65]

---

64. It may be that a *sociopathy* (psychopathy) among capitalist elites leads them to uncritically accept principles such as those of Mankiw. This *is also part* of the problem of a lack of objectivity and of empathy which *Global Finance* has begun to recognize. See Benedicte Bull, "Combating Inequality: Is There a "Scandinavian Way" to Reduce Inequality in Latin America? *Iberoamericana—Nordic Journal of Latin American and Caribbean Studies*, 2019, 48(1), 53–66.

65. Angela Berg, "Commitment to Equality," *Global Finance*, February, 2021, p. 11.

Tiziana Barghini suggests what might guide such new and different actions. She points to how the Roman Catholic Church offers a new values-based screening tool for investors that gives added weight to environmental and social considerations.[66] Lonergan's own lifework was dedicated to adapting traditional value-based Christian perspectives to the complexities of modern life. Our effort to link Lonergan's economics with his other writings is centered upon his notion of the rhythms of production that respect while integrating in society traditional values such as that of the common good.

GEM-FS Policies: Tackling Pervasive Economic Problems

Today there is a need to recover the objective reality of the good. There was a strange transmutation that afflicted right-wing Roman Catholics who opposed the "dictatorship of relativism" in tune with Pope Benedict XVI's observations in 2005. The term referred to what Benedict perceived as the culture war that does not recognize anything as definitive and whose only goal is to satisfy the desires of one's own ego. It pitted traditionalist Catholics against a "liberal" agenda whereby a secular state imposes its values on citizens. Yet, these traditionalists have now turned a blind eye to the campaigns of their adherents that ignore (or downplay) the traditional Church teachings on social justice.[67] In the face of these two opposing views of moral relativism we pursue a middle course. With Pope Francis, we as Christians seek to reclaim the joy of the Gospel

---

66. Tiziana Barghini, "For Asset Managers, a New Ethical Benchmark," *Global Finance*, February, 2021, 13. Environmental, Social, and Corporate Governance refers to the three central factors in measuring the sustainability and societal impact of an investment in a business. Analysis of these criteria can help better determine the future financial performance of companies. https://en.wikipedia.org/wiki/ Environmental,_social_and_ corporate_governance. See also Georg Kell, "Five Trends that Show Corporate Responsibility is Here to Stay," *The Guardian*, Aug. 13, 2014. Some asset management funds now screen companies based on their carbon exposure.

67. The concern for the poor must be translated at all levels, national and international governments, into concrete actions. "The basic moral test is how our most vulnerable members are faring." (Paul VI, 1965, no. 27). Promoting true development of peoples requires the desire, the right and the responsibility to ensure justice for all people, especially the poor. https://mettacenter.org/definitions/gloss-concepts/rehumanization-2/

that calls us to serve others—not simply reject them for holding contrary views. Analogously, we argue that a GEM-FS notion of justice provides a basis to restore an appropriate middle course within the democratic process that enforces needed governmental measures. This requires the ability and willingness to discern justice issues.

Reflecting on a world in which millions are unemployed—having to bear the brunt of the global economic crisis—Pope Francis, in his exhortation *Evangelii Gaudium*, wrote: "Just as the commandment 'Thou shalt not kill' sets a clear limit in order to safeguard the value of human life, today we also have to say 'thou shalt not' to an economy of exclusion and inequality. Such an economy kills."[68] Reminding us that living and sharing the joy of the Gospel necessarily demands that Christians be concerned for the plight of the poor who suffer many injustices in an economy that puts profit above people, the Pope lamented: "Today everything comes under the laws of competition and the survival of the fittest, where the powerful feed upon the powerless. As a consequence, masses of people find themselves excluded . . . , without work, without possibilities, without any means of escape . . . Human beings are themselves considered consumer goods to be used and then discarded."[69]

We have drawn on the Judeo-Christian prophetic tradition running from the Old Testament struggles for justice to those of Jesus. Today Christians have to deal with many ideologies of left and right that keep on distorting democratic processes. We have noted some of the distortions of economic principles evident in Adam Smith, Ricardo, Marx and modern economists. Lonergan did integrate the valid points of their insights along with those, for example, of Jane Jacobs, who worked along very different lines of research in urban economics. We have sought to show how Lonergan integrated such diverse views within his own systematic theology. Nor did he hesitate to confront the general and the particular implications of ongoing complicated issues

---

68. No. 53. The pope adds: Debt and the accumulation of interest . . . make it difficult for countries to realize the potential of their own economies and keep citizens from enjoying their real purchasing power. To all this we can add widespread corruption and self-serving tax evasion, which have taken on worldwide dimensions." No. 59.

69. Pope Francis, *Evangelii Gaudium*, November 2013, 46.

in economics. Lonergan linked the realities of starvation in some parts of the globe with misinterpretations that disregard economic realities. He did so in an original, "generalized-cum-particular" radical way. In *CWL* 15, Chapter 5, titled "Equilibria of the Mechanical Structure," for example, he links his general theorem of continuity with what has to be respected if one is to arrive at a correct interpretation of what happens with monetary accelerators. He manages to arrive at a generalization within the specialized ways of studying economic processes. He goes so far as to say that there is the need to understand and respect all the parts of an organic whole:

> To violate this organic interconnection is simply to smash the organism to create the paradoxical situations of starvation in the midst of plenty, of workers eager for work and capable of finding none . . . of everyone's inability to do what he wishes to do being the cause of everyone's inability to remedy the situation.[70]

Tad Dunne adds that for Lonergan, the theorem of continuity in economics

> is the abstract and formal aspect of such limitations in the economic order when the exchange process is static or expanding or contracting. We may like it so or we may wish it different. But in any case, there is some determinate range of values of the multipliers and of the monetary accelerators [...] that corresponds with such a decision. Moreover there has to be an internal coherence between these values, and to violate this coherence is to rout economic organization. Just as the movements of the controls of an airplane must be coordinated and all co-ordinations are not possible at all instants, so also the economic machine . . . can be moved only . . . in a limited number of ways at any given time.[71]

---

70. *CWL* 21, 74.

71. Tad Dunne, https://functionalmacroeconomics.com. "A New Paradigm: Bernard Lonergan's Macroeconomics' Foundational Theorem: a Purely Relational Foundation for Macroeconomics." Internet. In economics, a multiplier broadly refers to an economic factor that, when increased or changed, causes increases or changes in many other related economic variables. The term multiplier is usually used in reference to the relationship between government spending and total national income.

The Need for Public Benefit Corporations to Promote Strategic Values and Goals

In 21 of the states in the USA, there is a type of public-benefit corporation (PBC) that aims to have a positive impact on society, workers, communities and the environment in addition to its profit-motivation.[72] Its legally defined goals differ from the those of traditional corporations—that of making a profit. A PBC differs with regard to its purpose, accountability and transparency; it seeks to create a general public benefit—defined as fostering a positive impact on society and the environment.[73] While Amazon's stated goal is "To be earth's most customer-centric company," and while several public organizations such as the World Bank define their mission as that of "'Ending extreme poverty," in a PBC, the leader's job is to ensure that the purpose of the organization be anchored in common values. Evidence shows that purposeful companies have higher employee engagement, greater customer satisfaction, tighter supplier linkages and better environmental stewardship.

The pay-offs of PBC's are superior share price and operational performance, lower costs of capital, smaller regulatory fines and greater resilience in the face of shocks. We may contrast such pay-offs with how former Google CEO Eric Schmidt faced a backlash in 2022 when it was reported that he indirectly funded and wielded unusually heavy influence over the White House Office of Science and Technology, an important White House office tasked with advising the Biden administration on technical and scientific issues. OSTP has a meager $5 million annual budget. There are ethical concerns when a technology billionaire with an obvious personal interest in shaping government tech policy gives money to an independent government agency devoted to tech and science by way of his private philanthropic foundation.

---

72. These states are: Arkansas, California, Colorado, Delaware, Florida, Hawaii, Illinois, Louisiana, Maryland, Massachusetts, Nevada, New Jersey, NY, Oregon, Pennsylvania, Rhode Island, South Carolina, Utah, Vermont, Virginia and West Virginia—plus DC.

73. See Wikipedia, https://wikipedia.org/wiki/Public-benefit_corporation. In the face of the refusal of large, profitable firms such as Amazon to allow unions, responsible people should push for more PBD-like firms.

It is playing with fire when a government office needs private help to fund its work. It creates a conflict of interests. Schmidt's private nonprofit, Schmidt Futures, supports initiatives that use technology to address "hard-to-solve" scientific and societal problems. There has been direct coordination between OSTP and Tom Kalil, a Schmidt Futures employee, to secure funding for the office staff. Kalil had also served as an unpaid consultant to OSTP for four months while still working for Schmidt Futures. He had left the agency after ethics complaints in October 2021. The ties between Schmidt, his foundation, and OSTP go even deeper. "More than a dozen officials in the [then] 140-person White House office have been associates of Schmidt's, including some current and former Schmidt employees."[74] Both OSTP and Schmidt Futures maintain that their connection has been misconstrued as nefarious; they say this sort of partnership is "par for the course." In a statement, Schmidt Futures highlighted how the OSTP has been "chronically underfunded," and said that it was proud to be among the "leading organizations" providing funding to OSTP. In other words, Schmidt Futures makes clear that it is not the only private organization to "charitably" provide much-needed monetary support to government agencies.

President Joe Biden Returns the U. S. toward Anti-Monopolist Policies

Nelson Lichenstein has argued that an executive order by President Biden has correctly declared that the generation of the conservatives "who influenced the Reagan administration has failed." For Lichenstein,

> Mr. Biden's executive order does something even more important than trustbusting. It returns the United States to the great antimonopoly tradition that has animated social and economic reform almost since the nation's founding. This tradition worries less about technocratic questions such as whether concentrations of corporate

---

74. See Whizy Kim, *recode*, March 30, 2022.

power will lead to lower consumer prices and more about broader social and political concerns about the destructive effects that big business can have on our nation.[75]

Reaching back into history, Lichenstein comments:

In 1773, when American patriots dumped tea from the British East India Company into Boston Harbor, they were protesting not just an unfair tax but also the British crown's grant of a monopoly to a court favorite. That sentiment flourished in the 19th century, when Americans of all stripes saw concentrations of economic power corrupting both democracy and the free market. Abolitionists drew on the antimonopoly ethos when they denounced the slave power, and Andrew Jackson sought to dismantle the Second Bank of the United States because it sustained the privileges of an Eastern commercial and financial elite. Threats to democracy became even more pressing with the rise of giant corporations . . . When Congress passed the Sherman Antitrust Act in 1890, its author, Senator John Sherman of Ohio, declared, "If we will not endure a king as political power, we should not endure a king over the production . . . and sale of any of the necessities of life"

In the so-called Progressive Era in the United States (1896–1920) the courts had ruled that a wide variety of corporations and industries "affected with a public interest" might be subject to the kind of governmental regulation—covering prices, products and even labor standards—that in subsequent years was restricted largely to electrical utilities and transport companies. Two decades later, the New Dealers sought to challenge monopoly power not only by a renewal of antitrust litigation but also by encouraging the growth of trade unionism so as to create an industrial democracy within the very heart of the corporation itself (ibid).

Lichenstein recalls that in his 1936 re-nomination acceptance speech, Franklin D. Roosevelt "echoed that sentiment when he denounced

---

75. Nelson Lichenstein, *New York Times*, July 13, 2021.

'economic royalists' who had "created a new despotism." He saw con-centrated industrial and financial power as an "industrial dictator-ship" that threatened democracy. Standard Oil and other trusts had already become the target of antitrust lawsuits not just because they crushed competitors and raised consumer prices but also because they corrupted politics and exploited their employees. Breaking these giant companies into smaller units helped, but few reformers thought that government antitrust initiatives offered the prime solution to the imbalance of power so increasingly prevalent in modern capitalism.[76] What was needed was greater governmental regulation and power-ful trade unions. Yet, that antimonopoly tradition faded after World War II, collapsing into an arid discourse that asked but one question: Would the prevention of a merger or the breakup of a company lower consumer prices? Lichenstein concludes: "Mr. Biden has now correctly declared that this 40-year 'experiment' has failed. 'Capitalism with-out competition isn't capitalism. It's exploitation,' he proclaimed at the signing of his executive order (ibid)."

SEVENTH FUNCTIONAL SPECIALTY: ADDRESSING THE SYSTEMIC SHORTCOMINGS IN SOCIETAL PRACTICES[77] ACROSS THE GLOBE

Lonergan offers a new standard model of the objective economic pro-cess.[78] He notes in *Insight* that "Economic process was conceived by the older economists as a generalized equilibrium. However, we are concerned, not with single schemes, but with a conditioned series of

76. Some question whether the two Roosevelt presidents, sufficiently opposed the huge conglomerates. See Michael Lind *The New Republic*, May 4, 2018 "The Myth of the Roosevelt 'Trustbusters.'"

77. According to The Economic Policy Institute, Aug. 18, 2020, "There are gross inequalities in tax law in the USA. For example, despite the fact that CEO compensation surged 14% in 2019 to $21.3 million, the U. S. Congress in 2021 considered proposals that would lift the cap on the state and local tax (SALT) deduction—a move that would largely benefit wealthy individuals."

78. https://functionalmacroeconomics.com. We argue that his explanatory systemat-ics is also a new model.

schemes."[79] Lonergan did not reject wholesale the old economics but he sought to improve upon it. If there is something of the old economics that he rejected, it is the claim that economics should operate independently of ethics. For him, there is no dichotomy between morality and economics as free-market advocates and some Marxists[80] would want us to believe. As to the question whether there are tensions or even a contradiction between economics and morality, for Lonergan, interiority, freedom, morality, and economics imply one another. A healthy, well-functioning economy and an adequate science both demand that a person observe the four norming processes or transcendental precepts that he names "be attentive, intelligent, reasonable, and responsible." Responsibility requires that one's decisions and choices evaluate short-term and long-term costs and benefits to oneself, to one's group, to other groups. In that spirit, we asked above whether and how the present "science of economics" could withstand an accounting of the application of ethical principles to the rough-and-tumble daily life of an economy, without the kind of state coercion exemplified in the former Soviet Union, or in contemporary Russia and Communist China. On the other hand, we have argued that people must find adequate means to counter the evils of finance-dominated capitalism.[81]

---

79. *Insight*, 141–42. Adrial Fitzgerald in a Lonergan discussion group insists on the absolute requirement of first establishing a system for allocating the controlling ownership of assets not antithetical to the realization of a pure-cycle uniform economic expansion. He asserts that no such system now exists on any significant scale—certainly not on the global context. For him, 1) democratization is needed to meaningfully implement the type of reform this book is advocating; 2) while countervailing forces have decreased the efficiency of capitalism's pursuit of profit, thus mitigating the effects of injustice, the global context must not be neglected.

80. Marxist ethics describes morality as a property of one's behavior conditioned by socio-historical existence, that is, as those moral values that bring together (or force apart) living individuals. See https://penelopethemovie.com/is-marxism-moral?

81. As did the Old Testament prophets and Jesus, we must struggle against the ideologies of left and right that keep on distorting democratic processes. Jane Jacobs' research in urban economics could be integrated within a systematic theology as Lonergan himself suggests in *Healing and Creating in History*. Both thinkers argued that 1) the same dynamic principles that govern the functioning of natural ecologies are also to be found when human social and economic systems function well, but are absent when human systems go wrong; 2) the violation of principles that pertain to natural ecologies is destructive not only

The study of business ethics has grown enormously over the past decades. Usually, a "code of ethics" consists of rules employees should apply in their work. This ignores the fact that such codes, even the most enlightened, do not harness the real power of ethical decision-making in a firm: the employees' ability across the board to be attentive, intelligent, rational and responsible. In the face of such a quandary, some Lonerganian ethicists have proposed an approach to corporate ethical decision making (EDM) which would serve as an alternative to the imposition of codes to address the ethical consequences of grand challenges such as Covid-19. Their alternative approach to EDM

> embraces the concept of reflexive thinking and ethical consciousness among the individual agents who collectively are the corporation and who make ethical decisions, often in isolation, removed from the collocated corporate setting. This focus on individual decision-making agents' engagement in self-appropriation articulates a normative transcendental standard which delivers the critical moral realism needed to address the grand challenges of our time . . . Ongoing crises have left many of the most vulnerable to bear the health, economic, and eco-logic burden of others' hubris, greed, and denial . . . Lonergan's teachings provide an alternative restorative human paradigm of business, portraying the corporation as a community of persons nurturing authentic ethical thought, decision making, and action . . . It may also

---

of the natural environment, but also of communal and economic well-being. See Patrick Byrne, "Ecology, Economy and Redemption as Dynamic," 5. Jacobs extended her analyses to the unique characteristics of urban economics. In her *The Nature of Economics* (2000), she drew the results of some of her previous work on urban economic patterns into a synthesis with insights into biological systems. She argued that the same processes "that sustain vital, evolving natural ecologies also underpin robust and dynamic economies." Byrne notes that while Jacobs gave detailed accounts of the processes shared by both natural and human systems, "Lonergan developed a parallel, integral account of natural processes, human social and economic organization, and the 'economy of salvation.'" Byrne stresses that "the dynamics of human innovations and self-correction correspond in striking ways to the emergence, growth, development, and decline in the natural order." As we noted in Part I, Lonergan defined the negative effects of biases in human relations that distort genuine development, but he did not elaborate at length on how caring love can help heal the distorted dynamics of natural and human ecologies—nor on its relevant ethical aspects.

present a new dawn: one in which businesses have the opportunity to foster cognitive operations among their employees so that the ethical criteria of sustainability and self-transcendence pervade decision making.[82]

Toward Remedying Problems Relating to Fair and Unfair Taxation

Oxfam International has stressed that a global tax reform framework pushed by the USA and other countries is far from adequate. Hailed as an "important step" by President Joe Biden, the proposal includes a 15% global minimum tax rate[83] on multinational corporations and new rules aimed at closing loopholes. A proponent of a global minimum tax said that this means that multinational profits would be subject to a 15% minimum effective rate. For example, a German multinational that books income in Ireland, taxed at an effective rate of 5% would be subject to an extra 10% tax to arrive at a rate of 15%—same for profits booked by German multinationals in Bermuda, Singapore, etc. Other nations would do likewise. But a company such as Amazon might still be able to keep dodging its obligations because one of the framework's pillars would apply only to "profit exceeding a 10% margin for the largest

---

82. Patricia Larres & Martin Kelly, "A Framework for Authentic Ethical Decision Making in the Face of Grand Challenges: A Lonerganian Gradation. *Journal of Business Ethics* (2021). https://doi.org/10.1007/s10551-021-04974-2. Larres and Kelly have also written on Lonergan's stance on neoliberalism—a stance that we endorse. See their "Banking for the Common Good; A Lonerganian Perspective," https://pureadmin. qub.ac.uk/ws/ portalfiles/portal/159141064/Banking_for_the_Common_Good.pdf. They conclude that "the common good is superior to the public interest insofar as the former incorporates a moral dimension which is absent from the latter." It is such a broad view of the common good which helps lay a ground for six GEM-FS turnarounds.

83. Lawrence H. Summers, wrote in *The Washington Post*, Oct. 31, 2021, that the decision of the Group of 20 nations to impose a corporate minimum tax is a positive step: It would "create a more worker-centered global economy . . . arguably the most significant international economic pact of the 21st century." It is built around a profoundly important principle: countries should cooperate to raise corporate taxation, not compete to reduce it. "It demonstrates the power of ideas to shape economic policy" as has been advocated by tax scholars for years to fix present conundrums.

and most profitable multinational enterprises." While backed by more than 130 countries, the global tax idea remains a long way from enactment, given that national legislatures . . . must ultimately approve laws implementing the new digital tax rules for tech giants and the minimum corporate tax. Some critics say the tax rate should be higher than the proposed 15%. "A global tax rate of 25% would raise nearly $17 billion more per year for the world's poorest countries than a 15% rate."[84] These facts summarize some dilemmas in trying to reconcile GEM-FS reforms and the present injustices and sufferings of the poor in both rich and developing nations. We acknowledge that there are limits to what can reasonably be done even with the best of intentions. The growing horrors of climate change compound the dilemma. Still, there are some clear signs of possible incipient moves towards turnarounds in economics and environmental policies.

In pursuance of such goals, we as Christians invoke values and the virtues of faith, hope and love that secular capitalist and communist regimes have tended to reject. This is a dilemma that the Berrigan brothers and liberation theologians began to address in the 1960s. As a minimum, Church leaders must seek to restore hope so as to viably deal with the dilemma which calls for a turnaround insistence on justice toward the disadvantaged. On the margins, there are brave people working with the poor. True, there are limits to what can be done such as budget limitations and threats of inflation. Yet we should not misinterpret Jesus' statement, "The poor you will always have with you" (Matthew 26:11). All too often, this verse is interpreted as saying, "You can't overcome poverty. It's a hopeless cause." Or worse: "If they're poor, it's their fault." Lonergan's view of economics makes a difference. His GEM-FS ethical concerns in philosophy and in economics reinforce one another. Both are integral to sound social policies.

---

84. Oxfam International, July 1, 2021.

EIGHTH FUNCTIONAL SPECIALTY:
SHARING UNIVERSAL VALUES WITHIN A JUST
AND FUNCTIONALLY VIABLE ECONOMY

We have argued for a GEM-FS alternative to standard economic texts—one based on two circuits where the re-distribution function plays a key ethical role in promoting a sane global economy. Our effort has been inspired by those who struggle to bring justice in the world. There is required a sense of community—both local and global.[85] GEM-FS unfolds through sensitivity, intelligence, rational reflection, and responsible deliberation; it asks how individual persons come to know and act before trying to apply the method to communities. It can help provide a common basis across the globe to tackle social inequalities, climate change, etc. No man is an island. We need one another if all our needs are to be met—not only "our needs" but those of all people across the globe. Lonergan does indicate in Insight that his method is applicable to communities as well as to individuals, but it is in MiT and afterwards that he began to apply GEM's four basic differentiations of consciousness to the eight stages of functional specialization—thus providing a common base for interdisciplinary collaboration. Our book extends this agenda to the controverted field of economics. We have argued that without some understanding and acceptance of a spiritual foundation[86] in one's life, one cannot really account for the amplitude of Lonergan's overall achievement. In a parallel way—faced with today's extremes of secularism and doctrinaire approaches to faith—Pope Francis has also tackled the two extremes quite effectively. Such an attitude is at the heart of effectively sharing the message of the Good News today. In his account of the eighth FS, Lonergan writes that traditionally, society has been conceived as the organized collaboration of individuals for the pursuit of common aims.

---

85. See our comments on glocalization above.

86. Apophatic mysticism can help persons achieve self-transcendence. This is so because it "touches on the infinite," on the limits to which humans are subject. But it can also be a way whereby leaders and practitioners of the world religions can be brought into effective contact with one another and with people without faith." See Gordon Rixon, "Bernard Lonergan and Mysticism." *Theological Studies* 62 (2001), 479–97.

On the basis of this very general definition various kinds of society are distinguished and, among them, the church and the state which are named 'perfect' societies on the ground that each in its own sphere possesses ultimate authority. It is to be observed that on this view church and state are not parts within a larger whole but simply instances within a larger class.[87]

Lonergan adds that for sociologists or historians, "anything that pertains to the togetherness of human beings" is deemed to be social. "Society must always be conceived concretely and, indeed, the fewer the groups of men living in total isolation from other men, the more there tends to exist a single human society that is worldwide."[88]

IN CONCLUSION

Our study has argued that practicing economic justice based on enduring values can best occur within the frame of the conversion-turnarounds outlined in GEM and expanded into eight stages of healing and creating. Humanity has to adapt to the laws of economics, but only the optimum functioning of an economy can ensure the practice of justice. Some may say that advocating the need of policy changes in economics for the environment is unrealistic. But proposing concrete ways to achieve a higher standard of living, to reduce inequalities, while dealing effectively with climate change is more than "wishful" thinking. Preserving the status quo can only lead to endangering both planet earth and the human race.

The major crises of our time are all intricately linked to the economy. The climate crisis, the divisions across the world and unprecedented levels of income inequalities threaten the viability of democracies. The threats of an even worse repeat of the financial collapse of 2008, the pandemic that has killed millions as supply lines back up and rampant inflation now threaten humans. Adequately addressing these challenges requires the cooperative turnarounds we have insisted on. This is not a pipe dream; it is a way to survival. Lonergan was remarkably

---

87. *MiT*, 331. *CWL* 14, 331.

88. *MiT*, 331. *CWL* 14, 331.

forward-looking. He realized that a new form of economics based on both traditional and emerging notions of values is indispensable. In Parts III and IV, we have outlined how short-sighted views on maximizing profits could be overcome, lest the planet burn and children starve. Coercive regimes like the ones led by Vladimir Putin and Xi Jin-Ping severely limit citizens' creativity. This may prove to be their undoing. Lonergan's solution requires "the creative imagination of all individuals in all democracies,"[89] which could enable humanity as a whole bring about a new more just, cooperative world order.

This new order is feasible. It is intensely practical. It must be established—the sooner the better!

---

89. *CWL* 21, 37. For a perspective on how the development of blockchain technology might help implement democratic economics, see Appendix H.

APPENDICES

Appendix A

Linking Lonergan's Important Notion of Operator with his Views of Economic Processes

For Lonergan, the notion of operator (as potentially self-transcendent subjects) is at the center of how he would help us modify economic processes for the better. Understanding this means that GEM-FS operators help foster conversions and needed horizonal transformations. It also implies the need to integrate fresh data within new discoveries. There are many traditional and modern philosophical notions that Lonergan helps us consider anew. Two key such notions are those of process and of GEM-FS operators that foster dialectic and foundational conversions and integrate fresh data within new discoveries. Our text links these various notions to include dynamic economic processes.

Appendix B

A New Paradigm:
Lonergan's Macroeconomic Field Theory

Our attempt to integrate Lonergan's achievements in the fields of knowledge, ethics, spirituality and economics relies on the hope that GEM-FS' eight specialties might speak to economists in a more convincing way and to general audiences in a clear manner. Obviously, we cannot change the economy without some governmental regulations. In order to change the market, a government must seek to regulate it through democratic processes, and not allow it to be dominated by the oligarchical control of a few extremely wealthy individuals and corporations. Lonergan insisted that the whole process had to be democratic lest we fall victims to bureaucratic control as in China or to robber-baron, finance-dominated capitalism.[1] In "A New Paradigm: Bernard Lonergan's Macroeconomic Field Theory," Philip McShane helps us reconcile Lonergan's notion of pure cycle with his diagram. McShane writes:

> One formula is worth a ton of prose. Our purpose . . . is to remove the reader from the verbiage and allow him to concentrate solely on the relationships in the equations which explain the concrete economic process. Among these *Topics in Functional Macroeconomics* are four treatments which concentrate on the explanatory mathematical formulæ, but present them in different orderings.[2]

---

1. See Lonergan, *CWL* 21, 95–96. On government deficit spending and debt servicing, *CWL* 21, 200–01: "The effects of deficit government spending, then, have to be the compound resultant of both the spending itself and the debt servicing.

2. See https://functionalmacroeconomics.com/welcome. In his meetings with economists and entrepreneurs, Pope Francis has proposed a pact for renewing the economy to

McShane remarks that commentators should strive to understand the concise, precise mathematical forms which are isomorphic with the patterns of the dynamic process. He concludes:

> One's understanding should be comprised of purely relational functional aspects. Prices and quantities are defined implicitly by the interrelations within and between their functional flows rather than exogenously as a given . . . implicit definition of costs and profits. There is a sense in which one may speak of the fraction of basic outlay that moves to basic income as the "costs" of basic production . . . for the greater the fraction that basic income is of total income (or total outlay), the less the remainder which constitutes the aggregate possibility of profit.[3]

counteract the asocial aspects of modern business practices. He has discussed some of the most complex problems in today's world—from safeguarding the environment to committing oneself to rethink the economic paradigms of our time.

3. McShane, *JMDA*, Vol. 3, 2003.

Appendix C

Two Experts on High-Tech in Society who Advocate Closer Controls to Promote the Redistributive Function

Sam Altman, C.E.O of OpenAI, an artificial intelligence research laboratory, co-founded with Elon Musk, has argued that "the technological progress we make in the next 100 years will be far larger than all we've made since we first controlled fire and invented the wheel. . . . This revolution will generate enough wealth for everyone to have what they need, if we as a society manage it responsibly. Altman adds that if Musk is right, A.I. will generate phenomenal wealth largely by destroying countless jobs—a big part of how everything gets cheaper—and shifting huge amounts of wealth from labor to capital. "Whether that world becomes a post-scarcity utopia or a feudal dystopia hinges on how wealth, power and dignity are then distributed—it hinges, in other words, on politics."[1]

Linda Khan, appointed by President Biden to be chairwoman of the Federal Trade Commission, had a career of examining the limits of the current paradigm in antitrust law. She is now assessing that paradigm's corporate-based framework. She argues that as of 2021, the USA has betrayed the core of antitrust principles. Having focused on the shortcomings of dominant digital-era firms, she is said to be planning an antimonopoly approach that would address questions of power, distribution, and democracy. Khan has argued that the legal American antitrust framework, which focuses on keeping consumer prices down, cannot match the anticompetitive effects of platform-based business models such as Amazon's. As an alternative approach for doing so, she advocates "restoring traditional antitrust and competition policy principles

---

1. *New York Times*, June 11, 2021. Musk's takeover of Twitter is an instance of a concentration of power in the hands of a few elite—enabling them to impose their will.

or applying common carrier obligations and duties."[2] Our own plea for a political-civilian tool to control the excesses impeding fundamental exchange variables through the redistribution function as indicated in Lonergan's diagram of rates of flow (fig. 4–5) is in tune with Khan's policy. But one should beware. Recall, for instance, the inappropriate close FDA-Biogen collaboration—that suggested that "drug regulators surrendered their independence and objectivity, essentially working on behalf of Biogen" in what amounted to "a regulatory capture at the agency."[3]

2. Linda Khan, "Amazon Antitrust Paradox," *Yale Law Journal* , 126 (3), 564–67.

3. https://www.citizen.org/wp-content/uploads/2591.pdf

Appendix D

The Productive Process' Interrelated Stages[1]

Michael Shute notes that Lonergan studied the basic (real) variables so as to come to a clear understanding of basic productive rhythms without letting the often-obfuscating role of financial transactions get in the way. Lonergan wanted to understand what an economy actually *is*; he reached his goal by specifying a set of core variables for understanding economic rhythms.[2] He noticed that economic rhythms include both the processes of production, which provide goods and services, and the circulation of money. He realized that, because an economy provides for the material basis for a standard of living, production rhythms are the primary function of an economy.[3] In other words, the productive process consists of interrelated stages that include a *basic stage* and a series of interdependent *surplus stages*, i. e., a series of stages each "higher up" in producing

---

1. As the Occupy Wall St movement made clear in 2011, our global economic system is perceived as being vicious. Dark financial powers are guided by false theories *bereft of* a social dividend, (income over and above the standard of living) favored by Schumpeter and Lonergan. The redistributive function (RF) is ignored. It should be studied with new underpinnings on the analogy of mathematical physics which began with Faraday and Riemann. The RF touches profoundly upon the basic and surplus processes. Savings, loans and lines of credit, dividends, rents, interest, royalties, stocks and bonds, etc. In short, all exchanges that take place outside the productive process fall into the RF—which is also a process. The RF process-function normally serves the other two, providing loans and capital to producers, and managing income for the rest of us. The rise of massive income inequality is due to the usurpation of that role by financiers, those once called the "masters of the universe"—until they made an incalculable mess in 2008. Since we cannot get along ("do business") without some financial services, we are at the mercy of finance capitalism—a perverse form of capitalism that subordinates the processes of production to accumulating money.

2. Michael Shute, "Real Economic Variables," *Divyadaan*, 21, No. 2, 2010, 184.

3. Shute, "Real Economic Variables," 188. Shute compares this function to the movement of tides as a function of the phases of the moon.

the means of production. The difference between the two is functional: the goods and services of the basic stage enter directly into the standard of living, whereas those of the surplus stages enter into it only *indirectly*.[4] Surplus stages' production improve upon nature by increasing its efficacy. Thus, machines that make shoes are in the lowest surplus stage; the machine tools making the machines figure in the next higher stage, etc. Products of the surplus stages do not enter into the standard of living; yet they *are* related to it. The relation is determined by distinguishing between the productive process' short-term and long-term accelerations; the first increases rates of production due to fuller uses of existing capital equipment, the second due to innovations in product and newer, more efficient equipment. Both types of accelerations and the stationary phases must be monitored by fixing amounts of money circulating or being saved.

Since basic and surplus stages differ functionally in respect to standards of living, their relationships can lead to a *pure cycle*'s uniform expansion of an exchange economy. A pure cycle of the productive process is a matter of the surplus stage first accelerating more rapidly than the basic stage, then of the basic stage accelerating more rapidly than the surplus. Writing in Keynes' heyday,[5] Lonergan analyzed how stages can prevent recessions from turning into general collapse. The basic stage calls for more consumption; surplus stages need thrift and enterprise.[6] Fig. 5 illustrates how a GEM-FS ethical economics might work.[7]

---

4. Lonergan, *CWL* 21, 119.

5. Keynes sided with conservatives on the issue of maintaining the capitalist project. He argued that governments must come up with adequate policies to prop up aggregate demand during recessions. On Lonergan's suggested policies, see FS 6 in Part IV.

6. David Oyler https://www.davidoyler.org/ notes that Lonergan "simplifies the analysis by treating all of the "supplier" firms as an aggregate. Once the cycles are understood, companies could do their own strategic planning based on the functional analysis of their supplies . . . and markets with the statistics" provided via the proper appraisal of companies, consumers and the expectations of future flows based on political situations.

7. The US Congress is sometimes called upon to hold corporations accountable in shareholder resolutions which include the ability of investors, small and large, to file resolutions with Corporate America on issues such as the climate crisis, human rights, gender and minority pay disparity, corporate political influence, etc. See also Rickey Gard Diamond's *Screwnomics: How our Economy Works Against Women and Real Ways to Make Lasting Change* (Berkeley, CA: She Writes Press, 2018).

Its circles represent five monetary functions, namely, the basic and surplus *demand* income circles, I' and I", the *supply* outlay circles, O' and O" (basic functions bear a single prime; surplus functions a double prime). RF is the redistribution function.

Fig. 5 is *another snapshot at time t (based on Lonergan's diagram revised in 1981[8])*: Equilibrium if *i'fO' = c"fO"* (the crossovers)[9]

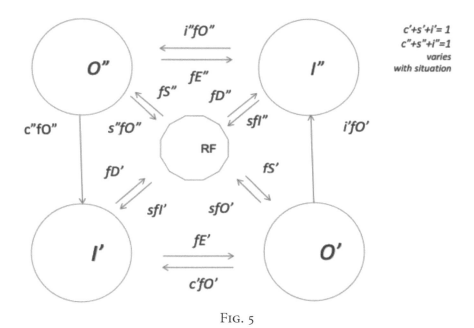

FIG. 5

Surplus outlay, O", divides into consumption, savings and investments; it is fed by surplus expenditures and withdrawals from RF.

Basic outlay, O', divides into *c'fO', s'fO',* and *i'fO'*; it is fed by *fE'* and *fS'*. Basic and surplus income contribute savings to the redistributional function and draw upon its facilities.

RF can be a *re-distributive* justice function on which GEM economics pivots. It can re-center the economy's channels[10] but is itself dependent

---

8. *CWL* 15, 192. This 1981 version somewhat emends those of 1978 and 1979.

9. Note that *f* refers to a *rate*, "a so much every so often." *CWL* 15, 46.

10. *CWL* 15, 37, 76.

on a holistic *episteme* where GEM-FS balances price-profit considerations with the "risks" of Kingdom-of-God justice[11] in the face of global needs. Since the RF rehinges monetary functions, it should be calibrated to serve as a tool for evaluating justice issues while effecting the productive process to maximum efficiency so as "to treat all with a generous hand."

A Note on Fig. 5, Quesnay's *Tableau* and Leontiff's Diagrams

As does François Quesnay's *Tableau*, fig. 5 correlates interdependencies; unlike the *Tableau*, it links these functions with two circuits and their crossovers; it is a simplified diagram of fundamental exchange variables for a dynamic macroeconomics.[12] Lonergan stresses Schumpeter's insistence on the merits of a diagram as a tool, e. g. in Quesnay's *Tableau*. Despite profound differences in their respective achievements, Leontieff's work may be viewed as a revival of the *Tableau*.[13] The *Tableau* was the first to make explicit the concept of *economic equilibrium*. All science begins from particular correlations, but *the Tableau's key discovery is the interdependence of the whole*. As figures 4–5 suggest, the interconnections of a few precise aggregates has important features that Quesnay's system

---

11. Acting on Tolstoy's conviction that "The Kingdom is within you" (Lk. 17: 21), Gandhi and Martin Luther King Jr renewed political systems—an indication that interiority is not just passive. While the economist, Daron Acemoglu, *New York Times*, Jan. 11, 2020, deplores the rise of technology and automation for provoking more inequality in society, Anne M. Carpenter, *The Church Life Journal*, June 25, 2021, praises "The extraordinary *delicacy*, the intimate intricacy and fragility of Lonergan's image of the human being. Every understanding is the opposite of automatic; it is an inviolable work that no one can do for someone else. It is an effort that often goes wrong, that must start again and again. The human mind is tasked with asking and answering every relevant question, with searching the luminous depths of experience and transfiguring it almost wholly into an interior world bent around the desire to know."

12. *CWL* 15, 53, referring to Schumpeter, *History*, 240–43.

13. Lonergan lauds the way Schumpeter showed how slumps and crises were related to contractions of plant and equipment, and that there were 'a hundred theories' on why, even though he could not explain why. Lonergan also praised Schumpeter's elucidation of Quesnay's *Tableau* which (1) allowed a theorist to correlate many things all at once, and to assign numbers arithmetically to the variables involved; (2) permitted insight into phantasm instead of mere speculation detached from the facts. Lonergan's five-point diagram indicates how he handled the need for adequate diagrams. *CWL* 15, 177–202.

of simultaneous equations" implies but does not manifest.[14] The aims and limitations of macroeconomics make the use of a diagram" very helpful, "for its basic terms are *defined by their functional relations.*"[15]

The Phases in a Pure Cycle

To reiterate, Lonergan's account of the pure cycle includes a stationary phase, a surplus expansion and a basic expansion. In the stationary phase, there is no appreciable growth. In the surplus expansion, there is a massive investment of pure surplus income in new production for the sake of innovation and more efficient production in the future. As the investment in the surplus expansion tapers to zero, the basic expansion gradually exploits the benefits of the surplus expansion, ideally returning to a new stationary phase with a higher standard of living. Fig. 5 shows how circulation and production interdepend. The functions are linked by rates of payments denoted as fE' and fE", referring to that income used for basic and surplus expenditure; and c'fO' and i"fO", the receipts of expenditures. *Per interval,* surplus demand, I", pays fE" for current surplus products and receives i"fO" dividends from surplus production and i'fO' from basic production. *Per interval,* basic demand pays fE' for current basic products; for its services it receives c"fO" from surplus supply, c'fO' from basic supply.

Various classes of operative and redistributive (RF) payments occur. RF, which links the other four functions,[16] is money held in reserve for

---

14. *CWL* 15, 179.

15. Tad Dunne, "Purely Relational Foundations for Macroeconomics: An Explanatory Systematics and a New Standard Model of the Objective Economic Process." Internet.

16. Lonergan, *CWL* 15, 34, 40–41; fig. 5's aggregate rates such as I', I" (basic and surplus income) O' and O" (basic and surplus outlay) describe the process, hold it together and relate secondary economic structures with primary knowing structures. The outlay of entrepreneurs becomes the income of workers and suppliers. Operative payments, a *boundary* class of aggregate receipts, become the expenditures of final buyers and of aggregate receipts. Suppliers' demand-income becomes basic and surplus outlay; without an exchange of money for produced goods, an element remains an *unfinished* product. Forming part of the productive process, these aggregate rates, distinguished from RF (a remainder class of *non-operative* exchanges), could also be, in our view, a possible ethical link—*if* unethical firms were indeed regulated.

payments to other functions. Basic outlay, O', divides into c'fO', s'fO' and crossover i'fO'; it is fed by fE' and fS' arrows (showing *rates* of payment)—basic expenditure and withdrawals from RF. Surplus outlay, O", divides into propensities to consume (c"fO"), save (s"fO"), and invest (i"fO"); each set of three together equals 1. O" is fed by fE" and fS", surplus expenditure and withdrawals from RF.

If the practice of capitalism often ignores ethics, GEM-FS calls for compassion—not greed. RF can reinforce the intentional aspects of a vigilant watch over the economy and serve as a conduit for revising values—just as the transcendental feedback nature of our intellect's four operations (attention, intelligence, rationality, responsibility) sublates John Rawls' "veil of ignorance"[17] in instantiating a viable ethics. We have relied, in part, on the work of such Lonergan experts as Phil McShane, Michael Shute, Peter Burley, Eileen de Neeve, and Tad Dunne who have advocated what we call "a GEM-FS economics."[18]

For McShane, operative payments are best understood in the context of chapter 16 of *CWL* 21, on "Monetary Flows." Long-and-short-term solutions, would involve the two-layered operative flows and their normative concomitance. The crossover channels (in fig. 5) transpose Keynes' national output model[19] by reversing net aggregate savings to zero during basic

---

17. See "Original position," https://plato.stanford.edu/entries/original-position/ For Rawls, *A Theory of Justice*, 143, the "veil" is a means to set up a fair procedure in one's principles of justice. It should be assumed that concerned parties "do not know the particular circumstances of their own society."

18. In *Journal of Macrodynamic Analysis* (2001), 3–8, Michael Shute, stresses the need to address social justice issues; but realizing that this need is being overlooked, Shute highlights Lonergan's shift toward dynamic analysis: "'Macrodynamics' pertains to the long-term, large-scale dynamics of human process, the elements of which are relevant to specific inquiries. Theoretic 'analysis' explicitly takes into account the intermeshing of the operations of the subject with the object of investigation. 'Macrodynamic analysis' explores the 'upper blade' (macro-context) governing 'lower blade' or micro-inquiry in any field. . . . 'Post-modern' carries with it a connotation deeply meshed with the contemporary academic disorientation . . . We aspire to being 'past-modern.' We envisage the emergence of macroeconomic dynamics as analogous to the shift in chemistry achieved with the discovery of the periodic table."

19. Keynesian economics is a "demand-side" theory that focuses on changes in the economy over the short term. Keynes was the first to sharply separate the study of economic behavior and markets based on individual incentives from the study of broad national economic aggregate variables and constructs. Stephanie Kelton, a leading exponent

expansions. The channels use a notion of pure surplus income, a monetary equivalent of new fixed investment in an expansion; it is money left over after paying bills—what drives an economy. It is the fraction of total surplus income of surplus expenditure that goes to new fixed investment. It is at the nerve center of free economies but subject to cyclic variations in the long-term acceleration of the productive process. The higher the rate of new fixed investment, the greater the rate at which long-term acceleration of the process is proceeding—and the greater is the rate of pure surplus income, first waxing and then waning to zero. In surplus expansions, dQ'', the rate of change in quantity, increases and in a basic expansion dQ' increases; in both cases an expansion begins with a short-term acceleration making full use of already existing resources and equipment. A movement toward long-term acceleration is marked by an initial increase of dQ'' alone, as efforts are concentrated on widening and deepening existing capital equipment and on training employees in new skills. As this process advances, the capacity for basic production keeps increasing; as the new capacity is more fully utilized, the increase of dQ' tends to far outstrip that of dQ''; for "surplus stands to basic as a flow to a flow of flows."[20]

---

of the Modern Monetary Theory, MMT, influenced by Keynes, argues that the government should pay for big-spending programs by printing more money. In her *Deficit Myth, Modern Monetary Theory and the Birth of the People's Economy* (Public Affairs, Sep., 2021), Kelton seeks to break free of fictitious constraints facing the USA. In her view, deficits can help us fight a myriad of problems that plague our economy–inequality, poverty and unemployment, climate change, housing, health care, and more. But we can't use deficits to solve problems if we continue to think of the deficit itself as a problem. However, on the basis of Kelton's ignoring the basic and supply circuits, we argue that MMT could lead to serious if not tragic consequences. For MMT, unemployment is evidence that a currency monopolist is overly restricting the supply of the financial assets needed to pay taxes and satisfy savings desires. It defines money as a creation of the government that derives its value from its status as legal tender. Adam Smith and Keynes both held that the State determines what can serve as money since it enforces its power through taxation. For the post-Keynesian economist Thomas Palley, MMT restates the principles of Keynesian economics, but is prone to "over-simplistic analysis" ignoring the risks of its policy implications. See www.boecker.de/pdf/p_fmm_imk_wp_ 44_2019.pdf

20. *CWL* 15, 129. One can hardly be economically just unless he/she had underdone the needed conversions. That is all the more difficult when dealing with groups, entities, corporations, communist states etc. Getting into the latter problematics needs a reliance on hope. We believe that the redistribution function could/should be adjusted to fit within *MiT*'s eight FS formula. Our arguments for social justice fit within this pattern. We argue

Basic and surplus income contribute savings to RF or draw upon it. Circulation, a circular series of relationships of dependence of one rate of payment upon another, is *not* a rotational movement of money; it is an aggregate of instantaneous rates of payment such as fS' and fS". In fig. 5, money only moves at the instant of payment; usually stationary, it may also be dynamically quiescent (held in reserve for a definite purpose). As in matrix language, so in a "GEM-FS economics," expressions can have any number of nested or recursive functions.

Our entire text has sought to integrate *CWL* 15, 21 within Lonergan's better-known works—a task that has not yet been attempted in sufficient depth.[21] Our approach to GEM-FS economics assigns ethical "functions" to Lonergan's circulation analysis; that is, we seek to integrate the power of human benevolence with GEM-FS's ability to ethically guide the exchange system. Besides the RF, we take other areas such as the crossover to be "functions" with ethical implications. GEM-FS economics balances crossover flows to maintain the dynamic equilibrium of the whole system, but this equilibrium is not automatic. Its functioning requires intelligent intervention based "on an understanding of crossover flows. The entire thrust . . . is towards an active and intelligent control of economic flows,"[22] thereby helping economists and ethicists suggest the movements of the productive and consumption cycles for the good of all within an overall democratic decision-making process. In dialectical fashion, let us evaluate how four crucial areas could help implement economic policies free of skewed premises so as to meet the world's larger needs.

The first crucial area is that of the two crossover ratios in the diagram, G' and G" which effect the transfers of money[23] between

---

with Lonergan that a surplus expansion requires capital; capitalism is a basic means of capital formation by private actors in a market economy. There is a great deal to be angry about in our current situation and much to fear for the future. Greed is not good; market regulations should restrain and punish greed. Remember the old Wall St adage that bulls make money, bears make money, but hogs get slaughtered.

21. We have only scratched the surface.

22. Michael Shute, *The Discovery of the Science of Economics*, 165.

23. Salaries and profits contribute to the standard of living, yielding a fraction heading to the surplus demand function (i'fO'); this is offset by amounts *per interval* surplus demand pays for current surplus products fE" and receives from surplus production, i"fO".

circuits; they link circulations of money between circuit-channels and the basic and surplus stages of production. A basic circuit of expenditure, fE', becomes basic receipts, c'fO', by moving through basic outlay, O', which becomes basic income, I', when allowance is made for the crossover difference, i'fO. The surplus circuit is parallel to the basic one: surplus expenditure, fE", becomes surplus receipts, i"fO", when it moves through surplus outlay, O"—with allowance made for the crossover difference, the fraction of O" moving to I', and basic demand via c"fO". Part of the income derived from surplus production is "spent on the standard of living" but *can* be socio-ethically adjusted by way of RF.

Crossover ratios help determine the portion of surplus income to be reinvested. Initial investment for long-term accelerations of the productive process occur at the surplus stage of production. Improving the capital goods sector increases the production of equipment and spurs surges in buying at the basic stage of the cycle. Analyzing the dynamic equilibrium of the pure cycle helps distinguish when prices express demand or when they fail to adjust income and savings needs. The pure cycle makes it possible for expansions to raise the standard of living in the long run without chronic unemployment or inflation. To achieve a pure cycle, leaders have to understand how the productive process and money circulation are interrelated and make needed adjustments in rates of savings-investment and consumption. Unless they do so, they will fail to make proper changes in subordinate rates of spending needed to adjust the rates of acceleration in production and to balance basic and surplus stages. The required decisions are hard to make because of our inability to gauge the meaning of systemic corrections—as in deficit spending or the balance of payments.

A second crucial area is that of the RF (the remainder function) that regulates transfers between circuits, between flows of money and between the basic and surplus stages of production. Money transfers are defined in the *dynamic functional* terms of how the flow of goods and services are interrelated. RF is an *external conditioning* that provides additions or subtractions from the stock of money available in the stages of production; *it stands outside the production of goods*. International balance of payments, deficit government spending, etc., are "superposed circuits" onto RF, as well.[24] The emergent standard of living and the basic stage of production are *directly* related through aggregate rates of production and *indirectly* related to successive surplus stages of production through other aggregate rates. The stages, along with the crucial RF, form a threefold process:

1) the basic process of production is an ongoing sequence of instances of so much every so often;

2) maintaining or accelerating the basic process depends on the sequence of surplus stages;

3) transactions that do no more than transfer title to ownership are confined to the RF whence "may be derived changes in the stock of money dictated by positive or negative accelerations."[25]

fD" are surplus-demand additions from the RF to I". A surplus expansion occurs when banks loan money to entrepreneurs, or investors place funds for production (fD").[26] RF, a template effecting complex economic transactions, breaks these down into manageable functional

---

24. In *CWL* 15, 162–63, Lonergan addresses sets of phenomena such as favorable and unfavorable balances of foreign trade, deficit government spending," and taxation, "that are analogous to the phenomena of the cycle of the basic price spread as "superposed circuits." It is possible that the RF become "a point through which a circuit regularly passes. . . . Such a circuit both presupposes and is distinct from the basic and circuits.

25. *CWL* 15, 42. The emergent standard of living and the basic stage of production are related by aggregates of rates summarized as double summations. "There is a first summation with respect to factors of production within a given entrepreneurial unit. There is a second summation with respect to the contributions of several entrepreneurial units towards the same product. . . . The second summation may emerge, not all at once, but gradually." Because the relation is a double summation, it is a matter of equivalent aggregates of rates," but *not* identical aggregates of rates. "Whether the second summation takes place gradually or all at once, it must be completed; else we are outside the supposition of an exchange economy."

26. RF could help Rawls' argument in *Justice*, 35, on ordering precepts on taxation or combining principles of fair equality and difference. Here, fD' , fD" demand undefined additions which play key roles. Unethical approaches to economics fail to "feedback-complement" persons' basic knowing-doing levels. The RF potential and monetary functions would help authorities oppose market manipulations.

units; it helps economists realistically gauge risks, the effects of taxation[27] or currency conversions on local markets.

A third crucial area is the way Lonergan measures[28] total sales in both the basic and surplus circuits. Differences between successive price levels lead Lonergan to define the conditions of accelerating the monetary circuits and the underlying productive process itself. He correlates variations in surplus income with variations in the basic price spread. He agrees with the commonly accepted significance of the distinction between the price level, P, and real income, Q. But his notions of basic and surplus production, which postulate national basic and surplus gross products, Y' and Y", allow him to distinguish between basic and surplus price levels P' and P", on the one hand, and basic and surplus real income, Q' and Q", on the other. Doubling turnover frequency may double production without any increase in the quantity of money in circulation. Due to inflation,[29] price levels fluctuate without change in the quantity or quality of goods or services. This process can restore an ethical role in economics downplayed in exchange value; it gives us ways to gauge where profits are going, or what is the fraction of GNP going toward production or consumption, enabling us to judge how and for what ends the economy is faring. (See below Appendix F: "The Mathematics of Circuit acceleration" for examples of Lonergan's version of econometrics).

A fourth crucial area distinguishes absolute rises and falls in prices from relative ones. The free economies must adapt to the pure cycle by distinguishing between the significance of a relative and an absolute rise or fall of monetary prices. A relative rise or fall calls for a relatively increased or reduced production; if a product i, has a greater increment,

---

27. Keynes, *The General Theory of Employment,* 321, contends that the redistribution of income through taxation is important but limited—acknowledging the importance of "significant inequalities in income and wealth." There are "valuable economic activities requiring the motive of money-making."

28. He does this using the vector magnitude known in mathematics as the dot product.

29. Lester Thurow, *The Future of Capitalism* (NY: Morrow, 1996) 164–93. Some predict that President Biden's economic policies will lead to (runaway) inflation.

positive or negative, in price than the product *j*, then more or less of the product *i* is needed than of the product *j*. As prices are in themselves relative (they express demand), so they must be interpreted relatively with regard to expansion and contraction. A fall and rise in prices may be general and absolute or real and relative. Change in demand does not cause a general absolute fall. Prices fall if income distribution fails to adjust to rates of saving or investment.[30] This interrupts the productive process' expansive cycle and converts a basic expansion into a slump. An inverse maladjustment occurs if rising prices in a surplus expansion are not real but stem from an absolute rise in prices that stimulates production. The egalitarian shift in monetary income required by a major basic expansion will not result from decisions that are only seeking ever higher incomes.[31]

A Surplus Expansion Giving Rise to an Increasing Price Spread

Besides these four crucial areas, Lonergan writes that a surplus expansion gives rise to an increasing basic price spread which may lead to a boom.[32] He uses a basic year with a standard price level of comparison

---

30. In "Income Distribution in Economic Growth: Ideas from Bernard Lonergan, *The Lonergan Review*, Vol. II, No. 1 - Spring 2010, Eileen de Neeve introduces Lonergan's theory of income distribution in the framework of his cycle of innovative growth. Changes in income distribution depend on the growth process and the phase in which the economy finds itself. She reviews how economists have measured income distribution, and relates Lonergan's equilibrium pure cycle and its phases to other economic thought. Lonergan's pure cycle of innovative growth is an equilibrium process in which production of new consumables lag the production of capital. The cycle of pure surplus income is driven by the innovative investment and the new money and credit it attracts. But economies in general have not adapted to changes in pure surplus income and tend to turn expansions into financial bubbles in the effort to maintain profit levels as the expansion matures. Income distribution does not become egalitarian enough to increase the demand for consumer goods and services. When demand is insufficient, prices fall. Lower prices discourage businesses, and a downward spiral of prices and incomes follows. De Neeve explores some policy-related questions that are raised by Lonergan's ideas on income distribution and growth.

31. See Fred Lawrence, "Commemorating 50 years of *Insight*," *Revista Portuguesa Di Filosofia*, 63, 4 (2007), 941.

32. Lonergan, *CWL* 15, 140.

to map economics as a domain of definition; it involves 1) a parameterization of the state space of economics in point-to-point or higher correspondences of the aggregates of rates of production with elements in the emergent standard of living; and 2) mapping difference curves to arrive at differences in price levels.[33] On the basis of *Circulation Analysis*,[34] free entrepreneurs should learn to distinguish between the two portions of income: "normal profit" (NP) and what Schumpeter called the "social dividend," (SD), that is pure surplus income which is income over and above the standard of living.[35] The entrepreneurs, oligopolies and multinationals that unilaterally and selfishly reject that distinction reduce SD to NP. As to how societies set prices, Lonergan has recourse to the cycle of the aggregate basic price spread that must be synchronized with the cycle of the productive process in such a way that the synchronicity will transform the trade cycle (with its slumps) to a pure cycle (without slumps).[36]

Teachers must devise methods of educating business people, traders, investors, bankers, financiers, butchers, bakers, etc. in the eighth functional specialty of communications. Artists could present the mathematics in animated cartoons that even a child can appreciate. Accountants must learn to use explanatory normative terms (instead of merely descriptive terms) in presenting their accounts.[37] Historians of economies (in the third FS) are indispensable in this process:

> The emergence both of new ideas and the concrete conditions for
> their practical implementation . . . gives rise to series of new pos-
> sibilities, and the realization of any of these possibilities has similar
> consequences; but not all changes are equally pregnant, so that eco-
> nomic history is a succession of time periods in which alternatively

---

33. *CWL* 15, 23–29.

34. *CWL* 15, 81, 116, 134–40.

35. Lonergan, *CWL* 15, pp. 81, 116, 135, n.186, 145, n. 201.

36. De Neeve, "Hayek," 109–10, stresses that Lonergan's pure cycle offers a general theory of innovative growth and fluctuations.

37. *CWL* 15, 26, note 26.

the conditions for great change are being slowly accumulated; later, the great changes themselves are . . . brought to birth.[38]

Arguing that current analysis fails to grasp the significance of distinguishing the two flows of money—consumer and capital investment flows, Phil McShane concludes that they cannot provide adequate explanations of business oscillations. Lonergan shows "how the distinction between the two flows can be carried forward empirically despite complexities of firms, secondhand trading, banking etc. Slowly, out of that there emerges his powerful and unique chapter 18, 'Cycles of Incomes and Prices.'"[39] He refers to Schumpeter's praise of John Bates Clark,[40] who "was the first to strike a novel note by connecting entrepreneurial profits, considered as a surplus over interest (and rent), with the successful introduction into the economic process of technological, commercial, or organizational improvements."[41]

Towards an "Eco-just" GEM-FS Social Equilibrium

Distinguishing between relative and absolute prices, as well as a sound analysis of cycles of incomes and prices, are helpful means to make judgments on a cooperative basis in determining economic policies. One should ask questions such as: On what criteria do Central Reserve Banks hold money in reserve? Do they seek to reward productive investment or just speculation? Do they adequately promote low rates of interest so as to foster production guided by sound policies? Do they resort to econometrics that are virtually divorced from the productive process?[42] Such

---

38. Lonergan, *CWL* 21, 243.

39. *CWL* 21, 285–307. See also *CWL* 15, Sec. 25, 26 on "Price and Quantity Changes" and "Cycle of Basic Income," 128.

40. The social dividend has affinities with Schumpeter's view of Clark's most important contribution. On this, see Israel M. Kirzner, "The Nature of Profits: Some Economic Insights and their Ethical Implications," p. 34, in *Profits and Morality*, edited by Robin Cowan and Mario J. Rizzo, Univ. of Chicago, 1995, 34.

41. *CWL* 15, 133.

42. Paul Felker, *privately shared with us* that business profits are of two kinds, those that 1) create new wealth and can be justified; 2) a "parasitic" decrease of the amount of

heuristic questions can guide GEM-FS in promoting self-transcendent *ideals* in economics. As GEM-FS links transcendentals with the transcendent, so it can link economics with the real economy, and so free us. Balancing our public and private lives, it points to concrete ways to a just standard of living for all, an economy in which each person has the freedom to be an actor in it. [43]

Mainstream economics has been based too long on the bottom line, *à la* Friedman.[44] To rehumanize that line, GEM-FS economics remaps the boundaries that can ethically re-center the economy. It seeks to create a "space" in which *virtues* can oppose inequalities.[45]

Can a GEM-FS process help us renegotiate group interests in favor of world solidarity? Yes, if self-transcendent actions are included in economic science. Just as we identify with characters in novels charting their way through life's complexities, fig. 5 reveals a moment of truth that should be self-evident but isn't at first: our knowing-doing operations *do affect* economic conditions for good and for ill.[46] This insight should lead to Lonergan's notions of the human good and of economic justice that are healing-creating vectors reinforcing an ethic based on human solidarity. Traditions of wisdom clearly criticize unaccountable

---

socially-needed products and services. If profiteers control vast wealth, "the value of paper money decreases because of the decrease in the amount of real tangible wealth they represent. As the real economy contracts, more people have to suffer increasingly lower standards of living."

43. Frederick Crowe, *Appropriating the Lonergan Idea*, (Catholic University of America Press, 1989) 141.

44. An organization should, of course, stand for more than just the bottom line.

45. Lester Thurow in his *The Future of Capitalism, How Today's Economic Forces Shape Tomorrow's World* (William Morrow, 1996) called for remaking the economic surface of the earth so as to combat surging inequality. This would involve a combination of a 'skill-intensive shift in technology" and overcoming the tendency to drive down the real wages of nonsupervisory labor.

46. Unfortunately, much reporting in the world is strained through the filters of corporate-dominated managerial classes in fields such as science, law, culture, medicine, and finance. This has been happening in both foreign and domestic news media, in non-governmental organizations, and in multilateral international agencies. The upshot is that directly or indirectly, almost all areas of reporting are beholden to corporate funding.

privatizations, for instance.[47] The question arises whether GEM-FS proponents have a strategy to implement the solidarity that begins from the necessary personal horizonal transformations that can lead to manifold types of cooperation to address the many outstanding global problems of climate degradation, vast income inequality, and the teetering world economy. In Appendix E, we follow up on this issue.

---

47. Privatize (from *privare*) deprives the public. Acting justly begs for revisions in the world's legal systems. In case of conflict between national and international law, U.S judges often ignore the latter in instructing juries on how to apply the rules of the law. But the Interfaith Center on Corporate Responsibility helped change the U.S. Securities and Exchange Commission rules (May 20, 1998) so as to allow social policy issues to be subject to stockholder votes. Only *caring* hearts intent on justice despite the reality of evil can build bridges.

Appendix E

Peter Corbishley's S-Shaped Curve:
Toward Ethical Treatment of the Two Circuits

Lonergan allows for general growth as reflected in the equilibrium of the crossover ratios between basic and surplus circuits. We think that Corbishley's notion of an S-shaped cycle helps clarify how it may be possible to work out how an ethical redistributive function (RF) could help rehinge the other four monetary functions. For Corbishley, Lonergan provides the fundamental insight into a sustained, ethical path for economic growth. This basic insight identifies an S-shaped economic cycle. With proper management of the economy, governments can help smooth out the cycle of 'boom and bust' into an S-shaped wave. Corbishley recalls that for Lonergan, a modern economy does not run through a single circuit from production to consumption, moving up and down like a roller coaster between boom and slump, but through two circuits. This yields an S-shaped curve consisting of the two circuits. The S-shaped curve is Lonergan's account of how we could link these two circuits together to smooth out the ride into a single upward movement:[1]

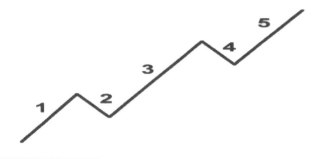

---

1. See Peter Corbishley, "Our Economic Problem—Greed or Ignorance," Oct. 17, 2008, peter@english-english.co.uk

The diagram describes a series of 2 booms and 2 slumps in a modern economy. The 5 phases do not form a cycle. Living standards do rise across time, but they are inequitably distributed. Lonergan's model of the economy enables him to smooth the sequence of booms and slumps into a single cycle based on the 's' or 'sigmoid' curve. The model has 5 phases (not marked here) where phase 5 at the top of the curve is equal to phase 1 at the bottom of the curve but clearly at a higher standard of living as indicated by the greater quantity of goods available in the economy which results in a single identifiable cycle:

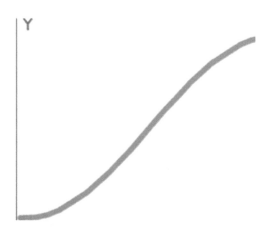

The redistributive function (RF) might equitably switch the focus of investment from surplus expansion to basic expansion over the longer term. In our view, this, in principle, would help economists make ethical judgments on the relative importance of supply and demand. If the ratio is positive, more is going to the surplus stage of production than to the basic stage; if negative, more is going to the basic than the surplus stage. Corbishley clarifies how it is possible to work out how the RF can help rehinge the other four monetary functions in ethical ways. Corbishley argues that Lonergan comes to this insight by recognizing that all economies, from earliest times have operated with two separate circuits, one related to consumption and the other to production. The S-shaped curve is one way to portray Lonergan's account of how we can link these two circuits to smooth out the ride into a single upward movement—thus providing an ethical underpinning for Lonergan's economics.

The initial distinction between basic and surplus circuits can be noted from the fact that from early on in history, humans have taken the time and effort to create new technologies. They have used available resources in developing a standard of living and devoted this surplus to developing technologies. In the basic circuit, people deliver a standard of living to each other, but in the surplus circuit of an economy they invest in developing new technologies which expand the means of production and provide the basis for a higher standard of living. Corbishley highlights that this requires literacy and education in modern economies. Young people could be taken out of direct production and placed within the surplus circuit so that at a future date society as a whole might reap the benefits of the higher standard of living that comes from higher educational standards. This means that individual persons could take time out from earning a living to undergo training or getting an education before returning to the work place to earn a higher standard of living. This is generally the case for many UK university graduates.

The surplus expansion of the basic circuit leads to a higher standard of living. This expansion expands capital formation to underpin higher standards of living in the basic circuit. Surplus expansion comes about through investment in human and technological resources. As investment in capital develops, a surplus expansion becomes increasingly complex. Corbishley observes that with a simple one-to-one investment in making a knife, one begins to realize

> Something of the complexity of the multi-levelled structure of capital development using the example of the clothing sector in an economy where innovatory investment is driven firstly by industrial and then by scientific revolutions.[2]

---

2. Corbishley, 3. He emphasizes the complexities of investing in the surplus circuit of production.

In the case of the 'pre-historic' form of leather manufacturing[3] as a knife culture in which a cutter uses a single knife to cut up an animal skin to produce a leather 'coat', one animal leads to one 'coat', but the one knife can be used time and time again.

Time, it is true, has to be taken out from hunting animals in order to make the knife in the first place, but once made, the knife increases efficiency. A technological innovation becomes part of an economy. Making the knife brings in a line of production—that of making knives—that is surplus to the basic stage of production in which we make and sell coats. . . . The knife improves the standard of living as the 'coat' is now no longer just something 'thrown together' across the shoulders. Equally importantly, there develops a secondary level of production which makes the machines that make the knives. In addition the machines that make the knives for cutting leather can also be used for making knives that do things other than cut leather or make clothes.[4]

Corbishley picks up on the notion that it is machines that make tools. In turn, machine tools are used to make machines. There is not only a basic circuit of production and consumption, but there are one or more secondary or surplus lines of production producing the machines that produce the machines. In the clothing industry, plantations produce cotton like hunting foxes produces the material for fur coats. But, as the industry develops, cotton gins clean cotton, spindles make that cotton into cotton thread, looms weave the thread into cloth, and sewing machines make the cloth into cotton dresses. One cotton plant is still made into one cotton dress, but time and money has to be taken out from making cotton dresses

---

3. Fast forwarding, Corbishley gives the example of leather manufacturers in the East End of London who can now only thrive by catering to the expensive end of the market. This is a telling comment on the great difficulty of dealing with poverty nationally and internationally. An area in the East End of London was chosen as the location for a program to reduce poverty, but ironically the program area mostly overlaps with another area mapped out for the past 150 years as "vicious and semi-criminal, as experiencing "chronic want." Relative poverty seems geographically affected and is hard to root out.

4. Corbishley, 4. Recall our initial starting point that the critiques of Heilbroner and Matson are similar to ours. They identify some of the imprisoning dimensions of the economic plight in which humanity has been caught since the Industrial Revolution. These dimensions can be alleviated through a GEM-FS process.

to make the machines that make the cotton gins, the sewing machines, the looms and so on. The introduction of different power sources—water, steam, electricity—further increases the possibilities for ranges of available machinery. So we can have a great number of levels of production, not all focused on the clothing industry, which are in a hierarchy of removes from the basic stage of making a dress or a suit purchased as part of a standard of living. Investment in the application of new power sources in new types of factories, or in investment utilizing new scientific knowledge leads to further expansion of the surplus circuit.

As to raising capital for the expansion of the surplus circuit, Corbishley stresses the importance of the sheer scale of the capital investment and the time required to invest in innovations that expand existing levels of surplus production in a modern complex society. The amount of money is one thing, but it may well be the case that years elapse before new goods are sold into either the surplus or basic circuits. If the benefits of new inventions are to be shared across the society, someone has to take the risk of investing in the latest wave of innovation, in a new level of surplus expansion. Historically, risk-taking individuals have invested in "a surplus expansion." Understanding the risks of such entrepreneurship is crucial to hopes of realizing a profit. Raising money for the surplus expansion is relatively unproblematic. For Lonergan, there is no difficulty is "in financing the surplus expansion. It is the first step towards increasing a society's standard of living,[5] a step about which financiers and engineers do not hesitate.

Lonergan signals the transition into the basic expansion by moving from investing in the expansion of a surplus circuit to investing in the expansion of a basic circuit. Corbishley notes that for Lonergan investing in a surplus circuit increases the efficiency of production. "Investment

---

5. *CWL* 15, 82. Corbishley, 4, adds that "The moral norms for the surplus expansion" are thrift and enterprise; those for the basic expansion are benevolence and enterprise.

Both require a technical understanding of where we are in the economic cycle before being applied. De Neeve, "Interpreting," 94, notes that the 19th century maxim of "thrift and enterprise" helped the surplus or capital expansions of that time. However, society as a whole did not benefit until later in the century "because profits were maintained by investing in other countries, or by exporting abroad the surplus expansions related, for example, to railway construction. . . . Lonergan pure cycle extends the general equilibrium theory of mainstream economics to include both growth and cycles."

in a basic circuit creates rising wages and falling prices. A critical mistake is to apply the rate of profit appropriate to risk-taking investment in the surplus circuit to investment in the expansion of the basic circuit. In that case, profit moves from being a motive to being a criterion of economic activity. Profit-making "as a motive for risk-taking investment in new technology is one thing, entrepreneurial rates of return as a criterion for low-risk investment is another."[6] If in fact we invest in advancing the benefits of new technology to new consumers in the basic circuit, but we continue to expect the level of profit that motivates a surplus expansion, then sooner or later this will lead to a slump. The slump begins when the providers of low-risk investment in the expansion of the basic circuit find that entrepreneurial level profits are not materializing; they use this fact as the criterion for diminishing their operations. To maximize the standard of living realizable within the possibilities of a given technology, we have to have economic reasons for changing the expectations about profit that currently surround investment in the basic expansion. For Lonergan the economic reasons are that first, 'profit' is a social dividend produced by the economic expansion of the surplus circuit; second, to avoid the bust that follows boom we have to learn how to manage the distribution of that dividend across the long term of an economic cycle.

The requirements for a 'normal profit' remain, but any excess over that is a social dividend. "It is not money to be spent. It is not money to be saved. It is money to be invested."[7] Lonergan is not focusing on an accountant's notion of profit or a demand for higher wages, but is pointing to "a social dividend that, at certain phases of the economic cycle, is available to invest in raising the standard of living of the whole population. The social dividend is founded on 'pure surplus income', namely the income over and above the income required for current consumption and the current replacement of what is required to produce that level of consumption." All organizations require the consumption and

---

6. Corbishley, 4.

7. *CWL* 15, 81–2. Corbishley, 5, comments that it may be what has happened in the UK in that the surplus income available for investment from the surplus expansion was spent through raising the standard of living directly, for example, by taking out credit against 'privately owned' but mortgaged houses.

replacement income[8] to keep people satisfied and happy. "In aggregate 'pure surplus income' is what is left over when normal profits have been made. Lonergan identifies pure surplus income with 'net aggregate savings', namely the money available to the whole economy that does not need to be spent to maintain the standard of living of that economy."[9]

Identifying Pure Surplus Income

Entrepreneurs are quite aware of the ideal of the successful man whose success is measured not by a high emergent standard of living nor by the up-to-date efficiency of some industrial or commercial unit but by increasing industrial, financial, and social power and prestige. In the old days when the entrepreneur was also owner and manager, pure surplus income roughly coincided with what was termed profit. Today, with increasing specialization of function, pure surplus income is distributed in a variety of ways: it enters into [the] very high salaries of general managers and top-flight executives, into the combined fees of directors when together these reach a high figure, into the undistributed profits of industry, into the secret reserves of banks, into the accumulated royalties, rents, interest, receipts, fees, or dividends of anyone who receives a higher income than he intends to spend at the basic final market.[10]

There are echoes here of the moral condemnation of windfall profits, excessive bonuses, high salaries, and the lifestyles of the famous and rich. However, Lonergan moves on from merely decrying individual "greedy bankers"[11] on Wall Street to an account of how we might promote an economic order that is both efficient and moral.

---

8. Corbishley, 6.

9. Corbishley, 6.

10. *CWL* 15, 153.

11. Lonergan foresaw the elements of the finance-based capitalism that is responsible for a great deal of the damage that perverse forms of capitalism are creating. "[the velocity of money] can become enormous when a number of men trade back and forth the same things with the same money, and this arises when the stock market becomes a gambling casino." He even refers several times to "Moneybags" in *CWL* 21, 61, 68, 88.

Corbishley on the Rates-of-flow Diagram's Redistribution Function

Lonergan's key distinction between surplus and basic circuits allows him to distinguish between two different types of growth or expansion. He uses his various versions of his rates of flow diagram to express mathematically the financial flows across production, consumption and redistribution circuits as *supply, demand and redistribution functions*.[12] For Corbishley,

> The redistribution function works through banks, investment companies, colonial powers . . . , larger firms and wealthier individuals who 'pitch' quantities of money into the circuits. Their actions accelerate and decelerate the movement of finance between the surplus and basic circuits, within and across economies, often further impoverishing the weaker. In the context of the contemporary crisis, the resale of houses is redistributive, whereas financial operations are partly redistributive and partly payments for services that are part of the basic circuit.[13]

Current liquidity problems in the redistributional circuit may spill over into a depression and to increasing unemployment leading to a real contraction in the basic circuit.[14] Lonergan has shown that the loss of liquidity may negatively affect entrepreneurial investments in such areas

---

12. Corbishley, 7; he adds that "Redistribution here does not mean giving from the rich to the poor, but models how financial institutions redistribute money between basic and surplus circuits; see our notes on Pigou's view on sharing wealth.

13. Corbishley, 8. Corbishley does suggest that investment cycles that produce a fundamental transformation of the capital equipment of an economy include long-term accelerations that prepare for the fundamental transformation, and long-term accelerations that realize the benefits of that fundamental transformation. See *CWL*, 15, 162. Here we may infer that Corbishley's Christian interpretation of the redistribution function could be modified in the manner suggested in Appendix D.

14. Roger Farmer, *How the Economy Works*, 120–21, argues that Bernanke and Paulson took the right action in not letting banks fail in 2008. He gives two reasons why the classical view of economics is wrong because it 1) ignores "the role of confidence as an independent factor that drives booms and busts"; 2) sees "the economy as a self-correcting mechanism in which market forces will restore full employment."

as the technologies of renewable energy, which in the UK are not currently regarded as commercially viable. This would lead to a failure to effectively confront changes in the climate.[15]

Research into Items Outlined in *CWL* 15, *Circulation Analysis*

Given the complexity of modern problems, Lonergan has provided just a beginning. We must delve further. So that his theoretical work can be applied, we need to identify which parts of an economy are in the surplus or basic circuits. We have argued, along with Lonergan and Corbishley that our present economic statistics are built on the belief that fundamentally there is only one circuit from production to consumption. Economists tend to measure what they can using descriptive categories to illustrate what ordinary people's buying and selling. Because Lonergan's categories are analytic, we need to develop his categories, using statistics to underpin the narratives of what we are up to. At present, Lonergan's analysis just provides what he called "rather convincing indicators."[16] Lacking statistically-based narratives, commentators will find it difficult to produce decisive policy statements, suggest relevant programs or support effective interventions.[17] Other interests and motives will remain dominant. Fortunately the task is not merely academic; given these pointers, it is now time to indicate some of the non-economic pre-conditions for managing a just economy in equitably distributive ways.

Towards a Just Democratic Economy

For Lonergan, one of the conditions for establishing an equitable economy is that we understand better how people live their everyday lives.

---

15. Corbishley, 8.

16. Corbishley quoting *CWL* 15, 72.

17. Compare the initiatives proposed by Pope Francis in his *Laudato Sì*: https://www.huffpost.com/entry/laudato-si-whats-missing-whats-not_b_7630516

Not being an advocate of bureaucracies,[18] he argues that the radical re-distribution implied in the basic expansion comes about through citizens, including business people, acting on a critically realist understanding of how an economy works. There is a role then for a Church with a world-wide educational system in preparing the ground for the reception of a critically realist account of the economy. Corbishley concludes his article by noting that the lack of sufficient investment in the UK may underlie its decline in manufacturing.

---

18. De Neeve, *Decoding the economy*, 131, notes that "More than half of all international trade takes place within global enterprises. This means that sales are not organized through market exchanges, but through a command system of accounting prices decided within the corporation." After commenting on the international financial and currency transfers that are part of the business of multinational corporations and international fund investors, she concludes this paragraph by saying, almost prophetically as regards the present situation, that "Regulating international financial transaction equitably remains an issue for world financial stability."

Appendix F

The Math of Circuit Acceleration and Lonergan's Version of Econometrics

The key to understanding economic acceleration and deceleration is price and quantity. We need to be able to measure the incremental changes in price and quantity at different intervals of time in order to have an overall insight into the changes of the economy—and eventually, to learn how to avoid booms and busts and promote pure cycles. What follows is the econometrics used by Lonergan and illustrated in the lawnmower business example we used above.

Rhoda the retailer sells quantity 1 mower to a customer at price 1 in month one, quantity 2 at price 2 in month two, and quantity 3 at price 3 in month three. These are final payments to Rhoda including Hannah's initial payments, William the wholesaler's transitional payments to Hannah the manufacturer, and Rhoda's transitional payments to William; the payments all involve quantities q at prices p.

If p_1, p_2, and p_3 are the same and q_1, q_2, q_3 are also unchanged, we are in a static economy. However, remember that the outlays O for all three all have prices p_i at quantities q_i as well. It is highly unlikely that the total expenditures E will go unchanged. For all the raw materials, labor, management, utilities, machine tools, costs of space, taxes, etc., will soon begin to vary at time intervals t_1, t_2, t_3 . . . How will we know whether we are in a boom, bust, or pure cycle acceleration?

Suppose that in month 1 Rhoda sold mowers i in the quantity q_i at price p_i, and in month 2 she sold mowers in the quantity $q_{i\,+}\,dq_{i,}$ at the price $p_i + dp_i$. Suppose further that there are n such sales for Rhoda, such that the aggregate payment in the first interval was Z, and in the second interval it was $Z + DZ$, so that

$$Z = \Sigma\, p_i q_i^{\,1}$$

$$Z + DZ = \Sigma\, (p_i q_i + p_i dq_i + q_i dp_i + dp_i dq_i)$$

for all instances of i from 1 to n.

The question arises: "Can one define two numbers, say P and Q, so that P varies with a set of numbers p_1, p_2, p_3, . . . and Q varies with another set of numbers q_1, q_2, q_3 . . . ?"

As we noted, if Rhoda sells quantity 1 mower at price 1 for x months in a row, this would be a static economic situation and the solution to the equations is that DZ is 0, and P and Q are invariant. Calculations for a dynamic situation can still follow this method, of course, though the numbers will be weighted averages.[2] However, for real precision, Lonergan also commends a standard economic mathematical tool, an n-dimensional manifold of vectors.[3] Here we quote at length a passage from *CWL* 15:

A universally valid answer may be had when P and Q are not mere numbers but vectors in an n-dimensional manifold. . . . Let *P* and *Q* be the vectors from the origin to the points $(p_1, p_2, p_3, . . .)$ and $(q_1, q_2, q_3 . . .)$ respectively. Then any variation in the price, that is, in any ratio of the type p_i/p_j, will appear as any variation in the angle between the projection of *P* on the plane ij and the axis j. Similarly, any variation in the quantity pattern will appear as a parallel variation in an angle made by the projection of *Q*. But besides such variation in price pattern or quantity pattern there may general increases or decreases in prices and quantities. The latter appear as either positive or negative increments in the absolute magnitudes of the vectors, for

$$P^2 = \Sigma\, p_i^2$$

$$Q^2 = \Sigma\, q_i^2$$

1. This is a basic equation in econometrics. See e.g., Christopher Dougherty, *Introduction to Econometrics*, 3rd edition (Oxford 2007) 38–39.

2. See *CWL* 21, 272, on weighted averages and its drawbacks.

3. See, e.g, Songzi Du, "Topology and Economics," https://www3.nd.edu/~mbehren1/18.904/ Du_project.pdf

that is, the length of the vector P is the square root of the sum of all prices squared, and the length of the vector Q is the square root of the sum of all quantities squared. Thus one may suppose two n-dimensional spheres of radii P and Q, respectively. The vector from the origin to any point in the first "quadrant" of the surface of such spheres represents a determinate price pattern or quantity pattern. On the other hand, variation in P or Q is variation in the size of the spheres.[4]

The dot product enables us to equate Z with P and Q. Hence,

$$Z = \Sigma \, p_i q_i = PQ \cos A$$

where A is the angle between the vectors P and Q. Thus variation in Z depends not only on the magnitude of P and Q but also on the price and quantity patterns as represented by the angle A between the vectors. This is evident enough, since it makes a notable difference in Z whether large or small instances of p_i combine with large or small instances of q_i, and such combination is ruled by the relative price and quantity patterns, to appear ultimately in the angle A.

Next, consider the second interval of time in which the vector P increases to $(P + dP)$, the vector Q to $(Q + dQ)$, and the angle A to $(A + dA)$. Then

$$(P + dP)^2 = \Sigma \, (p_{i\,+} \, dp_i)^2$$

$$(Q + dQ)^2 = \Sigma \, (q_{i\,+} \, dq_i)^2$$

$$Z + DZ = (P + dP) \, (Q + dQ) \cos(A + dA)$$

$$DZ = PQ[dP/P + dQ/Q + dPdQ/PQ) \cos(A + dA) - 2 \sin (dA/2 \sin (A + dA/2)]$$

Thus DZ depends not only upon the initial quantities P, Q, A, and the increments in absolute magnitude dP and dQ, but also upon changes in the relative price and quantity patterns as represented by the angle dA.

4. *CWL* 15, 73–74.

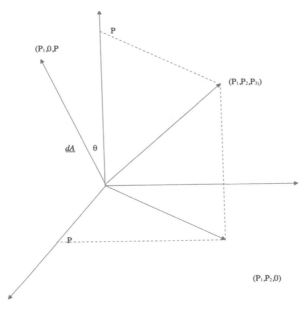

$$\text{Fig. 6}$$

[In this simplified example, P_1, P_2, and P_3 are prices at three consecutive intervals.[5]]

Lonergan continues:

The significance of the foregoing is purely theoretical. The question has been about the possibility of price and quantity indices. The only relevant common measure of tons of iron ore, ton-miles of transportation, kilowatt-hours, and so on, lies in their prices; but prices themselves are subject to change; hence if it is possible to measure the acceleration of the productive process, it has to be possible to differentiate between price variation, price pattern and quantity variation, and the pure quantity variation of the productive process.[6]

In *CWL* 15, Lonergan comments further:

---

5. *CWL* 15, 73, as interpreted by the abstract topologist Dr. Richard Schori. We thank him for his help, and David Bibby for sound advice.

6. *CWL* 21, 269–71

Admittedly we have not yet arrived at measurements but only at heuristic expressions . . . Many, no doubt, will urge that they prefer something less abstruse than an n-dimensional configuration space. But I would note that the configuration space, precisely because of its complexity, can represent all the qualitative differences from one interval to the next and thereby promote the modesty that befits appeals to price and quantity indices.[7]

In conclusion, we have shown that Lonergan's approach to economics was new and original. Now, several decades later, it is high time to study it in depth and to deploy it. Our "sandwich configuration" can hopefully bring a relevant perspective to this task.

7. *CWL* 15, 75.

Appendix G

Blockchains and Democracies

The basic question is how to implement pure surplus income as investment in innovative goods and services. Since it is savings above the profit necessary for a firm to operate, who will determine (a) what to invest in, and (b) how to collect the funds in question?

Dictatorships and robber-baron capitalists used force in the past to effect expansions—to raise a nation's standard of living and to enrich the rich further. "The surplus phase is anti-egalitarian, as much as in Russia and socialist countries as elsewhere; there was more . . . deliberatively inflicted suffering in Siberia at the base of the Russian surplus expansion than in the 19th century British expansion that so raised the explosive anger of Marx."[1] "Who decides" is a basic question of justice. "Who pays" is a further question. In both those cases there can be massive injustices. In any economic enterprise—beekeeping, lawnmower manufacturing, etc.—the attendant surplus manufacturers, wholesalers, retailers, there is risk. Bees may die off, aluminum become exorbitant due to disasters, currencies may devalue, interest rates rise, stock markets crash, and lawnmowers become as obsolete as buggy whips. Not to mention stupidity, criminality, and all the consequences of the seven capital sins.

It is enterprise that creates firms that make and raise (or lower) a society's standard of living; of course, enterprise needs investment. To improve the standard of living for all requires the pure cycle of a surplus expansion focused on innovations followed by a more expansive basic expansion. How to make this happen requires determining what innovations are worth investing in, as well as finding the needed funding. Lonergan argued that two conditions are necessary to establish a

---

1. *CWL* 15, 141–42, footnote 198.

just economy within a democratic framework: 1) decision-making that respects the "iron laws"[2] of economics, and 2) an appropriate, correct application of those laws. This is why he thought that the education necessary for such a sea change is the most difficult aspect of his approach. On this topic he wrote:

> To change one's standard of living in any notable fashion is to live in a different fashion. It presupposes a grasp of new ideas. If the ideas are to be above the level of currently successful advertising, serious education must be undertaken. . . . Coming to grasp what serious education really is . . . (and accepting) that challenge constitutes the greatest challenge to the modern economy. We have had the great surplus expansion of the industrial and scientific revolutions. . . . We have yet to master the basic expansion.[3]

That is as true today as it was in 1980. Income inequality has massively increased since then. Today there is far less confidence in democracy than there was in 1980. Dictatorships of a proletariat or an oligarchy of robber barons are not the solution for creating the conditions for a just economy. We believe that people would still be willing to participate in a democratically-organized economy *if they had a real say*—if they had reason to believe they will see a long-term benefit. As to the thorny problem of "having a real say," we have endeavored to relate a section of "The Method of Ethics," in *Insight*,[4] to how communities of thinkers might engage themselves in the FS. Lonergan's ethics requires that democratic control of an economy be guided not just by informed scholars but by informed producers and consumers as well.[5] Such an ideal political tool, may be helped by decentralized autonomous organizations (DAO's) which are, in effect, a development of the cryptocurrency revolution. "DAOs envision a collective organization owned and managed by

---

2. Ricardo's *laissez-faire* doctrine typically included his "Iron Laws of Wages" which held that any attempts to improve the real income of workers were futile.

3. *CWL* 15, 119.

4. *CWL* 3, chapter 18, 1, 1.4, 626–28.

5. There would be some overlap in relating surplus income to basic income.

its members with all of them having a voice. Many analysts and industry insiders affirm that this type of organization is coming to prominence, even potentially replacing some traditional companies."[6]

For example, the Ethereum website comments:

> The backbone of a DAO is its smart contract. The contract defines the rules of the organization and holds the group's treasury. Once the contract is live on [a blockchain], no one can change the rules except by a vote. If anyone tries to do something that's not covered by the rules and logic in the code, it will fail. Further, because the treasury is also defined by the smart contract that means no one can spend the money without the group's approval. This means that DAOs don't need a central authority. Instead the group makes decisions collectively and payments are authorized automatically when approved in a collective vote. This is possible because smart contracts are tamper-proof once they go live on [a blockchain]. You can't just edit the code (the DAOs rules) without people noticing due to the fact that everything is public.[7]

We suggest that DAOs could be organized and financed to invest pure surplus income in innovative ideas for the production of goods and services. Once a regional, national or transnational government had identified basic areas of development (e. g., activities reducing carbon emissions and other pollutants), it would ask specific DAOs to identify and eventually invest in concrete realizations of goods and services in

---

6. Cathy Hackl, "What Are DAOs And Why You Should Pay Attention," *Forbes Magazine*, June 1, 2021, www.forbes.com/sites/cathyhackl/2021/06/01/what-are-daos-and-why-you-should-pay-attention/ "Smart contracts and the metaverse have analogous functions in that smart contracts can be minted as a simple NFT (non-fungible token). Minting a NFT smart contract within a metaverse is considered a metaverse smart contract. Metaverse is an open source, decentralized, interoperable platform for programmable digit assets built on substrate. See https://mvs.org

7. https://ethereum.org/en/dao/. We substituted "[a blockchain]" for "Ethereum," since there is a swiftly-growing number of firms that use blockchain technology. It was invented to create Bitcoin, the first cryptocurrency, but it has wide applications well beyond finance. Firms such as Walmart have successfully adopted blockchain technology to solve supply-line problems. See e.g., https://www.hyperledger.org/learn/publications/walmart-case-study

those areas in the productive (surplus) economy. Savings (writ large) of firms, pension funds and insurance companies, as well as of individuals invested in the DAOs would fund them initially, perhaps with tax advantages. This would require that a government promote the good of *all* its citizens, which means first, that it would be truly democratic, and second, that citizens be sufficiently educated to demand of their elected representatives that societal economic goals intend the eventual raising of the standard of living for all—despite the initial anti-egalitarian investments in surplus firms.[8]

Returns from firms receiving such investments would repay the DAO over time. However, eventually there would be a tapering off of the surplus income (over average profit) as the surplus products fill demand. The DAOs would turn to financing the needs of the basic expansion so as to raise the overall standard of living by promoting consumption. Such a move would depend on the intelligent grasp not only of financing the surplus economy, but also on how to manage the movement of the productive process to the basic economy's expansion. This would require understanding and measuring the crossovers between surplus and basic circuits. In fact, we may say that Lonergan had diagnosed problems that impede the proper and just development of local and global economies and anticipated a solution:

> The dynamics of surplus and basic production, surplus and basic expansions, surplus and basic incomes are not understood, not formulated, not taught. When people do not understand what is happening and why, they cannot be expected to act intelligently. When intelligence is a blank, the first law of nature takes over: self-preservation.[9]

---

8. If DAO's are to be an answer, their members would need to be not only informed but morally converted as well. This is not easily done since we live in an age of great changes, many perils, much confusion, many uncertainties and glimmers of hope.

9. *CWL* 15, 82.

Appendix H

Are Economists Naïve?

To the question "What Can New Generations of Economists Learn from Henri Poincaré?"[1] commentators tended to agree that most economists are naïve in their uncritical use of mathematics. One participant distinguished between economic theory as a social philosophy which is an abstract discourse about wealth and about societies where wealth is considered as a quantity (of money or of labor), and economics as a set of tools used for policy or decision. The question arises, for example, as to how build a rational discourse in a supply-and-demand value theory[2] which would not be mostly mathematical in principle? Not a few mathematicians agree with Poincaré's viewpoint that mathematics in physics, economics etc. deal with a descriptive net formed of propositions and equations relating to various quantities. Mathematics is a way of communicating the description we have of reality but, as Gödel's theorem suggests, no matter how tight the net is it will always have holes. Poincaré seems to be saying "Mind the holes; rigor kills." The problem is that economists *mistake the net for reality and fall in love with their own* mathematical picture of the net. Humanity is too complex for such a picture.

Another discussion participant distinguished between economic theory as a social philosophy which is an abstract discourse about wealth and about societies "where wealth is considered as a quantity (of money, of labor . . . and economics as a set of tools used for policy or decision." For its part, value theory insists that mathematics should not be

---

1. See *Academia*, July 10, 2021.

2. See "Value Theory," Stanford Encyclopedia of Philosophy.

3. Interview with Professor Michael Roos, August 18, 2021, retrieved from his site.

the only language to which economists resort. They should be aware of the fact that the use of mathematics raises as many problems as the use of ordinary language.[3]

In his article, "Mathiness in the Economic Growth Theory," Paul Romer noted that what he calls "mathiness lets academic politics masquerade as science."[4] We have argued with Lonergan that economics is primarily a social science that should seek to discover the fundamental laws of the behavior of economies which should not be abstracted from the humans living in those economies. In this spirit, we have sought to discern[5] and spell out GEM-FS's relevance to the field of economics. We have argued that all of Lonergan's works can be approached as a process-based and a process-oriented method applicable to all domains of human activity including economics. We have sought to coordinate all of Lonergan's writings from a "GEM-FS-based process" standpoint— focused on discerning the roles of values and ethics which are all too often ignored in the "real-illusory"[6] world of economics today. It may be that many professional economists are hampered by their lack of a methodological approach needed to appreciate Lonergan's breakthroughs in economics, implying that

---

4. By "mathiness," Romer, a Nobel prize winner, meant a specific misuse of mathematics in economic analyses. See *American Economic Review: Papers & Proceedings* 2015, 105(5): 89–93. For Romer, an author committed to the norms of science should use mathematical reasoning to clarify, but "mathiness" misleads.

5. On discernment, Carl Sagan, in *The Demon-Haunted World: Science as a Candle in the Dark*, 1995 wrote: "Not explaining science seems to me perverse. When you're in love, you want to tell the world. But there is more. I have a foreboding of an America in my children's or grandchildren's time—when the United States is a service and information economy; when nearly all the manufacturing industries have slipped away to other countries; when awesome technological powers are in the hands of a very few, and no one representing the public interest can even grasp the issues; when the people have lost the ability to set their own agendas or knowledgeably question those in authority; when, clutching our crystals and nervously consulting our horoscopes, our critical faculties in decline, unable to distinguish between what feels good and what's true, we slide, almost without noticing, back into superstition and darkness."

6. We are reminded here of Orwell's *1984* and its "newspeak" through which Big Brother, wanting to limit free speech seeks to control all discourse. Lonergan died in 1984. We use his method to depict the exact opposite of what *1984* warns us of.

§ They don't know what they don't know.

§ They are not methodologists and don't know what constitutes good theory.

§ They have never read *CWL* 3, pages 3–172 or 490–97 and so they never studied the canons of empirical method, especially the Canon of Parsimony and the Canon of Complete Explanation; they lack a purely scientific and explanatory heuristic.

§ They do not adequately distinguish description vs. explanation.

§ They don't know what is a known unknown.

§ They do not put questions in the right order to discover basic terms of scientific significance—being mired in muddy premises and assumptions.

§ They are unable to employ a scientific, dynamic heuristic adequate for analysis of a current, purely dynamic process.

§ They don't understand what constitutes the normative system's requirement for concomitance, continuity, and equilibrium of flows.

§ Lacking a background in physics, they don't understand the principles and abstract laws of hydrodynamics, electric circuits, or field theory. Nor do they understand adequately the idea of continuity and the conditions of equilibrium in macroeconomic dynamics. They are unaware of analogies from physics applicable on the basis of isomorphism to the phenomena of functional macroeconomic dynamics.[7]

---

7. See "Why Macroeconomists Haven't Yet Flocked to Functional Macroeconomic Dynamics | A New Paradigm: Bernard Lonergan's Macroeconomic Field Theory" (functionalmacroeconomics.com).

Appendix I

Helpful Comments on Money Supply by Two Economists

In a 2021 article, "The Monetary Bathtub is Overflowing,"[1] the two economists John Greenwood and Steven Hanke, seemed to have found Lonergan."[2] Their evocation of the bathtub image is familiar to all of us: water flowing in and out of a bathtub. In our view, the simple image can represent monetary flows. The image attracts attention, which is a good thing; however, Lonergan's macroeconomic field theory presents a more adequate representative image of flows. In Lonergan's diagram of rates of flow, the rates are velocities and accelerations of *functionally interdependent* flows. Insight into Lonergan's diagram on rates of flow can yield an enriching explanation of the dynamics of the objective economic process.[3] Of course, Greenwood and Hanke's article had to be written so as to be understandable by laypersons; the *Wall Street Journal* commentator does make the following two points:

The objective economic process consists of two (or more) operative functional monetary circulations in circuits plus an accessible money pool of reserves situated in a "redistributive function." The circulations and the pool are functionally defined and have a role in any consideration of the money supply and its circulation.

In dynamics, the idea of money held for insurance claims, emergencies, a rainy day, retirement, personal wealth, or investment is better explained mathematically in terms of income strata and their average

---

1. *The Wall Street Journal*, 10/21/2021.

2. Commentary at https://functionalmacroeconomics.com/2021/11/12/john-greenwood-and-steve-h-hankes-the-monetary-bathtub-is-overflowing/

3. Continued commentary on Greenwood and Hanke article.

propensity to consume or invest.[4] Greenwood and Hanke do not explicitly analyze the functional dynamics of the current process and what constitutes continuity and dynamic equilibrium; they do identify recent and current flows that are presently intrinsically inflationary, even if it will take time for the actual inflation to work itself out through the supply chains, operative circuits, and stock and bond prices. Though it takes time for inflation to work through the long supply chain and the resistance of buyers and savers, Greenwood and Hanke measure and clearly point out what is implicit in recent Treasury, and Fed operations. Some observers have said that Greenwood and Hanke should have emphasized that excess money can result in inflation in present goods and services, in stocks, bonds, real estate, art, etc. The editors of the article conclude:

> So that they will gain a better understanding of how the production-and-sale process really works and thereby refine their arguments regarding how the monetary flows must properly conform to the magnitudes and frequencies constituting the dynamic economic process, we encourage Messrs. Greenwood and Hanke to study Lonergan's macroeconomic field theory . . . They should master the rate of flows diagram's scheme of functional interdependencies of the productive and monetary velocities and, thereby, gain a framework by which to critique, e. g., the Federal Reserve's alleged mismanagement of the process.[5] They should bring themselves to understand the diagram as a unified whole which would enable them to instruct on the good of order and "to soar to the top of their profession."[6]

---

4. *CWL* 15, 134–44.

5. The Fed's policy to counter the threat of inflation in 2022 is a source of concern for it may spark a recession.

6. Conclusion to the commentary on Greenwood and Hanke article.

Appendix J

Economics on Trial

Relying on Lonergan, Marybeth Gardam has suggested that the problem with the way our economy works is adhering to beliefs that limit our options. She argues that we must create for the public an alternative view of what economics should be measuring and analyzing: what is the real purpose of *the current* economic system (unfettered ruthless profit-over-people capitalism). We must put the role of economics on trial, testing whether it provides for the good of all. This would be an alternative view of how 'partnership economics' can and should work. As long as we continue to measure the economic health of a nation by looking with blinders solely at the GDP, the stock market, and measuring success only by the profits for those capable of buying, selling and holding stocks, we ignore the actual facts that truly measure economic health: the financial security of the poor, the ability of families to feel safe in their neighborhoods, access to education and healthcare that don't drive consumers of those services into crushing debt, the vitality of relationships, and the valuing of those relationships in communities.

> The facts that our economy is built on debt . . . that it only works for the small 1% group by deliberately denying fiscal security to the majority of people . . . are deliberately hidden. In this blinders-on reality the poor (and increasingly the poor middle class) are encouraged to believe that if they fail financially it is because of their own personal spending or their weaknesses. In fact, they fail most frequently because they are victimized by a system that unsustainably requires ever increasing profits at the top, gained largely by the suffering of the people at the bottom.[1]

---

1. Marybeth Gardam. Notes sent to a Lonergan discussion group: Lonergan_l@google groups.com in 2022.

Appendix K

Business Innovation Striving to Solve Environmental Problems[1]

Business innovation fosters progress around the world. It's becoming clear, however, that there are challenges that can't be solved by the pursuit of profit alone. In fact, many aspects of our existence—the environment, society, and corporate practice—are in a state of decay. If one is a business leader, one is legally bound to optimize one's strategy and resources to maximize shareholder return. This may lead one to assume that it's not your responsibility, or in one's best interest, to care about the environment, social, and governance issues (ESG). Although ESG is often seen as inhibiting profit, this is not so. Making ESG a part of one's business strategy can unlock growth opportunities, reduce costs, and be an incentive for one's brand in the eyes of an increasingly conscious public.

The Securities and Exchange Commission is reportedly putting pressure on asset managers by broadening its probe into environmental, social and governance funds and whether some are being mislabeled. The agency has been questioning firms for months about how they lend out their shares and whether they recall them before corporate elections, according to a recent Bloomberg article. In the exchange-traded fund world, the shifting tide is reflected in the emergence of so-called anti-ESG that recently sought to attract investors. The private sector is ready to supply the financing to set us on a course to avoid the worst effects of climate change. CEOs representing trillions in assets

---

1. Adapted from https;//gtmhub.com, https://home.treasury.gov/news/press-releases/jy0457, https://etfcom.cmail19.com/t/ViewEmail/y/D503E02B1059836D2540EF23F30FED-ED/2B0A9235B07A95F6FE6194DE962A274B?alternativeLink=False

have shown their commitment. Financial institutions with collective assets under management of nearly $100 trillion have come together under The Glasgow Financial Alliance for Net Zero. If these ambitions are realized, those portfolios will be carbon-neutral by 2050 and significantly reduce emissions. Questions do remain: Will enough investment opportunities materialize to absorb all this capital? How quickly can this reorientation occur? How can institutions transparently report on their commitments so we can hold each other to account on transition plans?

There are a number of actions governments can take to make sure we remain flexibly dedicated to a to net-zero path. First, we have an essential responsibility to ensure the resiliency of the financial system to climate-related risks. That is why in May, 2021, President Biden issued an Executive Order on Climate-related Financial Risks. In response to that Order, the Financial Stability Oversight Council issued a report on these risks and U.S. regulators' role in addressing them. This includes actions to enhance climate-related data and disclosures to improve the information available to investors, market participants, and regulators. The report's recommendations represent a vital step towards making the U.S. financial system more resilient to the threat of climate change." Treasury concludes: "We're working with our partners at the Financial Stability Board and elsewhere to support similar efforts on a global scale."

A Selective Bibliography

Anderson, Bruce, and Philip McShane. *Beyond Establishment Economics: No Thank you Mankiw.* (Vancouver: Axial Press, 2002).

Byrne, Patrick. *Worldviews*: *Global Religions, Cultures and Ecology* Vol. 7, No. 1/2, 2003.

————— *The Ethics of Discernment: Lonergan's Foundations for Ethics.* (Toronto: University of Toronto Press, 2017).

De Neeve, Eileen. "Suspicion and Recovery: Ethical Approaches to Economics," *Method Journal of Lonergan Studies* 15, 1997.

—————*Decoding the Economy.* Thomas More Institute Papers, 2008.

————— "Economic Dynamics: Does it Complete Hayek, Keynes and Schumpeter, *Journal of Macrodynamics Analysis*, 2010.

Descartes, Rene. *The Philosophical Writings of Descartes*, translated by John Cottingham et al. (Cambridge University Press, 1985).

Dunne, Tad. "Bernard Lonergan." *Internet Encyclopedia of Philosophy.*

Eldred, Michael. "The Notions of Exchange, Value, Justice in Aristotle, Adam Smith and Karl Marx." https://www.arte-fact.org/untpltcl/exchvljs.html

————— *Social Ontology: Recasting Political Philosophy through a Phenomenology of Whoness* (Berlin: de Gruyter, 2008).

Graeber, David. *Debt*: *The First Five Thousand Years.* (New York: Melville, 2013).

Husserl, Edmund. *Logical Investigations.* 2 vols. Translated by John Niemeyer Findlay. (London: Routledge, 2001).

Keynes, John Maynard. *The General Theory of Employment.* (London: Macmillan, 1936).

Lamb, Matthew. "Orthopraxis and Theological Method in Bernard Lonergan," *Proceedings of the Catholic Theological Society of America* 35, 1980, 66–87.

————*Solidarity with Victims: Toward a Theology of Social Transformation*, (New York: Crossroad, 1982).

Lonergan, Bernard. "Belief: Today's Issue." In *A Second Collection*, Edited by William Ryan and Bernard Tyrell, (New York: Paulist, 1985), 87–100.

————"Dialectic of Authority." In *A Third Collection*, *CWL* 16, edited by Robert M. Doran and John D. Dadosky (Toronto: University of Toronto Press, 2016), 163–176.

————*Early Works on Theological Method* 1, *CWL* 22, edited by Robert M. Doran and Robert Croken (Toronto: University of Toronto Press, 2010).

————*For A New Political Economy*, *CWL* 21, edited by Philip McShane (Toronto: University of Toronto Press, 1998).

————"Healing and Creating in History." In *A Third Collection*, *CWL* 16, edited by Robert M. Doran and John D. Dadosky (Toronto: University of Toronto Press, 2017).

————"Horizons," *Philosophical and Theological Papers, 1965–1980*. *CWL* 17, edited by Robert Croken and Robert M. Doran (Toronto: University of Toronto Press, 2004), 10–29.

————*Insight, A Study in Human Understanding*, *CWL* 3, edited by Frederick Crowe and Robert M. Doran (Toronto: University of Toronto Press, 1992).

————"Insight Revisited." In *A Second Collection, CWL* 13, edited by William Ryan and Bernard Tyrell (Toronto: University of Toronto Press, 2015), 221–234.

————*The Lonergan Reader*. Edited by Mark and Elizabeth Morelli. (Toronto: University of Toronto Press, 1997).

————*Macroeconomic Dynamics: An Essay in Circulation Analysis*, *CWL* 15, edited by Frederick Lawrence, Patrick Byrne and Charles Hefling, Jr. (Toronto: University of Toronto Press, 1999).

————*Method in Theology*. (New York: Herder and Herder, 1972).

————*Method in Theology*, *CWL* 14, edited by Robert M. Doran and John D. Dadosky (Toronto: University of Toronto Press, 2017).

———— "Moral Theology and Human Sciences," *Philosophical and Theological Papers* 1965–1980. *CWL* 17, edited by Robert Crocken and Robert M. Doran (Toronto: University of Toronto Press, 2004), 301–312.

———— "Natural Right and Historical Mindedness." In *A Third Collection, CWL* 16, edited by Robert M. Doran and John D. Dadosky (Toronto: University of Toronto Press, 2017), 163–176.

———— "A Post-Hegelian Philosophy of Religion." In *A Third Collection, CWL* 16, edited by Robert M. Doran and John D. Dadosky (Toronto: University of Toronto Press, 2017), 194–215.

———— *Verbum: Word and Idea in Aquinas*. *CWL* 2 (Toronto: University of Toronto Press, 1998).

McShane, Philip. *Pastkeynes. Pastmodern Economics*. (Vancouver: Axial Press, 2002).

————*Sane Economics and Fusionism*. (Vancouver: Axial Press, 2010).

———— "Grade 12 Economics: A Common Quest Manifesto," in *The Road to Religious Reality*. (Vancouver: Axial Press, 2012).

Mankiw, N. Gregory. *Principles of Macroeconomics*. (New York: Harcourt, 1997).

Marx, Karl. *Das Kapital*. (Dietz Verlag, English edition. Berlin, 1962).

Matson, Floyd W. *The Broken Image, Man, Science and Society*. (New York: Anchor, 1964).

Matthews, William A. *Lonergan's Quest: A Study of Desire in the Authoring of Insight*. (Toronto: University of Toronto Press, 2005).

Raymaker, John. *Empowering Bernard Lonergan's Legacy*. (Lanham, MD: UPA, 2013).

————*Theory-Praxis of Social Ethics*, Marquette Univ. Dissertation, 1977.

Raymaker, John, and Godefroid Alekiabo Mombula. *Bringing Bernard Lonergan Down to Earth and into our Hearts and Communities*. (Eugene, OR: Wipf & Stock, 2018).

Raymaker, John, with Ijaz Durrani. *Empowering Climate-Change Strategies with Bernard Lonergan's Method.* (Lanham, MD: UPA, 2015).

Ricardo, David. *On The Principles of Political Economy and Taxation.* 1817. Reprinted, digitalized by the University of Michigan, 2012.

Schlefer, Jonathan. "There is No Invisible Hand," *Harvard Business Review,* April, 10, 2012.

Schumpeter, Joseph. *The Theory of Economic Development.* (New York, and London: McGraw Hill, 1911).

Smith, Adam. *The Theory of Moral Sentiments.* The Glasgow Edition of the Works and Correspondence of Adam Smith. (Oxford University Press, 1984).

———— *The Wealth of Nations.* Edited by Edwin Cannan. (New York: Modern Library Edition, 1937).

Walras, Léon. *Elements of Pure Economics. Or, The Theory of Social Wealth,* Translated by William Jaffe. (Cambridge University Press, 2014—original edition 1874).

Whalon, Pierre. "Desperately seeking a macroeconomic theory that works," *The Huffington Post,* https://huffpost.netblogpro.com/entry/lonergan-economic-theory_b_1185449

———— "To Help the Poor," *Academia,* June 2015. https://www.academia.edu/19555839/To_help_the_poor

SELECTIVE INDEX